THE STATES AND THE NATION SERIES, of which this volume is a part, is designed to assist the American people in a serious look at the ideals they have espoused and the experiences they have undergone in the history of the nation. The content of every volume represents the scholarship, experience, and opinions of its author. The costs of writing and editing were met mainly by grants from the National Endowment for the Humanities, a federal agency. The project was administered by the American Association for State and Local History, a nonprofit learned society, working with an Editorial Board of distinguished editors, authors, and historians, whose names are listed below.

Oklahoma

A History

H. Wayne Morgan
Anne Hodges Morgan

**With a Historical Guide
prepared by the editors of
the American Association for
State and Local History**

W. W. Norton & Company
New York · London

American Association for State and Local History
Nashville

Authors and publishers make grateful acknowledgment to the Bizzell Memorial Library of the University of Oklahoma for permission to quote from the Ferguson Papers and the Lyle H. Boren Papers, Division of Manuscripts, Western History Collections.

Published and distributed by W. W. Norton & Company, Inc.
500 Fifth Avenue
New York, New York 10110

Library of Congress Cataloguing-in-Publication Data

Morgan, Howard Wayne.
  Oklahoma: a history

  (The States and the Nation series)
  Bibliography: p.
  Includes index.
    1. Oklahoma—History. I. Morgan, Anne Hodges,
1940–   joint author. II. Title. III. Series.
F694.M8175 1984   976.6   84-2927
ISBN 0-393-30181-8

Printed in the United States of America
1 2 3 4 5 6 7 8 9 0

To
Rennard Strickland

Contents

Historical Guide

TO OKLAHOMA

prepared by the editors of the
American Association for State and Local History

Introduction

The following pages offer the reader a guide to places in this state through which its history still lives.

This section lists and describes museums with collections of valuable artifacts, historic houses where prominent people once lived, and historic sites where events of importance took place. In addition, we have singled out for detailed description a few places that illustrate especially well major developments in this state's history or major themes running through it, as identified in the text that follows. The reader can visit these places to experience what life was like in earlier times and learn more about the state's rich and exciting heritage.

James B. Gardner and Timothy C. Jacobson, professional historians on the staff of the American Association for State and Local History, prepared this supplementary material, and the association's editors take sole responsibility for the selection of sites and their descriptions. Nonetheless, thanks are owed to many individuals and historical organizations, including those listed, for graciously providing information and advice. Our thanks also go to the National Endowment for the Humanities, which granted support for the writing and editing of this supplement, as it did for the main text itself.   —*The Editors*

Chickasaw Council House

Tishomingo

★ The Indian Territory of nineteenth-century Oklahoma was originally set aside for the Five Civilized Tribes: the Cherokees, Chickasaws, Choctaws, Creeks, and Seminoles. Removed from their homelands in the southeastern United States in the 1830s and 1840s, these Native Americans preserved their distinctive heritages and cultures by establishing separate tribal nations within their new western home. Among these was the Chickasaw National Council, whose first and last council houses still stand on Court House Square in Tishomingo. These structures reflect the growth and development of the Chickasaw nation prior to statehood and commemorate the broader Native American experience in Oklahoma's Indian Territory.

Original log Council House

The infamous Indian removal policy of Andrew Jackson's presidency forced thousands of Native Americans to migrate to a newly established Indian Territory west of the Mississippi River. From Mississippi came the Choctaws, from Alabama and East Georgia the Creeks, from northern Mississippi and western Tennessee the Chickasaws, from Georgia the Cherokees, and from Florida the Seminoles. Although some went peacefully and others resisted the white man's coercion, all ended up following the "trail of tears" to the West. When the Chickasaws arrived in present-day Oklahoma, they found that they were to share the southeast part of the Indian Territory with the Choctaws. Although the tribes were related, co-occupation did not work out. For one thing, the Choctaws had arrived first and established farms and settlements in the eastern portion, forcing the Chickasaws to settle to the west, where they were more exposed to hostile Plains Indians. Furthermore, attempts at unified government proved unsuccessful, for each nation insisted on maintaining its separate identity and tribal organization. In 1848 the Chickasaws wrote their own constitution, and then in 1855 the two tribes officially parted ways, each setting up independent governments. The treaty also divided the lands, giving the Chickasaws control over 4,707,903 acres.

The elective council of the Chickasaw Nation first met at Post Oak Grove but in 1855 established its permanent capital at Good Spring on the Pennington Creek—the present site of Tishomingo, named for the last Chickasaw war chief in Mississippi. The first Council House or capital was a simple one-room log house, but in 1858 the council moved into a more substantial two-story brick building. That building burned down in 1890, however, and the Chickasaw National Council erected a third capital at Tishomingo. The council occupied the new Victorian stone structure in November 1898 and continued to meet there until 1907, when the independent Chickasaw nation came to an end with Oklahoma statehood.

Just as the Indian removal policy reflected the interests of white Americans, so statehood reflected the influence of white settlers in the Oklahoma region. In 1889 the federal government yielded to demands that the Indian Territory be opened to white settlement and allowed homesteaders to establish claims in an area known as the Unassigned Lands. Situated in the heart of the Indian Territory, this white enclave organized the Oklahoma Territory the following year. In the decades that followed, additional sections in the western part of the territory were opened up as part of an allotment process that eliminated lesser tribal nations. Then in 1898 Congress passed the Curtis Act, which authorized allotment of the remaining portion, the lands of the Five Civilized Tribes, and dissolution of the Indian Territory and the tribal nations. Native American leaders still hoped to avoid absorption by the white-led Oklahoma Territory and petitioned Congress for the Indian Territory's admission to the union as the state of Sequoyah. Their appeal was ignored, however, and in 1907 the Oklahoma Territory and the Indian Territory were joined as the state of Oklahoma. Under the new state government, the former capital of the Chickasaw nation became the Johnston County courthouse.

The first Council House was moved in the late nineteenth century from its original site to the country home of R. M. Harris, then governor of the Chickasaws. In the 1930s it was moved back to Courthouse Square in Tishomingo and then in 1964 relocated to its present site, a few hundred yards east of its original location. The Oklahoma Historical Society acquired the historic structure in 1969 and subsequently erected a cover structure to protect the deteriorating building and provide space for exhibits on the tribal culture and the Chickasaw Nation. Nearby stands the three-story granite Victorian structure that served as the Chickasaws' last capital. Although there has been some modernization to accommodate the county government, this edifice also remains much the same as in the period before statehood. Together these structures reflect the growth and development of the Chickasaw Nation and call to mind the larger Native American experience in the Indian Territory of nineteenth-century Oklahoma.

Historic Guthrie

Guthrie

★ In 1889 the United States Congress yielded to pressure from both land-hungry white settlers and railroad and financial interests and authorized the first land run into Indian Territory. Thousands joined the race to claim homesteads on April 22, and by that afternoon a small stop on the Santa Fe Railroad had become the city of Guthrie, Oklahoma's largest settlement. Although made up of

Gray Brothers Building

only tents and temporary structures at first, Guthrie blossomed over the next two decades as territorial and then state capital. The Guthrie Historic District preserves the turn-of-the-century city and brings to life the Oklahoma experience in the critical transition from settlement to territory to statehood.

In the first Oklahoma land run on April 22, 1889, thousands of homesteaders rushed to claim farm land, but an equally impressive number headed for a townsite about eight miles south of the Kansas border. Named Guthrie in honor of a director of the Santa Fe Railroad, the townsite had only one complete structure when that day began: a small frame station that served as a watering stop and section house for the railroad. Construction had begun nearby on a federal land office, but the building was not complete by the time the first train rolled in packed with eager new residents. Others followed on subsequent trains; some came by wagon, horseback, and foot; and by sunset the town claimed a population of fifteen thousand. The federal government had restricted the new town to a half-section of land or 320 acres, but that area could not begin to satisfy the newcomers' demand for town lots. The shortage was quickly eased by simply establishing four adjoining townships. Thus, until consolidated over a year later, the new city of Guthrie actually comprised four separate legal entities.

The new residents wasted little time. Construction of more permanent buildings began that first afternoon with lumber brought in by rail, and within the month the first brick edifice was occupied. Following the city's most well-worn path, a central business district soon developed from the railroad station east to the land office. Oklahoma and Harrison avenues became the two principal commercial arteries, lined with a variety of stores, businesses, banks, hotels, boardinghouses, and saloons established by ambitious entrepreneurs catering to the needs of the booming territorial society. Among the most successful was Frank Greer. Greer arrived in Guthrie on the opening day, set up business in a tent, and that same afternoon published the territory's first newspaper, the *Oklahoma Daily State Capital*. He also took on job printing and soon moved into a small frame building on Oklahoma. As business increased, Greer's State Capital Company moved to a third and finally in 1902 to a fourth larger home on Harrison. By the early twentieth century he owned Oklahoma's three most widely circulated newspapers and one of the largest printing and bookbinding operations in the Southwest.

When Congress authorized the land run in 1889, no provision was included for organizing and governing the territory. Consequently, for the first year the residents governed themselves. When the territory was finally established in May 1890, Guthrie was designated the capital. The first territorial legislature convened that fall, and one of the first bills to gain approval called for relocating the territorial government to Oklahoma City, a rival city also established in the 1889 land run. The territorial governor vetoed the proposal, but the controversy over the capital's location continued for decades. When Oklahoma secured statehood in 1907, Congress temporarily settled the issue by designating Guthrie as the capital until 1913, when a popular referendum would determine the permanent location. Oklahoma Democrats, whose power base was further south around Oklahoma City, viewed that clause in the enabling act as an attempt by Republicans in Washington to control the state's politics. By 1910, the Democrats, led by Governor Charles N. Haskell, and the Republicans, led by Guthrie newspaperman Greer, were openly at odds over the issue. Haskell finally decided to take action and convinced the legislature to hold a referendum on the capital location in June 1910. Voters could choose among Guthrie, Shawnee, and Oklahoma City. Just after the polls closed, Haskell declared Oklahoma City the winner and had the state seal secretly transferred there. Greer and other Guthrie residents challenged the validity of the referendum, but the United States Supreme Court upheld Haskell's action.

Guthrie's growth and development ended with the capital's relocation in 1910. As a result, few of the buildings were significantly altered, and the city today appears much as it did in the first decade of the twentieth century. In fact, the city was placed on the National Register of Historic Places as the only intact territorial and state capital remaining in the United States.

Of particular interest in the historic district are the Oklahoma Territorial Museum and the State Capital Publishing Museum, both administered by the Oklahoma Historical Society. The Oklahoma Territorial Museum occupies the old Carnegie Library and a modern adjoining building. The library, constructed in 1902 and 1903, was the site of the inauguration of the last territorial governor and the first state governor and of Statehood Day ceremonies on November 16, 1907. This last included the symbolic wedding of Mr. Oklahoma Territory and Miss Indian Territory. Visitors can now see portions of the historic library as well as exhibits on Oklahoma's territorial period. The State Capital Publishing Museum occupies the last home of Greer's famed printing business. Erected in 1902 according to a design by Joseph Foucart, the structure contains many original furnishings, vintage letterpress printing equipment, and exhibits on the company and the printing industry. In addition to the museums, visitors to the district can see a rich assortment of historic structures erected during the city's heyday. These include the Gray Brothers Building, home of the Bank of the Indian Territory until 1905; the Logan County Court House, constructed in 1902 and used as the state capitol until 1911; and the Atchison, Topeka and Santa Fe Railway Company Station, built in 1902 on the site of the original Guthrie Station. These and the other historic buildings in the district effectively recall Guthrie's pivotal role in Oklahoma's transition from territory to statehood.

Frank Phillips Home

Bartlesville

★ Oklahoma's most famous resource is oil. First commercially tapped in 1897, the state's oil reserves fueled the dramatic growth and development of the Oklahoma economy in the twentieth century. A leading figure in the establishment of the petroleum industry was Frank Phillips, founder of the Phil-

Frank Phillips Home

lips Petroleum Company at Bartlesville. His home still stands there as a monument to him and the other oil entrepreneurs who played such pivotal roles in shaping the twentieth-century Oklahoma experience.

The town of Bartlesville was established toward the end of the nineteenth century in northeastern Oklahoma, between the Osage Hills and the Caney River. Its founder was Jacob Bartles, who purchased a grist mill there in 1875 and operated a trading post on the north bank of the river. The town remained a relatively insignificant rural settlement until 1897, when the Cudahy Oil Company drilled Oklahoma's first commercial oil well, the Nellie Johnstone No. 1, on the banks of the Caney. The arrival of the Santa Fe Railroad two years later led to expanded operations in the oil field, but full exploitation was hindered for a time by legal technicalities related to Indian land allotments. Determined entrepreneurs secured leases one way or another by 1901, and the oil boom spread from Bartlesville throughout Indian Territory. By 1905, 255 producing wells had been drilled in the territory, and by 1907 the new state of Oklahoma led the Southwest in the production of crude oil—a position it retained until 1928 and the Texas oil boom.

One of the early entrepreneurs in the Oklahoma petroleum industry was Frank A. Phillips. He was born in rural Nebraska in 1873 and grew up on his family's farm in Creston, Iowa. His education ended at the age of 14, when he began working in a local barbershop. Ambitious and determined to make his way in the world, Phillips purchased that barbershop and the town's other two as well by his early twenties. In 1897 he married Jane Gibson, daughter of Creston banker John Gibson. Phillips' new father-in-law persuaded him to try his hand at bond sales, and he again demonstrated an amazing entrepreneurial talent in moving bond issues that had frustrated more experienced salesmen.

Just after the turn of the century, Phillips heard about the oil strikes around Bartlesville. He and his brother, L. E. Phillips, traveled to Oklahoma and investigated the investment possibilities in 1903 and 1904. Convinced of the potential for enormous profits, the Phillipses decided to join the oil boom. John Gibson and several associates provided capital for the organization of the Anchor Oil and Gas Company, and by early 1905 the young entrepreneurs had settled in Bartlesville, opened an office, and hired a driller. Oil drilling lacked the scientific exactitude of present-day operations, and the Phillips' first three wells proved dry. With only enough money for one more try, the brothers drilled a fourth well near the Caney River on property leased from Anna Anderson, a young Delaware Indian girl whose grandfather had secured the land for her as her allotment in the division of tribal property. On September 6, 1905, the Anna Anderson No. 1 came in, yielding two hundred fifty barrels of crude oil a day. The Phillips brothers made eighty more consecutive strikes after that and soon had Anchor Oil and Gas on a sound competitive footing within the developing petroleum industry.

By 1915, the price of crude oil had dropped from $1.05 to $.35 per barrel. Phillips, still active in banking and finance, decided to sell most of his oil holdings. Then with increased demand during World War I, the per-barrel price of crude oil shot up to $3.50. The remaining tag ends of the old oil leases became valuable again and the brothers resumed oil drilling operations. On June 13, 1917, they incorporated the Phillips Petroleum Company, using as assets $3,000,000 in oil leases. The company expanded dramatically over the next decade and in 1927 diversified with the purchase of a refinery in Texas. That in turn led to direct marketing, and in November 1927 the Phillips company opened its first service station in Wichita, Kansas. Marketed at first in the Midwest and West, Phillips 66 products were on sale in all fifty states by 1968. Frank Phillips died in 1950, but the company he founded remains an innovator and leader in the energy and chemical industries.

The Frank Phillips Home at 1107 Cherokee Avenue in Bartlesville was erected by the oil entrepreneur in 1909. The two-and-a-half-story Greek Revival building, designed by Walter Everman, is constructed of brick with sandstone trim and an imposing two-story portico supported by white columns. Its twenty-nine rooms include a gameroom, a library, a sunroom, and seven bedrooms decorated with the Phillips' furniture, art, and other decorative objects. Opened to the public in 1973 and administered by the Oklahoma Historical Society, the home serves as a monument to Frank Phillips and his pivotal role in the development of the Oklahoma oil industry.

Visitors to Bartlesville can see several other sites related to the oil industry as well. On the banks of the Caney River in Johnstone Park stands a replica of the wooden oil derrick that once marked the Nellie Johnstone No. 1, the state's first commercial oil well. Southwest of the city is the Woolaroc Museum and Ranch, a museum of Southwestern culture located on Frank Phillips' four-thousand-acre ranch. And in downtown Bartlesville on the second floor of the Phillips Building is the Phillips Exhibit Hall, which depicts the company's history, activities, and products. Still headquartered at Bartlesville, the present-day Phillips Petroleum Company testifies to the impact of the oil industry on twentieth-century Oklahoma.

Other Places of Interest

*The following suggest other places of
historical interest to visit. We recommend that
you check hours of operation in advance.*

BOGGY DEPOT SITE, *fourteen miles southwest of Atoka.* Faint outlines of
streets with building foundations, abandoned wells and cisterns, and ceme-
tery of 1838 settlement by Chickasaws; important in the days of the California gold rush and Butterfield Overland Mail.

CHEROKEE NATIONAL HISTORICAL MUSEUM, *Cherokee Heritage
Center, Tahlequah.* Village museum with recreation of villages from the
1600s and late 1800s; Cherokee culture and history.

CHEROKEE STRIP HISTORICAL MUSEUM, *one-fourth mile east of Fir
Street exit off I-34, Perry.* Exhibits on the agriculture and culture of the
Cherokee Strip.

CHISHOLM TRAIL MUSEUM, *605 Zellers Avenue, Kingfisher.* General history museum with exhibits on agriculture and Indian life; information on
the 1892 mansion of Gov. Abraham J. Seay.

CREEK NATIONAL CAPITOL, *Old Creek Indian Council House, Okmulgee.* Displays of Indian craftwork and weapons and the history of the Creeks
since their removal from Georgia and Florida; in the 1878 Victorian capitol.

DAVIS GUN MUSEUM, *Fifth and U.S. 66, Claremore.* Besides guns, swords,
and knives, includes saddles, steins, animal horns.

FERGUSON HOUSE, *521 N. Weigel Street, Watonga.* Clapboard house built
about 1902, and home of Thompson Benton Ferguson, newspaperman and
governor of Oklahoma Territory; where Edna Ferber worked on novel *Cimarron;* state-owned.

FIVE CIVILIZED TRIBES MUSEUM, *Agency Hill on Honor Heights Drive,
Muskogee.* Art in traditional style by Cherokees, Choctaws, Chickasaws,
Creeks, and Seminoles; housed in 1875 Indian agency building.

FORT GIBSON, *Fort Gibson.* Reconstructed log buildings and stockade and
restored original stone buildings from fort of 1837–1857 used in Indian
conflicts and as a trade center.

FORT WASHITA, *southwest of Nida on state 199.* Restored buildings from
an 1842 fort established by Zachary Taylor to protect Chickasaws; a stop
on the Overland Trail.

GILCREASE INSTITUTE OF AMERICAN HISTORY AND ART, *1400 N. 25 West Avenue, Tulsa*. Displays on the Five Civilized Tribes and other Indians from Alaska to Mexico, the American frontier, and American art.

MARLAND MANSION, *Monument Road, Ponca City*. Coursed stone house with Mission Style elements, built 1928–1941 for E. W. Marland, wealthy oil man; with a museum.

MURRAY-LINDSAY MANSION, *south of Washita River, Erin Springs*. Vernacular Neoclassical Revival house built in 1880 by a cattle king.

MURRELL HOME, *Park Hill*. Clapboard house built 1843–1844 that was social center and school for the community; with a museum.

MUSEUM OF THE CHISHOLM TRAIL, *U.S. 81 and state 70, Waurika*. Exhibits on pioneers and the famous cattle trail through the area.

MUSEUM OF THE WESTERN PRAIRIE, *1100 N. Hightower, Altus*. General museum with early farming implements and cattle-ranching equipment.

NATIONAL COWBOY HALL OF FAME, *1700 N.E. 63rd Street, Oklahoma City*. Collection of Russell and Remington art and displays on cowboys and historic trails.

NELLIE JOHNSTONE NO. 1, *Johnstone Park, Bartlesville*. Replica of the 1897 oil well that was the first commercial well in the state; first oil well on private land near Wapanuck, drilled 1885–1888.

NO MAN'S LAND HISTORICAL MUSEUM, *Sewel Street, Goodwell*. Collection of Indian artifacts and exhibits from anthropology, archeology, agriculture, and natural sciences.

OKLAHOMA STATE MUSEUM, *Historical Building, Oklahoma City*. Galleries on the Plains Indians, Five Civilized Tribes, pioneer, territorial, and statehood aspects of Oklahoma, transportation, military life, Indian art, and aviator Wiley Post.

OLD TOWN MUSEUM, *Pioneer Road and U.S. 66, Elk City*. General museum with restored first house in Elk City, early school, wagon yard, chapel, and rodeo setting.

OVERHOLSER HOUSE, *405 N.W. 15th Street, Oklahoma City*. Built 1903 by rich pioneer and merchant.

PRICE TOWER, *Dewey Avenue and Sixth Street, Bartlesville*. Office building housing headquarters of the Phillips Petroleum Company; designed by Frank Lloyd Wright, built 1953–1956, showing adaptation of skyscraper for open-space setting.

SOD HOUSE, *four miles north of Cleo Springs on state 8*. Frame and sod house built by homesteader, the only existing homestead sod house in Oklahoma, with furnishings of the 1890s era.

THORPE HOUSE, *704 E. Boston Street, Yale.* Clapboard house built 1916–1917 where Jim Thorpe, first competitor to win both pentathlon and decathlon in the Olympics (1912), lived; state-owned.

TOM MIX MUSEUM, *Dewey.* Memorabilia of the famous movie star, who was once a Dewey marshal; with a silver-studded black leather saddle on a life-size replica of Mix's horse, "Tony."

WESTERN TRAILS MUSEUM, *2229 Gary Freeway, Clinton.* Exhibits from anthropology and archeology.

WILL ROGERS MEMORIAL, *one mile west of Claremore on state 88.* Grave and personal belongings of the famed humorist.

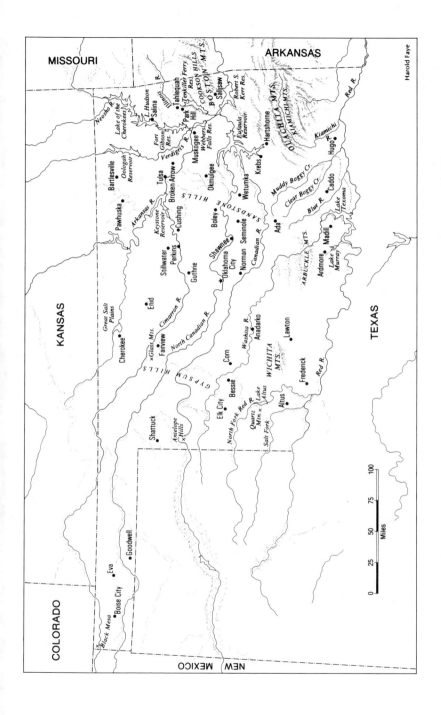

Invitation to the Reader

IN 1807, former President John Adams argued that a complete history of the American Revolution could not be written until the history of change in each state was known, because the principles of the Revolution were as various as the states that went through it. Two hundred years after the Declaration of Independence, the American nation has spread over a continent and beyond. The states have grown in number from thirteen to fifty. And democratic principles have been interpreted differently in every one of them.

We therefore invite you to consider that the history of your state may have more to do with the bicentennial review of the American Revolution than does the story of Bunker Hill or Valley Forge. The Revolution has continued as Americans extended liberty and democracy over a vast territory. John Adams was right: the states are part of that story, and the story is incomplete without an account of their diversity.

The Declaration of Independence stressed life, liberty, and the pursuit of happiness; accordingly, it shattered the notion of holding new territories in the subordinate status of colonies. The Northwest Ordinance of 1787 set forth a procedure for new states to enter the Union on an equal footing with the old. The Federal Constitution shortly confirmed this novel means of building a nation out of equal states. The step-by-step process through which territories have achieved self-government and national representation is among the most important of the Founding Fathers' legacies.

The method of state-making reconciled the ancient conflict between liberty and empire, resulting in what Thomas Jefferson called an empire for liberty. The system has worked and remains unaltered, despite enormous changes that have taken place in the nation. The country's extent and variety now surpass anything the patriots of '76 could likely have imagined. The United States has changed from an agrarian republic into a highly industrial and urban democracy, from a fledgling nation into a major world power. As Oliver Wendell Holmes remarked in 1920, the creators of the nation could not have seen completely how it and its constitution and its states would develop. Any meaningful review in the bicentennial era must consider what the country has become, as well as what it was.

The new nation of equal states took as its motto *E Pluribus Unum*—"out of many, one." But just as many peoples have become Americans without complete loss of ethnic and cultural identities, so have the states retained differences of character. Some have been superficial, expressed in stereotyped images— big, boastful Texas, "sophisticated" New York, "hillbilly" Arkansas. Other differences have been more real, sometimes instructively, sometimes amusingly; democracy has embraced Huey Long's Louisiana, bilingual New Mexico, unicameral Nebraska, and a Texas that once taxed fortunetellers and spawned politicians called "Woodpecker Republicans" and "Skunk Democrats." Some differences have been profound, as when South Carolina secessionists led other states out of the Union in opposition to abolitionists in Massachusetts and Ohio. The result was a bitter Civil War.

The Revolution's first shots may have sounded in Lexington and Concord; but fights over what democracy should mean and who should have independence have erupted from Pennsylvania's Gettysburg to the "Bleeding Kansas" of John Brown, from the Alamo in Texas to the Indian battles at Montana's Little Bighorn. Utah Mormons have known the strain of isolation; Hawaiians at Pearl Harbor, the terror of attack; Georgians during Sherman's march, the sadness of defeat and devastation. Each state's experience differs instructively; each adds understanding to the whole.

The purpose of this series of books is to make that kind of understanding accessible, in a way that will last in value far beyond the bicentennial fireworks. The series offers a volume on every state, plus the District of Columbia—fifty-one, in all. Each book contains, besides the text, a view of the state through eyes other than the author's—a "photographer's essay," in which a skilled photographer presents his own personal perceptions of the state's contemporary flavor.

We have asked authors not for comprehensive chronicles, nor for research monographs or new data for scholars. Bibliographies and footnotes are minimal. We have asked each author for a summing up—interpretive, sensitive, thoughtful, individual, even personal—of what seems significant about his or her state's history. What distinguishes it? What has mattered about it, to its own people and to the rest of the nation? What has it come to now?

To interpret the states in all their variety, we have sought a variety of backgrounds in authors themselves and have encouraged variety in the approaches they take. They have in common only these things: historical knowledge, writing skill, and strong personal feelings about a particular state. Each has wide latitude for the use of the short space. And if each succeeds, it will be by offering you, in your capacity as a *citizen* of a state *and* of a nation, stimulating insights to test against your own.

James Morton Smith
General Editor

Preface

PREFACES are places where authors say what their books are and are not about. This one is no exception. This brief history of Oklahoma is not a narrative account, nor does it pretend to be encyclopedic. We have chosen to treat a set of themes in roughly chronological order. But the account is not inclusive, and readers desiring more information can easily consult the works of Angie Debo, Edward Everett Dale, Edwin C. McReynolds, Arrell M. Gibson, and others cited in the bibliography.

Within the limitations of our design and the space allotted, we hope to present some new views of the forty-sixth state. We hope these ideas interest both Sooners and outlanders, since each in our judgment needs a clearer image of the state. Oklahoma has passed through several stages in the national consciousness. It began life as almost the last truly wild-west frontier, where all the elements of pioneering were worked out dramatically in the glare of national publicity. Its image then changed under a series of intense events such as the discovery of oil, the Great Depression, and the booms of two world wars. In the course of its relatively brief history, Oklahoma has been a place where national ideals matured with singular suddenness and vivid imagery. There is much truth in the warning that Edna Ferber gave readers in the preface to her novel about Oklahoma, *Cimarron:* "In many cases material entirely true was discarded as unfit for use because it was so melodramatic, so absurd as to be too strange for the realm of fiction." [1]

In the popular imagination, Oklahoma remains a land of cowboys and Indians, of oil derricks and multimillionaires. Yet there is a corollary vagueness about its history and unique quali-

1. Edna Ferber, *Cimarron* (New York: Doubleday, Doran and Co., 1930), p. ix.

ties. It is one of those states without any intense sense of place in national thinking. Too often, it is described as north of Texas, south of Kansas, or west of Arkansas. We hope that our account alters such misconceptions without denying the color and excitement of the state's past. As Edna Ferber intimated, in this state's case, the truth was both stranger and more interesting than the fictions that often pass for history.

Like all states, this one is complex and not easy to generalize about. In the national stereotype, for instance, it is probably seen as a plains state, where cattle graze and wheat grows in abundance on a flat landscape. That, of course, is true only of parts of its western marches. Its topography is as varied as the nation's, encompassing forests, mountains, and rivers, as well as flatlands. For the sake of convenience, we have thought of the state in two ways: first, as a set of quadrants intersecting at Oklahoma City; and second, as two halves, with a north-south line running through Oklahoma City. We hope the reader understands this convenience when we generalize about Oklahoma's varied parts.

We are especially concerned that the reader perceive the dimensions of the Indian contribution to the state's history and recognize the difficulty of generalizing about native Americans. The tribes settled in Oklahoma came from the three great divisions of Indian culture, those of the woods, the plains, and the plateaus. They shared some attitudes, but their cultures were as different as those of the nation states of Europe. Our generalizations about Indian life, therefore, are just that—generalizations.

We have tried for simplicity in citing sources and in suggesting further reading, noting only a fraction of the materials actually consulted. That is especially true of the abundant information on Oklahoma in the national press and periodical literature. The state's historiography deserves and surely will receive renewed attention. In our judgment, the state is poised to enter the nation's mainstream, and an understanding of its history is vital, both for its residents and for other Americans elsewhere.

* * *

It is a pleasure to thank the people who helped us in this work. The staff of the Western History Collections at the University of Oklahoma Library were consistently cheerful and efficient. We owe special thanks to the Collections Curator, Professor John S. Ezell, and to Mr. Jack Haley and Mr. Glenn Jordan of his staff. We thank the following members of the University Library's reference services: Mrs. Becky Haddad, Dr. Orlando Hernando, Mrs. Claren Kidd, Mrs. Patricia Simpson, and Mrs. Mary Esther Saxon. Mr. Carter Blue Clark, now of the University of Utah, was helpful in discussing the role of the Ku Klux Klan in Oklahoma. Mrs. Margaret Heisserer furnished some unusual information about the oil industry. At Oklahoma State University Library, Miss Vicki Withers gave important bibliographical and reference materials. Professor Paul Bonnifield of Panhandle State University kindly lent us a copy of his paper on the Dust Bowl, which added much to our knowledge of that disaster. Mr. Arnold Young of the Oklahoma Industrial Development Commission went out of his way to supply information on the state's economy.

We owe a profound debt to five special friends. Professor S. Louise Welsh of the University of Oklahoma history faculty read the manuscript carefully in the light of her lifetime study of the state's history. Professor William A. Settle, Jr., of the University of Tulsa Department of History also criticized the work with great care. Our special friends Professor Max L. Moorhead and Amy Moorhead of Norman read the manuscript for both content and style and improved it in many places. Rennard Strickland, John W. Shleppey Research Professor of Law and History at the University of Tulsa College of Law, brought to bear on the work a detailed knowledge of Indian history and of the state's other affairs. He has been an unfailing source of wisdom and encouragement, and we dedicate this book to him in gratitude.

H. WAYNE MORGAN
ANNE HODGES MORGAN

Norman, Oklahoma
November 1976

Oklahoma

A History

1

The Land

THE history of Oklahoma is an integral part of that peculiar phenomenon of restlessness that pushed people across the North American continent in unending pursuit of richer soils, better opportunities, and the chance to begin anew. The first white men entered this new land from two directions—the Spanish from the south, the French from the east. The Spanish adventurers moved out of their Mexican possessions in the 1500s in search of fabled kingdoms of sun and gold. But the future Oklahoma disappointed them. It held no gold or jewels, no exotic races of people, no prospects for the instant wealth so dear to the Spaniards' ambitions. Although the Oklahoma plains area was a logical extension of New Spain, in the end the conquistadores hurried elsewhere. They left trails and names on the land, but no permanent imprint.

With the growth of French influence in the Mississippi valley, after La Salle's explorations in the 1680s, traders moved up the rivers of Oklahoma in search of pelts for the St. Louis and New Orleans fur trade. There were traces of the French contact in French-Indian bloodlines and in some place names, but little permanent influence remained. Like the Spanish who preceded them in this new world, the French were soon overextended. By 1803, Napoleon was ready to abandon France's costly North American empire, more productive of risk than riches. With the Louisiana Purchase, modern Oklahoma, except for the Panhandle, became a part of the territorial United States. Despite a profitable fur trade with indigenous Indian tribes and the potential for even richer commerce with the Plains Indians and the Spanish borderlands, Oklahoma languished for eight more decades. It was an irony of her history that, despite expectations of being among the first of the new states fashioned from the Louisiana Territory established in 1805, she was the last.

The explorers, adventurers, and traders who touched Oklahoma prior to the nineteenth century made the nation conscious of the territory. Permanent settlers were needed, however, to make a new civilization from the contact of people and land. The pioneers who finally came entered from three directions, east, north, and south. Indian tribes from the southeastern part of the United States were resettled in Oklahoma prior to the Civil War. White ownership of land was not officially permitted until the end of the 1880s. But in varied ways the landscape reminded all of these settlers of their former homes.

To the Five Civilized Tribes—the Cherokee, Chickasaw, Choctaw, Creek, and Seminole—entering Oklahoma from the east, familiar vistas helped ease the wrenching experience of removal. Eastern Oklahoma was a leafy bower that could nourish the Indians' mystical attachment to the earth, just as the woodlands of Georgia, Alabama, and Mississippi had done. The hilly terrain and forests of pine, oak, hickory, cypress, and even magnolia were reassuring. The Indians regarded the green hills, lush valleys, rivers, and abundant wildlife as friends and providers, not as property. That concept appealed to few whites and underlay much of the later tension among varied groups of settlers.

To the "Jayhawkers," Unionist guerrilla bands who came from the north, the grass-covered, windswept prairie, with its extremes of heat and cold, drought and flood, was reminiscent of their previous experiences in the Dakotas, Kansas, and Nebraska. And settlers coming from the south through Texas found native pecan trees in the bottomlands of the Red River and many places that reminded them of former homes in the South. Moving north and west, they found an extension of the higher, drier lands characteristic of the greater Southwest. It seemed that the remnants of both geography and people came together in Oklahoma. In spite of their differences in origin and in time lapsed between their arrivals, both Indians and white settlers were refugees. Whether driven westward before governmental decrees, drought, or wanderlust, all came to Oklahoma in search of new roots and with hopes of success.

Oklahoma looked very different when settled in the nineteenth century from the way it would look in the twentieth. An arcadian quality, a sense of pastoral innocence about the land caused a Cherokee to write to Chief Dennis Bushyhead in the 1880s: "There is no better country in the west than this, you can picture any kind of land and location for homes and find it here. Rich loamy prairie or timbered bottoms and black limestone valleys and uplands . . . well watered and timbered." [1] Richard Harding Davis, glamorous correspondent for *Harper's Magazine,* traveled through Oklahoma in 1891. Despite an eastern heritage, Davis caught something of the new land's spirit and potential. Its soil was "rich and black and soft, and looks like chocolate where the plow has turned the sod." [2]

The interior plains of Oklahoma remained basically unchanged for centuries until white settlers came in the later 1880s. As a pioneer and historian wrote later, "pitted with the wallows of the vanished buffalo and broken in the distance by irregular green lines of timber that marked the courses of streams," the land had absorbed generations of red men. [3] Because the Indians lived *from* the land, not *on* it, they did not destroy the prairies.

To the first white settlers, the land's most striking quality was a mantle of luxurious grasses. Able to withstand recurring cycles of drought, wind, and extreme temperatures, the vegetation held the plains together. Bluestem grass, native to central Nebraska, spread across Kansas and spilled into central Oklahoma as far south as the Canadian River. It was the dominant prairie covering, and settlers were fascinated by its height, density, and constantly changing hues. It appeared a light green in the early spring, looked at with the wind, and dark green, seen

1. Richard M. Ketchum, *Will Rogers, His Life and Times* (New York: Simon and Schuster, 1973), p. 51.

2. Richard Harding Davis, *The West from a Car-Window* (New York: Harper and Bros., 1892), p. 96.

3. Angie Debo, *Prairie City* (New York: Alfred Knopf, 1944), p. 3.

against the wind. In summer the bluestem took on a reddish-brown cast. By autumn its purple and copper tints contrasted with the red, gray, white, and silver tones of dropseed, switch grass, squirreltail, and Indian grass.

Where the soil remained moist, bluestem formed a continuous sod, creating a limitless sea of grass interlaced with creek beds boasting borders of trees and shrubs. Early settlers often described the terrain in nautical terms. The breeze shifting the grass made it resemble waves and the ocean's gentle heaving. And the canvas tops of pioneer wagons were often compared to the sails of ships.

The grass grew so tall along creek bottoms that it hid all but the tops of wagons. Tiny islands of settlement on the prairie were sometimes engulfed in the tall grass. And the prairie chickens and fleet deer so necessary as food in early days of settlement abounded, but were often swallowed in the waves of bluestem before a man could shoulder his gun.

But the rich grasslands of northern and central Oklahoma did not shape her image to the rest of the world in later times. The land's comfortable, fecund look disappeared rapidly, as industrious farmers burned, plowed, and grazed hundreds, then thousands, of acres. Yet the memory of that verdant scene lingered for the pioneers. During the depths of the Dust Bowl days of the 1930s, a Panhandle farmer accidentally pulled up the cornerstone of an original land survey while contour plowing. The incident reminded his neighbor, Caroline Henderson, an early settler devoted to the land, of the time when the earth was fresh and untouched. She wrote a friend in Maryland that, for her, the cornerstone

> always . . . has suggested the beauty of the untouched prairie as it
> was when the surveyors set the stone, the luxuriant turf of native
> grass—grama grass, buffalo, and curly mesquite—the pincushion
> cactuses, straw-color and rose, the other wild flowers which in their
> season fulfilled the thought of Shakespeare:
> > The summer's flower is to the summer sweet
> > Though to itself it only live and die.[4]

4. Caroline A. Henderson, "Letters from the Dust Bowl," *Atlantic Monthly* 157 (May 1936): 545.

The first waves of settlers flowing into Oklahoma with the land opening of 1889 were as captivated with the climate as with the scenery. Compared to winters on the northern Great Plains, Oklahoma weather was temperate. Ruth Gage, a homesteader weary of battling twenty-below weather in the Dakotas and Nebraska, recalled "this 'Promised Land' of Oklahoma beckoning us on to further adventure." [5] Early territorial newspapers boasted of "a country which for several months in the year holds winter in its hand, spring in its arms and summer in its lap, all at the same time." [6] Yet even the most optimistic or gullible newcomer quickly learned the statement's implications. In Oklahoma, winter seldom melted into spring, and Indian Summer did not necessarily come in October. Like everything else in Oklahoma, the seasons overlapped and competed with each other. Nor was the daily weather any more predictable than the actions of people who lived with it. May might bring snow or heat; fall might come in October or December; and it could rain a year's quota in one week, or not rain for months.

Located in the transition zone between the humid, subtropical climates of the south and the colder climates to the north, with humid lands on her eastern borders and semiarid lands to the west, Oklahoma experienced turbulent weather. Nature did everything on a grand scale and with intemperate mixtures. Wide, shallow rivers were torrents one day, then sluggish, meandering streams with treacherous quicksands, or broad strips of blowing sand on still another. Dry air often evaporated rainfall quickly, so that one could experience a downpour and a sandstorm almost simultaneously, if the wind was strong enough. Summers were hot and long; winters were usually windy and cold.

Drought alternated with flood. Early settlers knew from experience in the Dakotas, Nebraska, and Kansas that the only safe prediction about plains weather was that dry years followed wet ones in both long and short cycles. Early white settlers came to the plains in a wet cycle and willingly allowed it to convince them that the territory would support most kinds of farming.

5. Lucy Gage, "A Romance of Pioneering," *Chronicles of Oklahoma* 24 (Autumn 1951): 292.

6. *El Reno Democrat,* September 26, 1891.

Reluctant to admit that there was no escape from nature's caprice, thousands of farmers reared in the practices of humid agriculture settled on the area's marginal lands. They were at the mercy of a rainfall pattern that varied widely.

But more than the vagaries of seasons, rainfall, and temperature, the strong wind was the most difficult feature of the region's climate to tolerate. As with other aspects of the weather, the booster territorial press concentrated on the wind's gentle moods. The editor of the *Watonga Republican* in 1893 described a December wind as "a balmy mellowness . . . in the air. Light zephyrs like the airy undulations of sweet softness that fan the sylvan bowers of fairyland, gently but voluptuously filled the earth." [7]

Because of the great variations in the temperature and humidity of air masses colliding over Oklahoma, winds frequently whipped up violent tornadoes or electrical storms that scattered hail or sand in their wake. Sometimes the atmosphere was so charged with electricity as thunderstorms raged over the prairies that "the points of the horns of cattle would at night blaze with tiny tapers of light." [8]

The Oklahoma settler learned to read the wind and sky with a concerned accuracy. Windmills turned away from the wind and shut off when it blew at twenty to twenty-five miles per hour. If hawks rode the air currents, while smaller birds were juggled like balls, the breeze was nearing thirty miles per hour. At about that speed, Russian thistles uprooted and became tumbleweeds that raced across the land. Driven along at sixty or seventy miles per hour, masses of them easily flattened fences. The winds were a necessary part of the plains' subtle ecology, since they reseeded grasses; but they equally foretold danger or death for man and animal when they became tornadoes, or took on hurricane force. When the winds were most savage, horses and cattle turned tail and drifted away; but the pioneer who survived in Oklahoma learned to interpret the air's moods, and like the

7. *Watonga Republican,* December 13, 1893.

8. Edward Everett Dale, *Cow Country,* 2nd ed. (Norman: University of Oklahoma Press, 1965), p. 9.

lordly bison that preceded him on the prairies, he faced into the storm.

So pervasive were the effects of climate on daily life that settlers quickly resorted to the ironic frontier humor that blended understatement with hyperbole. There was the story of a man plowing with a team in summer when one of the horses overheated and died. Before he could remove the harness, the wind shifted and the other horse froze to death. The newcomer who asked with irritation, "Does the wind blow this way all the time?" got a ready answer: "Hell, no! It blows the other way about half the time." [9] And if a man lost his hat in the gale, he was told not to chase it, since he could grab the next one blowing by. Even Oklahoma houses supposedly had special features called "crowbar holes" to gauge the wind. "You shove the crowbar through the hole; if it bends, the wind velocity outside is normal; if the bar breaks off, it is better to stay in the house." [10] And of course there were inevitable comparisons with Texas. A farm wife who lived in Old Greer County, an area both Texas and Oklahoma once claimed, hoped that the boundary commission would draw the state line to place her home on the Texas side, because she had heard that the Oklahoma weather was so terrible.

Yet even the climate had its blessings and its partisans. Summers were hot, but the wind offered some relief. The cool fronts of autumn and winter turned the sky brilliant blue and the air crystalline. And, later, people would offer ironic thanks for the wind, which kept smog from accumulating over the state's cities.

The climate joined with the terrain of western and central Oklahoma to reinforce the impression of a land of infinite possibilities. The opulent vastness made people revise their sense of proportion and standards of measurement: they learned to think in terms of miles, instead of the inches and feet that had once sufficed. Farmsteads became ranches, acres became domains. Plans and ambitions expanded in an environment where even

---

9. Dale, *Cow Country*, p. 9.
10. John Gunther, *Inside U.S.A.*, rev. ed. (New York: Harper & Row, 1951), p. 967.

the most monumental task seemed possible to fulfill. Such an enlarged viewpoint gave the settler a sense of importance and compensated for many drawbacks and disappointments. The Oklahoman further learned to exaggerate the sense of scope so common to Americans of all eras. In time, he pitied those too timid to face the beckoning distances of the great frontier and the arching sky: "He believed they were cramped by a narrow life and earnestly urged that they come out and join him in the development of a new country." [11] Yancey Cravat, fictional hero of Edna Ferber's *Cimarron,* spoke for thousands of real-life settlers when he declared: "Here everything's fresh. It's all to do, and we can do it. There's never been a chance like it in the world. We can make a model empire out of this Oklahoma country, with all the mistakes of other pioneers to profit by." [12]

The optimism of those early settlers did not diminish with time. In an environment where everything—climate, soil, vegetation, topography, scope, and isolation—combined to make achievement difficult, people endured. Second-generation Oklahomans born and reared on the open prairie loved the land so intensely that, when visiting the wooded areas their parents had left, they felt stifled and shut in.

Profound attachment to the land characterized both Indians and whites. But there were striking differences in their attitudes toward land use and toward the larger natural sphere of which it was a part. To the Indian, the land was one component of a great order of trees and streams, wind and rain, man and beast. He was but one part of a harmonious, unending cycle. The most remarkable feature of the Indians' relationship to land was the lack of any sense of private ownership. The land was for use and sustenance, but not for exploitation and profit. It belonged to all, whatever individuals used it. An Indian tilled only the soil needed to grow food for his family, not to sell to a neighbor or to feed a process that sustained distant people. His livestock grazed freely and he hunted in open woods and plains; he fished the streams to fill his stomach, not his purse. He had little desire

11. Edward Everett Dale, "From Log Cabin to Sod House," *The Journal of the Illinois State Historical Society* 38, no. 4 (December 1945): 406.

12. Ferber, *Cimarron,* p. 116.

to conquer the sod, drain marshes, or change land that nature had made inhospitable to cultivation. He accepted nature as it was. The Indian often lived a life of violence and insecurity, but not of conscious poverty, for he tailored his needs and desires to nature's apparent order.

For these reasons, Indian life left the land generally unchanged. The only scars were natural, marks of erosion, fire, or flood. If game overgrazed an area, hunger soon drove them to other pastures, and in time the grass healed the wounds. Even the industrious mixed-bloods among the Five Civilized Tribes, who engaged in plantation agriculture before the Civil War, used the land with care. Towns in Indian Territory were laid out neatly, and men built in accordance with the terrain, respecting streams and woodlands so that there was little sense of man's destructive impact, although a vigorous society flourished. No wonder the white settlers marveled at the beauty and the empty, undisturbed quality of this land they coveted.

Whatever the varieties or logic of nature's dispensation, the white settler, unlike the Indian, arranged the land to suit his preconceived purposes. Attitudes and practices that were natural and prudent to Indians seemed ''backward'' to the whites dedicated to earning more than subsistence from the land. The Indians' calmness toward nature often seemed apathy to those imbued with a different work ethic. And a willingness to take what nature gave without destructive effort seemed ''lazy'' in the eyes of many whites. This divergent view, reflected in many social attitudes, underlay much of the tension between Indians and whites.

The pioneers who came to Oklahoma in the 1880s and 1890s did not differ from those who had moved west earlier in search of wealth and new life. They were part of the long drama of filling up the continent. They wished to establish homesteads, rear families, develop a society, and attain economic security. The ideal was praiseworthy, but the pioneer psychology was not. The white settler believed firmly in dominating the land. Man clearly came before nature in his priorities, a view that religion, history, and human desire seemed to certify.

In subduing and arranging the land, the pioneer did untold harm to the natural order. His first act was usually to plow a

fireguard around his claim, then burn off the grass surrounding
his dwelling. To ease the task of planting, he often burned off
whole fields before plowing. Those burrowing creatures and
other wildlife who survived this fiery carnage soon fled before
the cutting, probing plow. Determined to mine the prairie environment with habits of farming learned in other climates,
the first settlers turned the light, rich soils, then exhausted
them with too many crops. The soil that did not blow away
in dry times washed off in rainy seasons. Human energy, self-
deception based on the desire for security and gain, and mechanical inventions broke the balance of nature that had sustained the complex ecology of plains life.

The Oklahoma settler was no more greedy or profligate than
other American pioneers. He sincerely believed in his right to
this vast, promising cornucopia. After he slashed the timber, destroyed the watershed, burned the grass, and mined the soil, he
could move on, like other generations. Indifference and simple
negligence accounted for as much of the devastation as did ignorance. By the time Oklahoma was settled, agriculture was a
business rather than a way of life. It was a risky business, with
high stakes, and everyone gambled. As one plains farmer admitted during the devastated 1930s: "We know how to farm better
than we do. We simply take chances, winning in good seasons
and losing when it fails to rain or the wind blows out our
crops." [13] Territorial journalists and agricultural experts
preached the need for windbreaks, contour plowing, stubble
mulching, and terracing in the 1890s, as their later counterparts
did after the great dust storms of the 1930s. But what did timid
men or "hifalutin' experts" know, when wheat was selling at
two dollars a bushel in Chicago? Or when corn-fed cattle
brought record prices and the chance to pay off the mortgage
beckoned the man willing to plow up another quarter-section
even if it was a dry year? Only fools planted grass, when wheat
and cotton turned to gold.

The farmer was not alone in violating the natural order. The
coal operators and later the oil producers each left ugly legacies.
Soil soaked with petroleum and brine became badlands, while

13. W. I. Drummond, "Dust Bowl," *Review of Reviews* 90 (June 1936): 39.

the patterns of gouging and filling the earth made while strip-mining created desolate areas that looked like "a giant's plowed field." [14] Early timber cutters did not bother to replant the forests that made them rich. The devastation of the landscape was usually the work of unthinking people caught in an exploitative ethic they took as natural, based on reigning national models, steeped in history and respectability.

By the time most '89ers reached middle age, erosion had scalped much of Oklahoma. Networks of gullies and sandy, scrubbed wastes replaced grass and forest lands in many sections. The rich cinnamon-colored clay that pleased the eye, especially against the green backdrop of spring vegetation, was a warning of erosion. Clear streams became silted, choked with debris, or stagnant. The fearful experience of the Dust Bowl was necessary to halt the chaos that threatened to destroy the land forever. It was a message written on the wind, echoing the older Indian ethic that not even the most optimistic agrarian could ignore. After more than forty years of slow, careful efforts at conservation, the land has been revitalized. Tree belts, dams, contoured fields, and greater care in plowing and grazing have softened the sinister look of ruined areas. But old-timers still recall the days when "the land was fresh," understanding the poignancy of Will Rogers's remark: "We spoiled the best Territory in the world to make a State." [15]

In modern times, an awareness of their treatment of the land has been an important key to understanding the cultural heritage and attitudes of Oklahomans. Like every other state, Oklahoma was a congeries of topography, people, and customs, settled at different times for varied reasons. Larger than any state east of the Mississippi, Oklahoma drew both geography and settlers from states on her borders. The eastern and western halves of the state varied almost as widely in terrain, vegetation, and rainfall as Colorado and Missouri. And the length of the growing season and topography of the northern and southern extremes were as disparate as Kansas and Texas.

---

14. Angie Debo, *Oklahoma, Footloose and Fancy-free* (Norman: University of Oklahoma Press, 1949), p. 104.
15. Ketchum, *Will Rogers*, p. 49.

Stretching east from the southwestern corner of Oklahoma, the land resembles Texas. The Red River drains the sandy soil there and forms the state's southern boundary. Intensive cotton cultivation and the neglect characteristic of tenant farming sapped this once-fertile area. The short grass native to the region now sustains limited grazing, and modern methods of irrigation, soil conservation, and crop rotation have rejuvenated the land. Peanuts, melons, and vegetables lend variety to an agriculture once limited to cattle, cotton, and sorghum. Despite the growth of trade centers such as Altus and Frederick, there is still a limited quality to life in the southwestern corner of the state that contrasts sharply with the vast sunny sky. The taciturn and wind-burned farmers live with the fear that deep wells may run dry, resulting in disaster for crops, animals, and men.

Farther east, the granite outcroppings of the Wichita Mountains rise above the surrounding plains as weather-sculptured domes. They witnessed several frenzied gold rushes that spawned dozens of ghost towns like Wildman, noted for its post office on wheels. In 1905, President Theodore Roosevelt designated the area a national wildlife preserve. Congress later provided funds to purchase seventeen buffalo from the New York Zoological Society in an effort to preserve the nearly extinct species. A large number of old Indians in traditional dress camped near the specially constructed receiving pens in the Wichita Preserve and awaited the return of the "Great Spirit's Cattle." It was a moving scene as the great beasts lumbered from the railroad cars back onto Oklahoma terrain. Deep emotions transformed the weathered faces of the Indians who pressed against the wire fences and "recalled the old days when the plains were black with buffalo." [16] Within a month, in 1907, two calves were born. In a land rich with Indian tradition, the arrival of the second calf, named "Oklahoma," on the day of statehood, November 16, 1907, was a good omen.

East of the semiarid Wichitas, the land is greener. Expensive herds of Santa Gertrudis and Charolais cattle graze placidly on

---

16. Jack D. Haley, "The Wichita Mountains: The Struggle To Preserve a Wilderness," *Great Plains Journal* 13 (Fall 1973): 70–99; and *Great Plains Journal* 13 (Spring 1974): 148–186.

well-tended ranches. The houses are substantial, well kept, but there is still some evidence of overgrazing and wasteful farming where the grass has yet to reclaim many deep red gullies and barren rises. In some places, fingers of the tangled, stunted forests of blackjack and post oak encroach on pasture and cropland. Known as the Cross Timbers, this miniature forest, varying from five to thirty miles in width, runs diagonally from the southwest toward central Oklahoma. It divides the bluestem prairies and rolling woodlands of the east from the shortgrass-covered, level plains of the west. Early travelers dreaded struggling through these "forests of cast iron," where masses of reeds and brambles snared the feet while bushes and limbs tore at the flesh of men and horses.[17]

A little farther east are the Arbuckle Mountains. Although very old and worn to a height of only six hundred to seven hundred feet above the surrounding plains, they are a geological textbook. The top of the range looks as if some ancient cataclysm had pulled a plug of earth from a horizontal position and tilted it upward. These richly textured, exposed strata now fascinate travelers on Interstate 35.

Still farther east, the land begins dramatic changes. Broken cotton stubble dots the fields, and unpainted shanties blend with the dull colors of the earth. Children, pigs, dogs, and chickens share yards littered with rusting car hulks and cast-off furniture. The habit of parking cars in the yard rather than on the street is hard to break, even in Oklahoma's modern cities. The sounds of speech become slower, movements more deliberate. Fundamentalist religious groups meeting in one-room churches, billboards announcing visiting evangelists, and other signals suggest the placid calmness, if not the torpor, of the rural South.[18] Heat, humidity, and a watchful attitude toward strangers evoke some of the darker qualities of the Louisiana bayou or Mississippi delta. Near the town of Hugo the population is so sparse and vegetation so dense that two elephants es-

17. Washington Irving, *A Tour on the Prairies* (1835; reprint ed., Norman: University of Oklahoma Press, 1956), p. 125.

18. See Michael Frank Doran, "The Origins of Culture Areas in Oklahoma, 1830–1900" (Ph.D. diss., University of Oregon, 1974), p. 11.

caped from a circus in 1975 and eluded their keepers there for two weeks—an event that received national news coverage. Another bizarre Oklahoma story, it belied the state's stereotype as a windswept plain. There is a slow quality about life in "Little Dixie," a moist, wooded section that contrasts sharply with the rest of the state.

Part of "Little Dixie" is mountainous. The rough, wooded terrain of deep, narrow valleys reinforces a sense of isolation. The Ouachita Mountains near the southeastern border with Arkansas are composed of high, almost parallel ridges. They have romantic, fanciful names typical of Indian Territory—Winding Stair, Blue Bouncer, Buffalo, San Bois. There is a tranquility in the rivers and deep shade uncharacteristic of the rest of the state. As the Choctaw name for the Kiamichi River and mountains implies, this part of Oklahoma is a refuge to many.

The Arkansas River valley separates the Ouachita Mountains and the old Choctaw plantation area of the southeast from the Ozark Plateau farther north. Once bordered with fine shade and sandy beaches, the Arkansas River, carrying about two-thirds of the state's runoff, is now navigable, moving through long stretches of man-made channels. An intricate system of dams and locks enables barge traffic to move between Tulsa and New Orleans. But even with increased commercial traffic and the promise of large-scale future growth, life here retains a slow and easy tempo.

The inhabitants have deliberately cultivated the area to make it appear more southern, more hospitable. On the land where the early Indian administrators had encouraged the tribes to grow cotton, the citizens of Muskogee have planted azaleas. These flowering shrubs have prospered, creating an impression of the more temperate Gulf Coast.

Crossing north onto the Ozark Plateau, a predominantly wooded region of moderate limestone hills, the land empties. At the extreme southern end of the plateau lie the Cookson Hills, an area of deep gullies, wild prairie, and oak-studded foothills. Primitive and inaccessible, this tract was the special refuge of outlaws from the 1870s to the 1930s. Illegal backwoods stills are not unknown, and strangers are not welcome, even today.

Beyond these hills, deep into the Ozark Plateau, lies the heart of the Old Cherokee Nation, now the last retreat of conservative full-bloods. Unobtrusive, quiet, and generally poor, their lives blend into the heavily wooded landscape. Everything seems to occur or grow on a small, gentle scale. Tiny bottomland plots characterize the agricultural system, and livestock range freely through the tangled woodland. Occasionally a log cabin or its modern equivalent, a mobile home, or a house, newly constructed with an Indian loan, is visible. But most dwellings are out of sight. The beauties of autumn and spring in these woodlands often camouflage the bleakness of human existence underneath.

Settled more than half a century before the west, eastern Oklahoma seems very old. It has a violent social history, including much destruction during the Civil War, and long-term conflict between whites and Indians, and whites and Negroes. There is also a sense that the land and the people are dormant, though here and there a town revives when a particular modern industry comes in, creating new jobs and incomes.

The images of Arkansas and Missouri fade beyond the Verdigris River, as the angle of vision curves westward again. The Sandstone Hills, a wide strip of land extending north and south through the east-central part of the state, supports little but the scrubby Cross Timber forests and a profusion of spring and summer flowers. But beneath the thin topsoil are deposits of oil, gas, coal, lead, and zinc that have enriched the state. The landscape is not as appealing as parts of eastern Oklahoma, but there is a great sense of vitality and activity.

Farther west, the land runs into vastness, and wheat engulfs the senses. It rolls to the distant horizon, replacing the sea of green with oceans of gold and russet. Most of this land is cultivated with modern, expensive machinery. Many older houses built at the turn of the century have been renovated, while newer ones bespeak prosperity. On many of these farms, a modern ranch-style dwelling stands near the old homestead as sons continue to work with fathers in the tradition of the frontier. There is a mood of profit about this wheat land, where people rest from hard work but are not idle.

Two tiers of counties west of Enid, the texture of the landscape coarsens. Here in the Gypsum Hills the climate is drier and the vegetation more ragged. Bands of red and white alternate in the soil. And in some places, sparkling crystals washed down from the Glass Mountains are strewn across the surface like false jewels.

As the "Gyp Hills" region rises to the High Plains, the growth declines to chaparral, sagebrush, and shinnery, so called because it scrapes the shins of a walking man. Tumbleweed drifts against fences. Near the far western boundary of the state are the barren Antelope Hills, a welcome landmark to early travelers on the way to Santa Fe. At the northwest edge of the Panhandle is Black Mesa, the state's highest point at 4,973 feet. Lava spilled from a New Mexico volcano formed this tableland where piñon trees and western yellow pines struggle against the wind and sun.

The Panhandle is shortgrass country, a place of wind-driven snow in winter and dancing mirages in summer. It is bountiful when the rains cover it with wheat and always attractive to those enamored of a big sky. In some places the land is so level that water will not drain. The few people in these counties, really immense fields, seem to take their temperament from the land: they are solid folk who persevere.

Crossing the Oklahoma landscape in a counterclockwise arc from southwest to east to north to west gives a profound impression of the changing look and mood of both land and people. The northwest resembles the nation's Midwest. The southeast retains the South's unhurried casualness. There is also a sense that physical geography exaggerates the ranges of poverty and wealth.

The importance of land, man's hunger for it, his attitudes toward it, his use and abuse of it, dominated Oklahoma history. Land for farms and homesteads, land that utilized human energy rather than capital, was the area's greatest lure. It represented the average man's last chance to make security if not a fortune for himself and family. Unlike the Indians, white settlers with no understanding for nature's balances or limits occupied this land and depleted its resources. The crisis came with the Dust Bowl of the 1930s and a realization that man's desires must conform to nature's plan. But man's ambitions and nature's systems, whether at war or in harmony, made a unique civilization in this last frontier.

2

Indian Culture

N the three decades after the Louisiana Purchase, Oklahoma followed the pattern of development typical of other frontier regions. Trappers and traders, restless adventurers or "Long Knives," flowed into the area, eager to participate in the profitable commerce in furs that early French entrepreneurs had established with the indigenous tribes. The region's river patterns allowed easy access to the plains tribes, the Kiowa and Comanche, with their buffalo robes and wild mustangs, and to the wealth of the Santa Fe trade beyond. People and goods streamed from St. Louis to Santa Fe, across Oklahoma and back to New Orleans. Soldiers mapped the area, searched out the sources of rivers, and chose sites for military posts needed to maintain peace and to establish American control over the land. Scientists also frequently accompanied these expeditions, to survey the flora and fauna, rocks and soils. Thomas Nuttall, famed British naturalist, traveled widely in eastern Oklahoma in 1819–1820. He recorded a vision of the land "beautiful almost as the fancied Elysium . . . now enamelled with flowers . . . Serene and charming as the blissful regions of fancy." [1] In the early 1830s, writers such as Washington Irving and Charles Joseph Latrobe often joined military entourages, during which the pleasures of the hunt for deer or buffalo frequently eclipsed the mission's official purposes.

1. Thomas Nuttall, *Journal of Travels into the Arkansas Territory During the Year 1819* (Philadelphia: Thomas H. Palmer, 1821), p. 208.

Gradually the transient quality of life in the new land changed, as tiny settlements grew up around trading centers and military posts. Some early settlements and families prospered and survived, such as the French-Indian Chouteau clan who produced merchant princes in the nineteenth century and prima ballerinas in the twentieth. As farmers followed adventurers and traders into the fertile valleys of the Grand, the Illinois, and the Kiamichi rivers, the rim of the frontier crept westward. New white and Indian settlements required military protection from the raids and reprisals of the indigenous Indians. In 1824, Fort Gibson, in the north, at the "Three Forks" of the Verdigris, Arkansas, and Grand rivers, and Fort Towson, near the mouth of the Kiamichi in the south, became twin sentinels to replace Fort Smith in guarding the widening gateway to the Pacific.

Congress sanctioned the settlement and located the extreme boundary of Arkansas Territory on a line from Fort Gibson south to the Red River. It seemed merely a question of time before Oklahoma entered the Union, either as a part of Arkansas or as a separate state. But thus situated midway between the Atlantic and Pacific coasts, Oklahoma was destined to play a different and poignant role in the drama of settling the continent.

From the beginning of the Republic, United States policies toward native Americans were a curious mixture of leniency and firmness. Many people had great expectations of the Indian populations, yet did not quite know how to achieve them. Planners and philanthropists of all persuasions alternated among desires to remake Indians in white images, to ignore them, or to preserve their culture.

In attempts to ameliorate conflict between two very different cultures, succeeding national administrations tried to fashion an environment where peoples lacking the concept of private property could coexist with European settlers for whom property, especially the real estate of farms and homesteads, was sacred. While the white population remained relatively small or sedentary, some accommodation was possible. The new continent was vast, with ample room for many conflicting peoples and ideals. But the hope of establishing an extensive separate domain for each tribe, with solemnly guaranteed treaty rights ensuring that whites would not disturb Indians, proved impossible to attain. Sometimes Indians who did not understand the concept of segregated lands strayed onto other tribes' territories or onto settled land in pursuit of game; but most such trouble came from the whites. Resentful of the government's attempts to restrict their movements and considering Indians unworthy of respect or concern, settlers everywhere simply ignored treaty obligations that interfered with "progress." As the white population increased and pressed against the borders of Indian nations, it was clear that some other solution must be tried.

On acquiring the Louisiana Territory in 1803, President Thomas Jefferson glimpsed an alternative—removal of the Indians beyond the Mississippi. Most whites and some Indians found the proposal attractive. For whites intent on expediency and movement, removal meant "out of sight, out of mind." Fertile, cotton-producing acreages in Georgia, Alabama, and Mississippi evoked images of great plantation-based fortunes and blinded men to the injustices of uprooting native people from their homes. Small landowners, conditioned to think of a homestead as an inalienable right and coveting just a few acres in the vast Indian hunting preserves, felt no remorse. Still other whites scented quick profits in government contracts to relocate the Indians. And many public officials, weary of balancing contradictory policies and of managing the human problems they created, embraced removal.

The idea of a permanent "Indian Country" also appealed to some Indians eager to preserve their way of life and culture. Among some tribes, the removal question caused bitter rifts and factionalism that lingered long after they reached Oklahoma. But many prominent Indian leaders ultimately accepted, however fatalistically, the futility of resistance to the white man's civilization and prepared their people for the march west.

But removal did not solve the Indian question. It was a typically American response to a complex problem, the usual compromise measure aimed at benefiting if not satisfying everyone involved. It only postponed the inevitable task of absorbing native Americans into national citizenship.

The voluntary removal of portions of the eastern and southern tribes was fitful during the first two decades of the nineteenth century; but the accelerated movement of white settlers and their pressure against the tribes combined with the election of Andrew Jackson in 1828 to bring events to a climax. Jackson shared the average frontiersman's hostility to Indians who blocked further white settlement. Early in his first term, Congress approved Jackson's requests for legislation to remove the Indians beyond the Mississippi.

While the national government forged a policy, Georgia, Alabama, and Mississippi busily harassed Indian governments within their borders. The experiences of the Cherokee people in Georgia typified the common fate of ancestors of the southeastern Indians who eventually settled in Oklahoma.

Under treaties negotiated in 1817 and 1828, about one-third of the Cherokees, eager to escape white civilization, exchanged lands east of the Mississippi for equal acreage in western Arkansas and later in northeastern Oklahoma. The majority of the tribe, however, remained in Georgia, where they prospered. With direction from various mixed-blood leaders, the eastern Cherokees emulated their white neighbors. Some owned slaves and extensive plantations; many raised livestock and abundant crops; others operated grain and lumber mills; most pursued the "civilized" life.

At the invitation of the Cherokee Tribal Council, missionaries established churches and schools on Indian lands. Every year the most promising mission-trained youths went to Connecticut to Cornwall Academy for more education. When Sequoyah, an uneducated traditional Cherokee, succeeded in "catching and taming" the sounds of his native language into a system of symbols, most of the nation became literate almost overnight. Sequoyah's remarkable syllabary enabled the divided tribe to communicate again through letters, or "talking leaves." Soon the Cherokees acquired a press and published a newspaper, as well as religious tracts, public laws, books of the Bible, and hymnals, all in the tribal tongue.

These progressive and industrious people, probably more literate than the white settlers encroaching on their lands, had begun to formulate a legal code in English in 1808. By 1828, the eastern Cherokees had created a constitutional system of tribal government modeled on the United States.

The white citizens of Georgia became alarmed at the developing Indian republic within their borders. Many feared that the federal government would not honor its long-standing promise to relocate these Indians in the west. Despite official assurances from Washington that removal would come when it could be effected peacefully and on terms reasonable and acceptable to the Indians, the clamor intensified. The Indians' various successes also illustrated possibilities for whites. When gold was discovered in the northern mountains of the Cherokee Nation in the 1820s, simple greed overwhelmed reason. Thousands of intruders stampeded onto Cherokee lands, staking out mining claims, trampling fences, stealing livestock, and looting households. Forbidden to prospect for or mine gold on their own lands and denied redress for damages in the state courts, hundreds of frightened Indians abandoned their homes and fled to other parts of the Cherokee domain.

Then, through a series of repressive laws, the Georgia legislature extended the state's jurisdiction over all Indian lands and voided the Cherokee consititution. All Cherokees became subject to Georgia law, but were prohibited from testifying in court. Their tribal council was not to meet except to ratify land cessions. State officials, convinced that the missionaries encouraged Indian resistance to removal, required all white persons living among the Cherokees to obtain residence permits from the state on threat of imprisonment. These confiscatory measures and repressive personal restrictions were Georgia's official revenge upon a people who had tried to follow the white man's way without abandoning their own culture.

The Cherokee Nation's conduct during the agonizing struggle to retain their lands and homes evidenced their political maturity. Legend taught that in early times the Cherokees were given the book and the bow, but did not use the book and thus were left with only the bow. The tribal elders said that was why Cherokee civilization languished so long. But by the 1830s, these people had abandoned the bow for the law in settling disputes; their native belief that the American legal system's promise of due process was a guarantee of justice was as mistaken as it was touching.

The United States Supreme Court ultimately denied that the

Cherokee Nation was an independent foreign state, and defined their relation to the United States as that of ward and guardian. In 1832, in the famous case of *Worcester* v. *Georgia,* the high court declared all of Georgia's laws extending over the Cherokee Nation "repugnant to the Constitution, laws and treaties of the United States," hostile to the will of Congress, and in violation of presidential authority. But the Cherokee victory was an illusion. The missionaries imprisoned under the nullified Georgia laws remained in jail. And Georgians continued to plunder Indians with the silent approval of the president whom the Indians called "Chicken Snake."

In that worsening context, an influential group of predominantly mixed-bloods gradually became convinced that flight from the whites was the Cherokees' only hope of salvation. Known as the Treaty Party, the group included Major Ridge, the full-blood speaker of the Cherokee National Council; his son John Ridge; Elias Boudinot, editor of the *Cherokee Phoenix,* and his brother Stand Watie. The Treaty Party, fearing the horrors of the removal, contended that only in the west could the Cherokee Nation escape white encroachment, become united, and develop a prosperous, progressive society. But most of the tribe looked upon the prospect of leaving their lands in Georgia as equal to abandoning the mother who gave them life. John Ross, the Cherokee Nation's principal chief and the leader of the antiremoval forces, was a Scotsman of one-eighth Cherokee blood, but his views reflected those of the most conservative and tradition-minded full-blood. Better to suffer at home, they stoically maintained, than die in exile. After repeated efforts to treat with the Ross element failed, federal officials negotiated an agreement with the minority Treaty Party.

The men who signed the Treaty of New Echota in 1835 sincerely believed that removal was the only option if the Cherokee Nation were to survive. Major Ridge, author of an earlier statute that decreed the death penalty for any Cherokee deeding away tribal land, signed the treaty aware that he was assenting to his own demise. Aware of the risks, he simply believed resistance to white civilization and power was futile.

Opposition to the treaty was so persistent that, by 1838, the date anticipated as the end of removal, fewer than two thousand of the almost seventeen thousand Cherokees had started west. General John Ellis Wool, commander of troops concentrated in the Cherokee country to prevent armed resistance to the treaty provisions, reported that ragged, starving Cherokees attended tribal councils to denounce the treaty. They consistently refused supplies from government agents lest they seem to accept the treaty proposals. Heartsick with the disagreeable task, Wool wrote Representative Horace Everett of Vermont: "If I could, and I could not do them a greater kindness, I would remove every Indian tomorrow beyond the reach of the white men, who, like vultures, are watching, ready to pounce upon their prey and strip them of everything they have or expect from the government of the United States." [2]

When it became clear that force was necessary, the War Department dispatched Major General Winfield Scott to supervise the evacuation. Stockade forts were erected and Indians herded into them to await the forced march west. Some Cherokees found refuge in the North Carolina mountains, but soldiers found most of them hidden in the forests. "Families at dinner were startled by the sudden gleam of bayonets in the doorway. . . . Men were seized in their fields or going along the roads, women were taken from their wheels and children from their play." [3]

Often before the Indians were even out of sight of their homes, looters drove off cattle and burned the cabins. Not even Indian graves were safe from people who robbed the dead of silver ornamentation. A Georgia militiaman recalled years later: "I fought in the Civil War and have seen men shot to pieces and slaughtered by thousands, but the Cherokee removal was the cruelest work I ever knew." [4]

The first contingent of Cherokees started west in June of 1838. Hundreds died from the unsanitary conditions in camps, an unfamiliar diet, and the heat. Grief also claimed many. Appalled at the mortality rate and resigned to the inevitability of

2. James Mooney, *Myths of the Cherokee,* Smithsonian Institution, Bureau of American Ethnology, 19th Annual Report, 1897–1898 (Washington: Government Printing Office, 1900), pt. 1, p. 127.

3. Mooney, *Myths of the Cherokee,* pt. 1, p. 130.

4. Mooney, *Myths of the Cherokee,* pt. 1, p. 130.

going, Chief Ross persuaded General Scott to permit tribal officials to conduct the migration. But the physical exertions of the journey and a severe winter continued to decimate the tribe. For Chief Ross, the trek to Oklahoma was doubly painful. He had failed to prevent or control removal and had lost his wife during the journey. She was buried in a shallow grave, and the sorrowing cavalcade moved on. More than four thousand Cherokees ultimately died on the Trail of Tears. No set of memories ever remained more vivid, or with more compelling reason, than did the tragedies of this march among the Cherokees.

The other four of the Five Civilized Tribes, the Choctaws, Creeks, Chickasaws, and Seminoles, shared the anguish and pathos of the Cherokees. Factionalism over removal threatened old bonds of respect and affection in all the tribes. All endured harassment and physical abuse from the states and citizens who coveted their lands. The Mississippi Choctaws acknowledged the futility of resistance early, and sullenly accepted the inevitable. Still, heavy casualties, primarily from cholera, thinned their ranks on the removal march. Creek Indians in Alabama and eastern Georgia, who resisted rapacious white settlers and federal troops, walked to Oklahoma in chains and shackles. For the Chickasaws of Mississippi, removal was less difficult than for other tribes. With a shorter distance to travel than the Cherokees or Creeks, this small tribe benefited from the experience of their kinsmen the Choctaws, who were already in Oklahoma. The Seminoles, the least modern of the tribes, did not reach Oklahoma until 1842.

The eviction of the Five Civilized Tribes from their homes in the Gulf and southern Appalachian regions was a tragedy exceeding the much-sung exile of the Acadians. A people of fixed habits and tastes, the southern Indians were not nomads like their Plains counterparts. Neither were they restless wanderers seeking a moving dream, like so many whites. They felt rooted in the land, with attachments to trees and watercourses, mists and skies that most whites either never understood or dismissed as mere "backwardness." The white settler accepted the unfamiliar, adapted readily to hostile circumstances, and was at best casually attached to any place. He did not understand or sympathize with the grief and desolation that engulfed the Indians so violently uprooted and sent to a strange environment. They were the stagnant past, in the frontiersman's imagination, and must now yield to the buoyant future he was so sure he represented. But the Indians, as Choctaw Chief Pushmataha pointed out, "had grown up as herbs of the woods, only to be broken off like a dead branch from an old tree." [5]

Those Indians who survived the rigors of the overland trek on short rations, or escaped the pestilence of passage in the packed and stinking steamboats still faced the ordeal of pioneer life in Oklahoma. The Choctaws originally shared title with the Creeks and Cherokees to most of present-day Oklahoma. The Panhandle was a no man's land, and the northeast corner belonged to the Quapaws and some Senecas. The lower third of Oklahoma, from the Red River north to the Canadian and Arkansas rivers, belonged to the Choctaws. The Creeks were in the middle, with their northern boundary beginning just west of the Arkansas River and extending to the one-hundredth meridian. The land east of the Arkansas and above the northern Creek boundary belonged to the Cherokees. The Creeks later were to share their territory with their kinsmen the Seminoles. And the Chickasaws were to join the Choctaws under one tribal government.

The political union of the Choctaws and Chickasaws was turbulent and short-lived. By mutual consent, in the mid-1850s, the Chickasaws established a separate nation in the western half of the Choctaw territory. At the same time, the Choctaws leased a large tract west of the ninety-eighth meridian to the federal government as a home for the Wichitas and other Plains Indians. The Seminoles, belligerent at having to acknowledge the supremacy of Creek law and angered at finding Creeks squatting on land promised to them, resisted absorption into the Creek Nation. The Creeks, with a repressive slave code modeled on that of the Deep South, accused the Seminoles of harboring runaways. Paralleling the action of the Choctaws, the Creeks finally relinquished western lands for an independent Seminole Nation. That total area, plus other lands in Nebraska and Kan-

5. Faubion Bower, "Oklahoma, OK!," *Holiday* 43 (May 1968): 121, 124.

sas, became known as Indian Territory. When white settlement advanced into Kansas and Nebraska, the term was applied to Oklahoma alone.

The Indians' first concerns, like those of all new settlers, were food and shelter. Most of the money received for improvements on homesteads abandoned in the East and South was gone. Forced to pay "back rents" on their confiscated properties to the southern states, most Indians arrived penniless in Oklahoma. When bureaucratic lethargy in Washington delayed the subsistence payments promised as help in the first year of resettlement, charlatans typical of the frontier environment descended on the Indians with inferior goods. Whites from Arkansas and Texas sold whiskey to the tribesmen, and when soldiers or tribal leaders drove them away, enterprising Indians assumed the task of distilling and selling liquor to their fellows.

Although some seventy thousand square miles were available for Indian settlement in Oklahoma, the Five Civilized Tribes clustered at first in the eastern portion of their new domain. The fierce Osages and Plains Indians, who regarded this land as hunting domain, had roamed there freely in pursuit of game and did not understand the concept of ceded or reserved lands. They continued to raid both Indian and white settlements. The Chickasaws, who settled west of the Choctaws, were terrified at the sudden appearance of these awesome and hostile bands. Most of the Chickasaws refused to venture into their own district and mingled with the Choctaws along the Blue and Boggy rivers. Although Fort Washita was established in 1842 as protection against the war parties, most of the Five Civilized Tribes stayed east of the Arbuckle Range. The remaining Civilized Tribes also feared the Plains Indians, and the Osage were especially bitter enemies of the Cherokees. Although the Seminoles were entitled to all lands west of the Creek Nation, none settled beyond the Cross Timbers. Removal thus established a whole new set of frictions and anxieties to replace the familiar conflicts with the southern states.

The physical beauty of the wooded land, as well as fear of the western Indians, caused the Five Civilized Tribes to settle thickly in the eastern half of their territory. The climate was temperate and humid, with a long growing season and short, mild winters. The terrain was also comforting to the refugees. The soils resembled those of their former homes, red and yellow-brown clay in the hills and black earth along rivers; but most important was the protective forest covering. The open areas of the west at first disturbed these Indians, who ventured onto them only occasionally to hunt. They preferred the security of the mixed forest-prairie lands of eastern Oklahoma.

The task of beginning life again in a raw, untamed country was difficult enough for people living in harmony and united in purpose. But partisan hostilities festering from preremoval controversies threatened to destroy the Creeks and Cherokees. In the new Creek Nation, factions avoided violence by continuing the historic tribal division. This distinction of Upper and Lower Creeks originally arose from disparities in the life-styles between conservative full-blood town dwellers and less traditional mixed-blood plantation owners. In Oklahoma, it also involved removal politics. The Lower or western Creeks had arrived in Indian Territory in the late 1820s. They were prosperous farmers before the conservative Upper Creeks left Alabama. Wishing to avoid conflict over land and politics, the leaders of the two factions agreed that their peoples should continue to live apart. Theirs was a moderate political union in which, initially, the two groups retained separate governments, each with a principal chief and council, with representatives of both factions meeting periodically in a national council.

Among the Cherokees, however, internal strife flared again after removal. A dispute of Byzantine complexity arose over which faction—Old Settlers allied with the Treaty Party, or the Ross group—would govern the new nation. An intratribal war erupted in June 1839, after the brutal murders of Major and John Ridge and Elias Boudinot. The brilliant leadership of the Treaty Party was emasculated, as only Stand Watie escaped. That vendetta degenerated into civil war until the federal government forced the exhausted partisans to negotiate a truce in 1846. Fundamental differences remained, but submerged. Yet in the fourteen years before the Civil War, the resilient Cherokees entered a Golden Age.

Between removal and the Civil War, the Five Civilized Tribes prospered. Each tribe owned lands in common under patented titles, and every citizen was protected in his occupancy. Under the system, mixed-bloods among the Choctaws, Chickasaws, and Cherokees laid out extensive plantations with slaves and built richly furnished mansions. Chief John Ross of the Cherokees owned a great white house at Park Hill near Tahlequah. Named Rose Cottage, it accommodated forty guests comfortably. In a style befitting any national chief executive, Ross enjoyed all the comforts of a successful country gentleman.

Captain Robert Jones, a wealthy Choctaw, owned six cotton plantations before the Civil War. The Lake West plantation consisted of some five thousand acres and employed nearly five hundred slaves. For a single shipment of cotton to Liverpool, England, in 1859, Jones earned $80,000 in gold—a huge sum of money at the time.

Steamboats of shallow draft plied the Arkansas and Red rivers, bringing farm implements, printing stock, china, linens, and calico, as well as staples in exchange for cotton, corn, pecans, and furs. Farmers in Indian Territory grew a variety of agricultural products and livestock to feed and provision local military garrisons and growing towns. Gold-miners from the southern states bought supplies as they crossed Oklahoma enroute to California. The Texas Road conveyed homesteaders and traders from the Old Northwest through Indian Territory on the journey to the Southwest. And twelve stations along the Butterfield Stage route in eastern Oklahoma brought mail and travelers on a regular basis.

Except for the Seminoles, the Civilized Tribes adopted written constitutions. These documents were a blend of Anglo-Saxon usage and Indian custom. Each showed reliance on the separation of powers. The Choctaw, Chickasaw, and Cherokee constitutions contained bills of rights. The short Creek document echoed the preamble of the United States Constitution, but retained much of the traditional tribal town organization reflecting the confederate nature of the tribe. All provided for manhood suffrage, had an amendment process, and recognized Negro slavery.

The tribes also had orderly school systems. Various missionary societies established schools in Indian Territory, but most Choctaws, Cherokees, and Chickasaws were educated in tribal schools. There were one-room schools for primary education and imposing brick boarding schools for higher learning for both men and women. The sons of wealthy mixed-bloods usually completed their education in the East. On the whole, the children of the Five Civilized Tribes were better educated and more concerned about learning than were their white counterparts on the frontier.

The missionary societies that had worked among the Indians before removal continued their ministries in Oklahoma. Congregational missionary Samuel Austin Worcester, imprisoned in Georgia for his work among the Cherokees, joined the tribe in the West in 1835. He brought a printing press, one of the few items salvaged when a steamer carrying his personal effects and supplies sank in the Arkansas River. His print shop at Park Hill Mission near Tahlequah resumed the Cherokee publications that removal had interrupted. In addition to a bilingual newspaper, *The Cherokee Advocate,* he published religious tracts and an annual *Cherokee Almanac.* In his spare time, Worcester, a classical scholar, supervised translation of most of the Bible into Cherokee and printed materials for other tribes. The Park Hill press published more than eleven million pages of material for the Choctaw Nation alone.

During the early years in Oklahoma, profound social changes occurred in each of the Five Civilized Tribes. For many years before removal, the hunter and warrior had been yielding to the farmer and mechanic. Forced expatriation hastened the process. As a later observer noted: ''Torn from their native streams and mountains, their council fires extinguished and their townhouses burned behind them, and transported bodily to a far distant country where everything was new and strange, they were obliged perforce to forego the old life and adjust themselves to changed surroundings.'' [6]

The shock was not easy, and many did not desire new opportunities. Those unwilling to imitate the white man's ways simply settled in remote areas. They cultivated small patches of corn or squash, taking the rest of their food from the forests and

6. Mooney, *Myths of the Cherokee,* pt. 1, p. 146.

streams. They avoided settled areas except to trade furs for powder or shot. They desired and received few possessions and no new habits. Speaking only their native tongues, they wore traditional dress and secretly bowed to the nature gods of the fathers. Such full blood communities prospered among all the tribes, but were strongest among the Creeks and Seminoles.

The ambitious mixed-bloods in every tribe saw removal as a chance for survival, then a fresh start, then success modeled on the white man's "progressive" ways. In some, that reflected candid ambition. In others, it bespoke homage to the reality of changing times and new orders of civilization. In Oklahoma, they settled the fertile river valleys and purchased slaves to work farms or plantations. They first adopted the dress of white frontiersmen, then that of the southern planter and small-town merchant. They comprehended the white man's law, language, and attitudes.

And yet, in many respects, they remained Indian. Their attitude toward land, their concepts of punishment, their belief in shared obligation for their fellow tribesmen was decidedly Indian. For that reason, tribal society rarely split into full-blood-traditional versus mixed-blood-progressive factions. Each seemed to understand and honor the other almost until the time that the white man began to force allotment and distribution of the shared tribal estates.

In the 1840s and 1850s, it seemed that the experiment of a separate Indian country might succeed. Tiny bands of Indians driven from the old Northwest trickled into western Indian Territory, but there was plenty of room. Few seemed aware that these refugees were harbingers of an ominous future. In spite of earlier experiences and growing cognizance of encroaching white settlement in Nebraska and Kansas, the Five Civilized Tribes believed that, as a unit, they could withstand any onslaught. Yet, while they grew and prospered in their sheltered island, believing that treaty guarantees and their impressive achievements were adequate defenses against greed, white settlement moved relentlessly toward the Pacific.

The Civil War was the first great interruption of Indian Territory's growth—a blow from which tribal government never completely recovered. Despite long and bitter debate over the extension of slavery into the territories before Lincoln's election in 1860, the question of slavery was not decisive in the Five Tribes' decision to ally with the Confederacy. Although some tribal leaders struggled to maintain neutrality in 1860 and 1861, the geographic location of the Indian Nations and their citizens' southern heritage and dislike of the national government tipped the balance toward the southern cause.

On the eve of war, Indian Territory felt the passions that tore the nation apart. On the southern border, Texas was strongly proslavery. Arkansas, on the eastern flank, was secessionist, and a divided Missouri pressed the northeastern corner. To the north, bloody violence convulsed the ardently Unionist new state of Kansas. And the lonely, unsettled, western and north-western reaches of Indian Territory seemed a vacuum waiting for disorder.

Events seemed to reinforce the Indians' fear that the United States had abandoned them. Early in the war, federal troops had withdrawn from Indian Territory into Kansas. Annuities that supported the tribal governments and schools were stopped, lest those funds fall into Confederate hands. Without a federal presence, it was impossible for the Tribes to oppose Confederate propaganda and pressure. And most Indian agents, holdovers from the Buchanan administration, were secessionists who tried to influence the tribes toward the South. When the Lincoln administration named new appointees, they remained in Kansas, out of touch with the Indians. And although there were abolitionists among the missionaries in Indian Territory, religious denominations had not escaped the sectional cleavages that divided governments and families.

Soon emissaries from the Confederacy swarmed over Indian Territory. They sought Indian allegiance for propaganda value, but they also wanted the territory for its strategic location and raw materials. These spokesmen reminded Indians of their southern heritage, while gently ignoring its adverse results. The area's slave economy and river transportation oriented toward the Gulf ports were also important. With remarkable ingenuity, these agents summoned up painful memories of the national government's perfidies without alluding to the crimes of Georgia, Alabama, or Mississippi. They played on the tribes' disgust with government laxity in making annuity payments and on the Indians' anxieties about invasions. Posing as an Indian protector, the Confederate commissioner Albert Pike negotiated treaties allying the Five Civilized Tribes to the Confederacy, while guaranteeing each tribe perpetual title to its domains. His report to Confederate President Jefferson Davis, however, made it clear that the rich Indian Territory would be "opened to settlement and made into a state." [7] In allying with the Confederacy, the Five Civilized Tribes traded one set of predators for another. Whatever their differences of ideology, southerners and northerners remained white.

The decision to fight with the Confederacy provoked as much dissension among the Five Tribes as the removal question had, a generation earlier. Only the Choctaws responded unanimously to the Confederate call. Wedged in the corner between Texas and Arkansas, they were the most southern in outlook. The Chickasaws had a strong pro-Union minority, while their government remained staunchly prosouthern. The three northern tribes fought civil wars of their own, often reactivating old quarrels from removal days.

Whatever the sense of ardor or inevitability that took the Indian nations into the conflict, the war brought results as unexpected and as terrible to Indian Territory as to South Carolina or Georgia. At the conflict's end, Indian Territory was "a vast scene of desolation where only chimney monuments are left to mark the sites of once happy homes." [8] Confederate and Union forces raided and sacked alternately; guerrilla bands plundered the charred remains. The three northern tribes lost almost one-fourth of their people. And nineteen thousand Indians were homeless, crowded into refugee camps at Fort Gibson, in Kansas, or scattered through the Choctaw and Chickasaw nations. Returning to weed-infested fields and ravaged orchards, many Indians found wolves and panthers where hogs and cattle had grazed. Some were left with a single hoe as the only farm tool for a whole settlement.

7. Angie Debo, *A History of the Indians of the United States* (Norman: University of Oklahoma Press, 1970), p. 171.

8. Edward Everett Dale and Morris L. Wardell, *History of Oklahoma* (New York: Prentice-Hall, 1948), p. 176.

The Civil War, like the War of 1812, marked another shift in federal policy toward the Five Civilized Tribes. Just as Indian alliances with Great Britain furnished a rationale for annulling earlier agreements, the Tribes' association with the Confederacy provided new reasons for abrogating treaties. Although there was much talk of opening all of Indian Territory to white settlement after the war, Congress resisted such an extreme proposal. It chose a simpler plan of concentration, the work of Kansas's two senators, James Lane and Samuel Pomeroy. The proposal reflected that state's vindictiveness toward the Tribes' southern favoritism. It authorized the president to cancel all treaties with the Five Tribes, who would then cede portions of their domain for Indians expelled from Kansas.

The new treaties imposed in 1866 varied according to the negotiating skills and strength of the tribes. As reparations, the government obtained land cessions and permission for railroads to cross Indian Territory. Each nation—except the Cherokees, who temporarily retained the long strip of land called the Cherokee Outlet—ceded western lands for the settlement of other tribes. Tribal annuities then resumed, and the Indians were paid for forfeited lands. Slavery was abolished, and freedmen were guaranteed property rights and certain aspects of citizenship among all but the Chickasaws. In the end, the Civil War proved more disastrous to the Five Civilized Tribes than to the Confederacy—for, despite the devastation and plunder of war, the southern states lost no land.

There was also an elaborate proposal for an intertribal council to meet annually to work toward a single government and, eventually, to an Indian State. During the deliberations over the joint Choctaw-Chickasaw Reconstruction Treaty, Choctaw delegate Allen Wright suggested that the chief executive of the proposed commonwealth be called "Governor of the Red People." In Choctaw, *Red People* was *Okla Homa*. No Indian commonwealth was ever formed, but an Indian chose the name of a new state half a century before it came into the Union.

As punitive as these treaties seemed, they did little immediate violence to the actual settlements of the Five Civilized Tribes. In some instances, the government's token payments for land cessions helped replenish depleted treasuries and hastened postwar recovery. But in acknowledging that the occupied lands of the Five Tribes were clearly east of the new national limits, the treaties made it apparent that dissolution of the Indian Republics was only a matter of time. Even more clearly than the land losses, the railroad provisions foreshadowed the inevitable penetration of white culture.

From the end of the Civil War to the early 1880s, the United States continued to remove eastern tribes from lands attractive to white settlers and subdued the turbulent Plains Indians. Scores of diverse native peoples found new homes in Oklahoma, whether as refugee, exile, or settler hoping for new beginnings. Many were once as powerful and important in their woodland, plains, and plateau regions as the Five Tribes had been in their southern domain. Most of these Indians, gathered from places as divergent as New York and Montana, were never truly at home in Indian Territory. The more sedentary bands— Delawares, Sac and Fox, Potawatomies, Shawnees, Peorias, Kaws, Otos, and others—resumed farming and herding livestock. But the nomadic hunters of the central and southern plains resisted confinement to reservations and rejected agriculture as a way of life. For these people, the government's removal and resettlement policies were especially inappropriate. In western Oklahoma, agents following the dictates of federal Indian policy attempted to stamp out all remnants of nomadic tribal culture with such ill-advised laws as those prohibiting tribesmen from herding and butchering rationed cattle in the old ways they had followed with the buffalo. The fear that the Kiowa Chief Satanta expressed, "when we settle down, we grow pale and die," was indeed prophetic.[9]

The Kiowas, Comanches, Cheyennes, and Arapahoes were especially troublesome to the white man. Forts Sill, Reno, and Supply were established in western Indian Territory to control these fierce raiders, but their resistance was not broken until the mid-1870s. Confinement and subjugation robbed them of both a food supply and a cultural sense. Their identity rested on motion, a life with no enclosures; the prairie was a habitat without

9. Arrell M. Gibson, *Oklahoma: A History of Five Centuries* (Norman: Harlow Publishing Co., 1965), p. 239.

walls. That way of life clashed dramatically with the sedentary ideals of the homesteader and rancher, who came in ever greater numbers. Within a few years, when the buffalo herds were annihilated, the source of their whole life—food, utensils, lodging, bedding, even religion—disappeared. Despair overtook them as they searched for deeper explanations than the white man's apparent greed and vengefulness. They reasoned that some offended spirit had trapped the buffalo underground, and they conducted elaborate rituals to coax back the great beasts. But the buffalo, like much of the Plains Indians' way of life, was simply another victim of encroaching white civilization.

In eastern Oklahoma, the Five Civilized Tribes recovered quickly from the war's ravages. In 1867, Saladin Watie, helping in his tribe's reconstruction, personalized the recuperative powers of his people when he wrote to a friend, "and better than all mama has grown to be stout and healthy. She steps about like some sixteen year old girl." [10] People rebuilt homes, planted gardens, fields, and orchards, and tended new herds. As usual, nature recovered quickly from man's catastrophes. Schools reopened with expanded curriculums, often offering classical languages, music, and mathematics, with teachers imported from the East. Printing presses clattered again, producing a variety of books and newspapers.

Although the loss of slave property and land titles impoverished the white aristocracy of the Old South, emancipation did not have the same effects on the upper classes in the Five Tribes. The system of common ownership of land insured every Indian citizen the ability to claim and utilize land as long as he did not infringe upon the rights of others. Each tribe still owned more land than its people cultivated. And the ambitious tribesmen worked their holdings now with hired hands instead of slaves. Most of these white tenants were Civil War veterans unable to find homesteads. The Five Tribes had always allowed certain kinds of noncitizens, such as skilled artisans, to reside within their domains, but permission to immigrate and settle was carefully guarded. After the war, demands for farm labor increased dramatically, and the number of permits issued to

10. Debo, *History of the Indians of the United States,* p. 183.

white tenants increased. These permits did not involve leasing lands to whites, which tribal constitutions prohibited, but were merely labor contracts between the parties. But many whites established footholds in Indian Territory, hoping to settle there permanently. With abundant labor and land, the Indian aristocrats soon dominated economic as well as political and social life in the Territory.

Except among the traditional full-blood communities, where people were content to practice subsistence agriculture and the old religion, Indian Territory was eager to become "modern" and "civilized." Postwar events increased the attraction of the white man's goals. As a contemporary observer noted: "Instead of ceremonials and peace councils we hear now of railroad deals and contracts with cattle syndicates." [11]

The coming of railroads accelerated the process of modernization. The first line in Oklahoma, the Missouri-Kansas-Texas system—the "Katy"—followed the old Texas Trail and had crossed the Five Civilized Tribes' land into the Lone Star State by 1872. The lines made a more sophisticated and complex economy possible and opened the Territory to a new kind of communication with the rest of the world. Unlike the erratic rivers, the railroads provided stable year-round transportation so necessary to planning and growth.

Within a few years, tracks crisscrossed the area. A lumbering industry developed in Indian Territory's southeastern forests to supply railroad construction needs and to build the towns that followed in the steam engine's wake. The railroads also opened new markets for the Tribes' products. Adequate transportation made it profitable to work the glistening black coal seams in the Choctaw Nation and to recover the lead and zinc in the northeast corner near the Missouri border. For a brief time, the rails distributed the products of a flourishing Cherokee tobacco industry into Arkansas, Missouri, and Texas. And the telegraph and telephone also linked Indian Territory to the white world.

Economic growth followed the railroads, but so did lawlessness and disorder. The Five Civilized Tribes had effective

11. Mooney, *Myths of the Cherokee*, pt. 1, pp. 147–148.

governments and courts before 1860, but the postwar problems facing freedmen and Indians created near chaos. Before the federal government resumed tribal annuities, Indian governments lacked the funds to maintain adequate law enforcement. And federal troops in the area were preoccupied with policing the western frontier. The atmosphere attracted renegades and desperadoes. Railroad construction, mining, and lumbering also brought in a turbulent work force. Drifters, gamblers, and prostitutes mingled with law-abiding townspeople. Cowboys, whom tenacious settlers forced from the dwindling range, and squatters on tribal lands were added problems. The tribal courts had no jurisdiction over the whites who crowded onto their lands. And many of them claimed Indian citizenship to avoid the jurisdiction of Judge Isaac Parker's federal district court at Fort Smith. Parker's district, which encompassed an area the size of New England, was too large for effective law enforcement. And the national government contributed to the chaos by pursuing a double standard regarding whites encroaching on Indian lands: the government did not hesitate to force Indians to cede land to railroads, but it ignored tribal demands to evict white squatters.

The presence of some whites in Indian Territory as agricultural tenants, as cattlemen in the Cherokee Outlet, as traders, or as workers on the railroads and in the mines and forests encouraged many others to drift in. After the 1880s, federal officials abandoned efforts to keep whites out, and many Indians suspected that they secretly encouraged white settlement. As the surrounding states' free lands filled up, frontiersmen looked toward Indian Territory as another last chance. The Indian populations were small and their land holdings enormous: surely they had no right to the land when whites could do so much more with it! Homesteaders barred from Indian Territory were incensed because cattlemen leased grazing land from the Indians at very low rates. And whites living among the Five Tribes, denied access to Indian schools and the right to own land or exercise political rights, joined the nesters and the railroad promoters in calling for the opening of all Indian lands to white settlers.

In 1889, the government finally permitted white settlement in the "Unassigned Lands." The decision temporarily relieved pressures on lands belonging to the Five Tribes. For the next few years, the Dawes Commission was busy determining allotments to the western tribes. And in successive land runs, whites staked out claims on former western reservations.

Tribe after tribe acceded to the inevitable as the century closed. According to the original terms of the Dawes Act, all allottees would become citizens of the United States and thus citizens of the newly organized Territory of Oklahoma as the ancestral Indian communities were liquidated. Only the Osage escaped the provisions of the act, which divided mineral as well as surface land rights individually. They managed to retain tribal ownership of minerals, and when each citizen received his allotted acreage, there was no surplus for white settlers. The terms of the Osage agreement took on great importance after the lucrative Burbank oil strike of 1920 occurred in their former reservation.

The sanctuary of the Five Civilized Tribes, all that remained of the old Indian Territory, was now a shrunken relic. Talk of eventual statehood dominated politics in the so-called Twin Territories. But Congress was preparing to extinguish the Indian treaties. A series of federal statutes in the 1890s systematically reduced the powers of Indian courts and councils. The Curtis Act of 1898 finally authorized allotment of the Five Civilized Tribes' lands, division of their properties, and the end of their government.

By 1900, most tribal leaders suspected that resisting allotment was as futile as opposing removal. But they bid for a separate Indian state to be called Sequoyah. When Congress rejected the eloquent Sequoyah Constitution in favor of combined statehood, Indian leaders simply entered the new society and system, determined to exercise their old powers in new names.

Both conservative mixed-bloods and traditional full-bloods, however, resisted allotment with a dignity that highlighted their tragic heritage. For them, the dissolution of the tribe was the end of everything. To divide the common land was as brutal as murdering one's mother. Chitto Harjo, the full-blood Creek leader of a resistance movement known as the Crazy Snake Rebellion, pleaded with a congressional committee in 1906:

"All that I am begging of you, honorable Senators, is that these ancient agreements and treaties . . . be fulfilled." [12]

As allotment proceeded remorselessly, the full-bloods withdrew to the forests. They hid from enrollment parties, refused to select acreages, and rejected any certificates and payments awarded them. As late as 1915, poverty-stricken Creek and Cherokee full-bloods refused allotments and proudly returned checks for their portion of per capita payments from the division of tribal funds. These protests were the Indians' only way of trying to retain a homeland and a way of life falsely promised them "as long as the sun rise and go down . . . as long as grass grew . . . as long as the water runs." [13]

The general attitude of both the federal government and whites toward the Oklahoma Indians was a mixture of idealism and pragmatism that dated from the nation's first encounters with the continent's indigenous population. Whites desired alternately to "civilize" Indians into their system and isolate or eradicate them if they resisted. Indians also alternated between accepting and rejecting the white man's "progressive" ways. In the end, as the entire nation became a self-conscious economic unity, the Indian civilizations seemed anachronistic. And given the white man's expansive ideals and expectations, not even the vast American wilderness afforded refuges for a people oriented toward the past.

Yet, despite all the sorrows and emotion-laden events in the Indian's history in Oklahoma, he gave the new state a unique heritage. Many of his attitudes persisted amid the burgeoning white civilization. His image and customs were more than quaint, as much a heritage of America's frontier civilization as those of the whites who displaced him.

12. Debo, *History of the Indians of the United States,* p. 310.
13. Debo, *History of the Indians of the United States,* p. 313.

3

White Settlement

$\mathcal{T}$HE era of Indian settlement lasted from the 1820s to the 1880s. White settlement, which technically began in 1889 with the first run into "Old Oklahoma," ended in 1906 with the auction of land in the Big Pasture. In that span of sixty years, from 1820 to 1880, Indian Territory existed behind the dike of a different culture, with the tide of white settlement constantly surging against it. The barrier eroded slowly, then finally collapsed.

Although white settlers were forbidden to live in Indian Territory, except with permits from the resident tribes, thousands of illegal intruders streamed into the domains of the Five Civilized Tribes after the Civil War. In the northern and far western parts of Indian Territory, Plains Indians, the open prairie, and cold winters all combined to discourage squatters. And the federal troops garrisoned to keep the peace among the reservation Indians evicted adventurers who tried to establish footholds. By 1883, there were fewer than fifteen thousand Indians living west of the Five Civilized Tribes in an area only slightly smaller than the state of Ohio. The Plains tribes were not large, and they usually lived in settlements along streams. They did not farm extensively or pasture large herds. Though they often roamed widely, these Indians did not in fact occupy much land area. Western Indian Territory remained a great hunting preserve and pastureland. The tall, thick grasses that covered the prairies and nourished the great buffalo herds before the Civil War became the foundation for the range-cattle industry of the 1870s and

1880s. Oklahoma, the Indian's final refuge, shortly became the ranchman's last frontier—a frontier fraught with both profit and legend.

The great Texas landholders returning from the war after 1865 found their state almost untouched. Their herds of cattle had multiplied, but local market prices for beef were low. Without a railroad to transport the animals to eastern markets, the ranchers faced financial ruin. Their response to such a risky but potentially profitable situation was typically Texan. They drove the cattle to northern railheads in great herds, following the Old Texas Road through the Five Civilized Tribes into Kansas, and it was a near disaster. In addition to the predictable dangers of bad weather and unknown terrain, there were other, human problems. Guerrilla bands left over from the war era demanded payment to help reassemble herds they had deliberately spooked. The Indians demanded cattle in payment for the grass consumed, or as a toll for crossing their lands. Settlers at the Kansas and Missouri borders feared that the Texas cattle carried diseases that threatened local stock. They tried to quarantine the offending herds, and when that failed, they attacked drovers and cattle alike to turn them south again. Only a small portion of the 260,000 cattle driven north in 1866 were sold at the railhead market in Sedalia, Missouri.

Despite these adversities and risks, the first cattle drives convinced ranchers that the enterprise would prosper under better conditions. Joseph McCoy, an Illinois stock-raiser, solved the problem of a hospitable market for Texas cattle when he constructed stock-holding pens and accommodations for cowboys at Abilene, Kansas. Located on the Kansas-Pacific Railroad, the town was well to the west of advancing homesteaders. It became the first of a series of legendary cowtowns—Newton, Ellsworth, Wichita, Caldwell, and Dodge City. Each became a fabled capital of the western empire of grass and longhorns that gave the entire region a distinctive flavor in the history books.

As the number of herds moving north increased each year, Indian Territory became the grassy highway connecting the Texas ranches to the stock-shipping yards in Kansas. Eventually, four major cattle routes developed, with the Chisholm Trail and the Great Western route carrying most of the traffic through western

Indian Territory. As the cattle crossed the prairies, enterprising drovers paused to let their stock drink and graze. Soon a tangled network of irregular leasing arrangements developed between the cattlemen and the Indians.

As homesteaders displaced stock-growers on the northern Great Plains, cattlemen in ever greater numbers swarmed into western Indian Territory. The competition among rival ranchers for grazing privileges was so keen that their intrigues with Indian leaders and government officials resembled those "of various European nations to gain or widen a sphere of influence among the savage peoples of Africa." [1] By the 1880s, large-scale ranching was established throughout western Indian Territory, with the most extensive enterprise located in the six million acres of grass in the Cherokee Outlet. The Cherokee Nation collected grazing fees, first from individual ranchers, and later from the Cherokee Strip Livestock Association. That group of stockmen and ranching corporations organized to gain exclusive use of the Outlet and to protect their cattle from rustlers.

Most ranchers and cowboys lived for the moment, dreamed of future profits, and thought this bonanza would last forever. One cattleman summed up the optimistic feeling: "This ain't no country fer little two-by-four farmers. . . . The big thing about the plains is that you don't have to feed stock. It can rustle for itself [and] the dollars crawl into yer jeans." [2] Most cattlemen did not believe the farther plains suited to agriculture and did not worry about encroaching farm populations around the territory. Nor did they really fear trouble from the federal government. Since the cattlemen said they had no interest in the Indians' land, but only in grazing and water rights, they believed their presence no threat to the tribes.

The lifespan of this Grass Empire was brief; yet it left indelible marks on Oklahoma's and the nation's history. Bridging the disappearance of the nomadic Plains Indian civilizations and the coming of modern white culture, these years were the middle ages of the frontier. A curious feudalism sprang up, strongly

---

1. Edward Everett Dale, "The Ranchman's Last Frontier," *Mississippi Valley Historical Review* 10 (June 1923): 42.

2. Ketchum, *Will Rogers: His Life and Times,* p. 30.

reminiscent of the feudal order of medieval Europe. Wealthy ranchers became "cattle barons" in the penny press and local politics. Rodeos and roping contests replaced jousts and tournaments of old. Brands were the frontier's heraldry. And cowboys arrayed in their colorful costumes, including high-heeled boots, broad hats, jingling spurs, and special trousers, were as splendid as Lancelot or Gawain.

Even the power and influence of the major livestock associations, who virtually governed in regions remote from the usual protections of laws and courts, paralleled the orders of chivalry. Despite these feudal trappings, the cattle empires were modern. Founded for economic rather than political reasons, they typified impersonality and bigness to the farmers who came later. Their success and scope paved the way for criticism of Big Business that seemed to threaten pioneer ideals of individualism and competition.

These associations also focused tensions between homesteaders and cattlemen, though that conflict was as old as the nation. Farmers in search of new or more fertile lands always pushed aside Indians and husbandmen when migrating across the continent. Before 1860, stock raising was a comparatively small enterprise, operating on the fringes of agricultural settlement. Hostile Indians to the west and poor transportation to the east confined it. In the two decades after Appomattox, as the Plains Indians were subdued and the railroad network burgeoned, stock-raising became a major regional industry in the West. The thinly settled area from the Dakotas to Texas was "Cow Country."

But as settlers ventured onto the plains, the fundamental antagonisms between farmer and cowman were starkly revealed. The nester-cattleman conflict had deeper roots than economics, and concerned psychology, life-style, and attitudes about the future. Life on the open range produced a rough, masculine society where men shunned fixed abodes. Campfire hospitality was boundless and money earned with difficulty during long stretches of isolation and hard work was spent quickly and joyously.

The sober, industrious farmer, with his heavy shoes, drab clothes, and dull routine looked uninteresting to the cowboy.

Only a man of small ideas, in his view, would be content with a mere 160 acres, a mule or plowhorse, and the endless chores of farming. The homesteader lacked the aura of action and risk that mythology accorded the cowboy. But to the nester, the cowboy was a vulgar, hard-drinking, improvident vagabond who let his herds trample crops, and had designs on farmers' daughters.

In this opposite view, the cowboy was a relic of America's adolescence. And the rancher who employed these men represented a last effort to perpetuate instability and get-rich-quick schemes at the expense of the sober, provident settler whose labor would have far more beneficial long-term effects. And yet, ironically, the rancher and his employee paid with dollars represented the future. The family farmer living on a combination of his own capital and his own labor was at odds with the coming economy of the factory and the impersonal hired laborer paid by the hour.

By the time this old struggle centered on Oklahoma, the seemingly endless frontier was almost gone. The Indian could move no farther; there was no great pasture left where ranchers could escape with their herds. Without new land, collision between the conflicting life-styles of the sedentary homesteader and the wide-ranging cattleman was inevitable. The inhabitants of Indian Territory rapidly became pawns in a struggle where greed or "progress" made treaty rights and sacred oaths mere technicalities.

The homesteaders eventually overpowered the cattlemen numerically and politically. Yet, in spite of their brief dominance, the cattlemen had great influence in Oklahoma. Just as the early wagon roads through Indian Territory became the route of the east-west railways, the north-south arteries followed the broad outlines of cattle trails. Ironically, the cattlemen who thought they had found a haven in Indian Territory were the unwitting advance agents of agrarian settlement. As explorers they made the area known, proved it could support life, and, in singing its praises, hastened their own demise.

While the cattlemen acted as if they were paying guests in Indian Territory in the 1880s, farmers along the Kansas border began noticing telltale signs of permanence. Rival ranchers stretched miles of barbed wire through the Cherokee Outlet to separate herds, and tribal officials acquiesced, since the fencing facilitated collection of grazing fees. Bunkhouses for cowboys, line camps, and corrals for sorting and branding stock dotted the landscape. Land-hungry farmers sanctimoniously protested that wealthy cattlemen profited from Indian Territory while men with homeless families were cruelly excluded. Many of these early "Boomers," professional promoters who advertised the merits of the country, were veterans of the earlier Black Hills invasion. They were sometimes allied with interests promoting railroads and town development. The Boomers became adept at manufacturing public opinion from the sacred images of the American dream, free land, the toiling farmer, hearth and home. That the native residents held similar values was of no consequence to prospective settlers.

In 1879, attorney Elias C. Boudinot, a mixed-blood descendant of the Cherokee Treaty Party leadership who represented various railroad interests, wrote an article in the *Chicago Times* arguing that some fourteen million acres in Indian Territory belonged in the public domain and were open to qualified homesteaders. Boomer propaganda quickly centered on a tract of nearly two million acres in the heart of Indian Territory, known as the "Unassigned Lands" or "Old Oklahoma." After the Civil War the Creeks and Seminoles had ceded these lands so that other tribes might settle there, but none did so.

Reams of literature advertising the bounties of this area flooded the surrounding states. A typical tract proclaimed: "Oklahoma! Well watered, well timbered, rich in soil, a most enchanting clime, may in the near future be your home." Another broadside envisioned a wine-producing area "not excelled by California . . . where the next generation will see the Canadian and Red River country as the Rhine of America." [3] Boomer propaganda mentioned no hardships. The new lands, whatever their origin or present status, thus appealed mightily to envious neighbors afflicted with chinch bugs and dashed hopes and contending grimly with drought, thin soil, and unpredictable rain.

---

3. A. P. Jackson and E. C. Cole, *Oklahoma! Politically and Topographically Described, History and Guide to Indian Territory* (Kansas City, Mo.: Ramsey, Millett and Hudson, 1885), pp. 150, 71.

During the 1880s, hundreds of pioneer families who had failed elsewhere flocked to the Kansas border, eager to start over again in Oklahoma. Local merchants had visions of mounting retail sales and spiraling real estate values. They made an incongruous alliance with railroad promoters, adventurers, and poor farmers, all clamoring for Congress to remove the barriers to settlement in Indian Territory.

Many were unwilling to wait for official sanction to homestead. Under the charismatic leadership of Captain David L. Payne, they invaded the forbidden area. Time after time, federal troops rebuffed Payne's efforts, uprooted the stakes marking townsites and farm boundaries, and escorted the colonists to the Kansas border. Judge Isaac Parker consistently ruled in favor of the Indians and imposed the stipulated fines when offenders came before his court at Fort Smith. But collecting a thousand dollars from such people was impossible, and reprimands were ineffectual. Having little to lose, the Boomers returned again and again, like drops of water wearing away rock.

The same conditions that made it easy for Payne and his followers to enter western Indian Territory were paralleled in the Five Republics to the east. The permit system, which authorized whites to enter as artisans, skilled professionals, and tenant laborers, was so widely abused that thousands of whites drifted in. And the Five Tribes' governments alleged that intruders were rarely removed. Yet, according to Union Agent John Tufts, the white intruders who were apprehended and taken across the border "took one or two breaths of state air and returned." [4] The inability of the courts to stop Boomers and Congress's unwillingness to strengthen the law created the impression that these people were acting rightfully. More and more law-abiding citizens consequently joined the extralegal efforts to settle Indian Territory by force.

Payne died in 1884, but his lieutenants continued the invasions another year. Then attention focused on Washington. The east coast metropolitan press joined the Boomer groups extolling the poor man, the common laborer trying to make a new

4. U.S., Congress, House, *Executive Documents*, 48th Cong., 2d sess., 1884, XII, H. doc. 2287, pp. 142, 143.

life in Oklahoma. Despite tireless efforts of delegations from the Five Tribes, missionary societies and other friends, the Indian cause was doomed. In 1889, Congress yielded. The United States government paid the Creeks and Seminoles for clear titles to the "Unassigned Lands," and President Benjamin Harrison proclaimed April 22 as the day the lands would open to settlement. Failing in their repeated invasions of Indian Territory, Boomers finally triumphed in the halls of Congress when their political strength gradually became a majority.

The earlier settlement of United States territory followed a pattern. A slow, steady infiltration of people drifted west, pushing native inhabitants and pioneer stock-growers to less desirable lands. But in Oklahoma the entire process was telescoped. Since the tribes in western Indian Territory were small, scattered, and poorly organized, the barriers to white settlement toppled there first. The fiction of a permanent Indian commonwealth was abandoned as, one by one, the western tribes were forced to take allotments of land in severalty and to sell the surplus to the government for homesteading. All the land the Five Civilized Tribes had ceded at the end of the Civil War as a refuge for other Indians soon became homes for white settlers.

Contemporary historian Edward Everett Dale employed a striking image to summarize this unusual process. The settling of other states resembled "the slow leaking of water into the hold of an old type [of] ship; [but] that of Oklahoma was like the sudden bursting of water into a modern vessel divided into many watertight compartments. The first rush filled one compartment, then the others were filled, one by one." For the Five Civilized Tribes, it was only a matter of time "until at last the interior walls gave way and the entire vessel was full." [5]

During the short time between Congress's decision to allow settlement on the Unassigned Lands and the formal opening, there was frantic activity as thousands prepared for "Harrison's Hoss Race." Government surveyors divided the two million acres into quarter-sections for homesteads and reserved larger tracts for townsites. Two federal land offices were hastily con-

5. Edward Everett Dale, "The Spirit of Sooner Land," *Chronicles of Oklahoma* 1 (June 1923): 173.

structed so that successful homesteaders could file entry claims at either Guthrie Station, where the Santa Fe Railroad crossed the Cimarron, or at the Kingfisher stage stop thirty miles west of Guthrie.

Preparations for the great race were frenzied. Men and boys whittled sharp-pointed sticks with the family's initials on the side to stake the precious claim. Women and girls stitched tents of canvas bits or of colorful quilts for shelter, and to give the appearance of an "improved" claim. And pioneer grand-mothers, veterans of other promising frontiers, prepared food to sustain the family until the first crop, doubtless wondering where they would go next if the new start in Oklahoma failed.

Frontier businessmen were as harried as prospective home-steaders. Contractors checked mounds of lumber and prefabri-cated buildings with which they planned to erect towns over-night. Merchants vied for freight space to ship the staples and luxuries that would bring rich profits in the new towns. Cabinet-makers also busily hammered together rough coffins of green wood—a grim necessity in any frontier settlement.

For weeks before the opening, people trained their swiftest, most surefooted ponies to endure the hard run. Some riders practiced taking spills, timing the seconds needed to remount. Others put their faith in modern technology and planned to ride bicycles. Those who made the run in wagons scrutinized axles, greased wheel hubs until they spun noiselessly, and devised ingenious ways to lighten loads and reduce wind friction. The race for Oklahoma land was to the swift, strong, and ingenious.

Three days before the opening, homeseekers were allowed to gather on the perimeters of the promised land, so that theoreti-cally each man would have an equal chance to stake a claim. Everyone was warned that any settlers who entered before noon of the opening day would be barred from holding a claim. Blue-coated soldiers were stationed at intervals along the boundary to guard against intruders and to keep the peace.

The majority of people in the run of 1889 came from the north through Kansas. Crossing the ranches in the Cherokee Strip or following the Chisholm Trail, they fanned out along the northern and western edges of the Unassigned Lands. Fewer came up from Texas. Because of the dangers in crossing the Canadian River during flood season, many homeseekers came from the south in railroad cars. The Santa Fe ran trains from both directions, holding their speed to that of a rider on horseback, as the rules prescribed.

April 22, 1889, was a brilliant, sunny day. Spring rains had turned the prairies green and brought out a myriad of wildflowers. A buoyant sense of optimism among the waiting crowds complemented the weather. Everyone seemed eager for the El Dorado that lay ahead. It did not matter that many of the land seekers would not succeed. No one consciously considered the possibility of failure.

Every aspect and aspiration of American society was represented in the first run. The typical frontier family consisted of a big-boned, shaggy father with a determined wife and several small children. Their prairie schooner bulged with chickens, farm implements, furniture and mattresses, and the ubiquitous family dog. A worn leather trunk or box might hold mementos of other and perhaps happier days, a few worn books, some fragile china, or a bit of wedding lace.

Next to such a family might be a span of prancing bays with a fine carriage, all shiny wheels and polished brass, in the hands of a more dapper pioneer. One man rode an ox. A girl in a billowing pink dress sat astride a spirited thoroughbred. But four circus midgets riding a single horse toward destiny surely provoked the most comment.

The European press as well as the great American dailies reported this novel event in some detail. The land run seemed to explain American character through a set of condensed images and larger-than-life events. The correspondent for *Le Figaro* was fascinated with American idiosyncrasies. ''In all the picturesque things that have come out of America nothing is more striking than the statement that 'there will be fights especially in those localities which appear suitable for the location of towns.' Here we seem to have returned to the heroic age!'' He also noted the American fondness for litigation. ''In each group of immigrants one will find at least two lawyers who are entrusted with the task of defending all claims to land regardless of the means by which the land was obtained.'' With wry Gallic humor, he concluded by anticipating ''the sudden appearance of a civilization. . . . In one rapid move modern culture will be brought to this wilderness." [6]

The reporter for *Le Temps* was a less sanguine but more profound observer of the run's meaning. "All these sturdy adventurers with their brawny arms, rude and simple manners, after a century or more, by a sort of providential irony, are still, wherever they go, the pioneers of that complicated and penny-pinching civilization and legality which they are attempting to escape by constantly moving farther and farther west." [7] There was a sense of finality about this day because, after Oklahoma, there was no place for most of them to go, except back.

As twelve o'clock approached, the waiting crowds became quiet, poised for flight. Horsemen strained forward in their saddles, checking cinches already checked a hundred times. Men in wagons daubed one last extra swath of grease on axles already floating in grease and prayed that their conveyances would survive the bumpy trip over the prairie. Engineers in the waiting trains gripped their throttles, and passengers clung to every space with any hold they could find. At high noon, the starting flag dropped, a bugle sounded, and cavalry guns along the line repeated the signal amid shouts of anticipation and relief.

The trains quickly surged ahead of the ragged lines of horsemen, and excited claim seekers jumped from roofs and doors of cars. Those not seriously hurt raced east and west of the tracks. When the thousands hurrying southward caught up with them, the crowds became a hopeless jumble. The trains finally stopped at Guthrie where hundreds more poured out in excited confusion, some looking for town lots, others seeking farm land on the edge of the proposed townsite.

Within hours, the "Magic City of Guthrie" was a seething, barely believable reality. What earlier in the day had been a plain with cottonwoods to the west and grass everywhere now presented the colors of the rainbow. Ten thousand people crowded into five hundred makeshift homes. "Tents of all colors, blankets of every shade, flags and streamers of every hue,

6. *Le Figaro* (Paris, France), April 22, 1889.
7. *Le Temps* (Paris, France), April 22, 1889.

coats, and in fact anything and everything that could be hoisted to the breeze,'' served both as shelter and as signs of habitation on lots.[8] Drinking water cost as much as beer, and long lines in front of a few pay toilets were proof of the opportunities open to imaginative entrepreneurs.

In spite of the prevalence of guns, knives, and other weapons, there was little violence during or shortly after the run. The character of the people accounted for a curious conservatism and orderliness amid all the expectancy and occasional foolishness. The conditions of settlement in Oklahoma did not attract desperadoes. The great majority of people making the run came for homes, farms, or business starts. Their life savings were tied up in farm equipment, piles of lumber, or drygoods and groceries. There were no great mining ventures, payrolls, or other treasures to attract gamblers and outlaws. Although the population was predominantly young and male, wives and children soon followed and stabilized the social structure. The men who came to Oklahoma were gamblers only in risking a last chance to settle and prosper.

The most worrisome immediate problem was an unprincipled minority known as "Sooners" who had managed to sneak in and settle claims before the run officially opened. Many were evicted, and the term *Sooner* remained one of disapproval —until the gridiron success of University of Oklahoma football teams made it palatable to the local population in the twentieth century. Many humorous tales survived in pioneer lore about the early settlers. In one account, two men on fast horses arrived in central Oklahoma at a desirable spot well ahead of anyone else. They were startled to find an elderly farmer peacefully plowing with a team of oxen. Onions stood four inches high in his new garden. When queried, the man swore that the soil was so rich that the onions had grown that much in the fifteen minutes since he planted them!

At sunset on April 22, 1889, practically every homestead and all the town lots in the virgin cities of Guthrie, Kingfisher, Stillwater, Oklahoma City, El Reno, and Norman were taken.

8. Marion Tuttle Rock, *Illustrated History of Oklahoma* (Topeka, Kans.: C. B. Hamilton and Sons, 1890), p. 21.

There had never been anything like it. People who made the run proudly declared years later, like one of Edna Ferber's barely fictional characters: "Creation! Hell! That took six days. This was done in one. It was History made in an hour—and I helped make it." [9]

As spectacular and thrilling as the first run was, there was a poignancy and sense of loss mixed with all the jubilation and pride. Every homesteader was not successful. Thousands lost a disputed claim in the toss of a coin, or had to sell to a later arrival with ready cash. For the men and women who failed, the beckoning prairies represented unfulfilled hopes.

Gone too were the age-old solitude and loneliness of the Indians' magnificent homeland. With astonishing speed, the new settlers destroyed the arcadian quality of the land in the name of triumphant progress and civilization. By twilight on the opening day, the feet of people and animals, the wheels of heavy-laden wagons, the new foundations of buildings, all had crushed the wild grasses and flowers. It was symbolic of the changes to come, as the new frontier entered an economic and social system based on national ideals rather than local needs or circumstances.

The scenes of the run of 1889 were repeated elsewhere as the western tribes were forced to accept allotments, and their surplus lands were surveyed and opened. The second run absorbed the Iowa, Sac and Fox, and Shawnee-Potowatomi reservations into the newly organized Oklahoma Territory. Nearly every tract was claimed the first day. But when the more than three million acres of the Cheyenne and Arapaho reservations were opened in April 1892, only 25,000 people participated. Most of the western land was thought unsuitable for farming. Thousands of acres remained unfarmed, until Russian immigrants settled there, transforming the economy and the landscape with their hardy Turkey Red wheat.

But the most famous land run occurred in 1893, as more than a hundred thousand people stampeded into the Cherokee Outlet at noon on September 16, while the thermometer registered 100 degrees. The editor of the *Arapaho Bee,* fearful of losing popu-

9. The character Yancey Cravat speaking, in Edna Ferber's *Cimarron,* p. 14.

lation to the Outlet, belittled the area as an "overrated cow ranch." [10] But nesters had coveted the fertile area since before the first cattle ranches developed. It seemed that everyone in Kansas wanted 160 acres in that 58-by-100-mile strip. "Bill thought about that place so much he expected to find a white house and red barn on it," a survivor recalled years later.[11] One pioneer woman was so eager for a claim that she wrapped herself in a feather mattress so her son could push her out of the wagon without having to stop and jeopardize his own chances for a good claim. The plan worked, but the son was never seen again.

The Cherokee Outlet contained some of the most desirable available land outside the domain of the Five Civilized Tribes. As desperate land-hungry men, many ruined in the drought of 1892–1893 on the Great Plains, competed for the dwindling public domain, violence often flared. One successful settler stumbled over the body of a man with a slit throat and crushed skull, hidden in a hollow soon after the opening. "Another . . . met a man who appeared demented, wandering around in a circle and asking helplessly, 'Where can I stake a claim? I want to get a home!' " Still another pioneer party boasted of frightening a Negro from a claim with threats of lynching. Their neighbors endorsed the act with cries of "That's right; we don't want any niggers in this country." [12]

The confusion and lawlessness in the Cherokee Run was greater than that of previous openings. The inspired pictures taken by the frontier photographer W. S. Prettyman captured all the vigor and turbulence, the sense of desperate exhilaration as men tried to claim the future. Success determined history; the losers were forgotten in short order. In 1945, *Time* magazine reported that "the glory of having been in the [Cherokee Outlet] Run cut a lot more ice in Enid than coming over in the *Mayflower*." [13]

10. *Arapaho Bee,* August 3, 1893.

11. Debo, *Prairie City,* p. 47.

12. Debo, *Prairie City,* p. 48.

13. *Time* 46 (September 24, 1945): 100, reviewing Marquis James's *The Cherokee Strip* (New York: Viking Press, 1945).

Other, final openings followed, in short order. The tiny Kickapoo reservation east of the original "Oklahoma Lands" was opened in 1895. In 1896, when the United States Supreme Court decided that disputed Greer County belonged in Oklahoma Territory rather than in Texas, it became available to settlers. Five years later, the surplus lands of the Kiowa, Comanche, Apache, Wichita, and Caddo reservations in the southwest corner of the territory were ready for opening. Because of recurring rumors of gold and silver deposits and tales of buried Spanish treasure in the Wichita Mountains, some 165,000 people registered for the 13,000 available homesteads. The government decided to avoid the inequities of a run and substituted a lottery, giving equal chance to speculator and homesteader alike. It was so hot on the day of the drawing, in August 1901, that pitch oozed from the pine boards of the officials' platform, but the heat did not wilt the ardor of waiting crowds.

The remaining reservation lands of the Poncas, Otoes and Missouris, and the Kaws were divided among the native inhabitants, many of whom became citizens according to the original terms of the Dawes Act. After 1890, the name *Indian Territory* referred only to the older eastern area that the Five Civilized Tribes owned and governed and additional land belonging to remnants of tribes living in the far northeast corner.

Oklahoma Territory continued to symbolize the chance to start again, or from the beginning. Men who knew "how rotten and narrow and bigoted the other way has been . . ." with its "ugly politics, ugly towns, ugly buildings, ugly minds . . ." were determined to forge a better society.[14] The early settlers were generally two kinds of idealists so familiar to the American scene: those who had failed elsewhere and started again, confident of success; and those eager to succeed the first time.

The American frontier was always the province of people oriented toward the future. Wagons with signs reading "Chinchbugged in Illinois, Bald-knobbed in Mizzouri, Prohibited in Kansas, Oklihonny or Bust!" carried people determined to make another try in a new place.[15] The faith and expectations of

---

14. Ferber, *Cimarron*, p. 116.

15. George Milburn, "Oklahoma," *Yale Review* 35 (March 1946): 522; and Debo, *Prairie City*, p. 12.

these new settlers were often astonishing. A pervasive sense of living through a new dispensation softened early hardships. Instead of prairie, they saw producing farms; where creeks turned, they saw cities and towns.

A certain self-righteousness tinged this idealism and fortified the settlers' persistence. They did not feel that a homestead was a gift from the government, but a chance to be independent in the larger social system. In due course, drought, winds, and grasshoppers—to say nothing of fluctuating prices—reduced these empire-builders to mere mortals. The depths to which their expectations fell caused many people to embrace radicalism ill-suited to their true beliefs. That was a response to hard times and specific grievances, but it also represented resentment at the society that had allowed them to believe and to try to practice such inflated myths.

Settlers in Oklahoma Territory represented every region and occupation. The new instant civilization boasted doctors and lawyers as well as farmers and merchants. But patterns established in the first land run in 1889 influenced political, social, and economic life in the forty-sixth state into the 1970s. More than any other factor, the previous residence of the Oklahoma pioneer shaped certain characteristics of the state's development. Since the greatest clamoring for new land occurred in states surrounding Indian Territory, they naturally contributed the largest number of original settlers. Residents of Kansas and Texas shared equally in the opening of the centrally located Unassigned Lands. In later runs, people from the state nearest the run predominated. Kansans outnumbered all other participants in the Cherokee Run, but below the Cimarron River, settlers were primarily of southern origin. Southerners claimed more than eighty percent of the homesteads in the Cheyenne-Arapaho opening. Texans in particular dominated the population in areas bordering the Red River and in Old Greer County.[16]

Although there were no runs into the domain of the Five Civilized Tribes, the basic patterns of white settlement there were similar. In 1900, people from Texas, Arkansas, and Mis-

16. See Solon J. Buck, "The Settlement of Oklahoma," *Transactions, Wisconsin Academy of Science, Arts and Letters* 15, pt. 2 (1907): 325–380; and Doran, "Origins of Culture Areas in Oklahoma, 1830–1900," p. 174.

EARLY OKLAHOMA · INDIAN TERRITORY
1866-1889

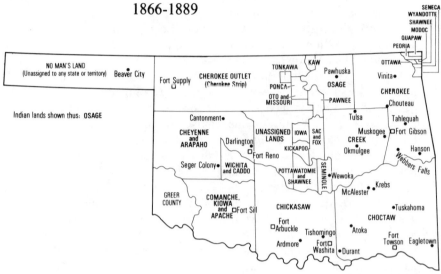

OKLAHOMA · LAND OPENINGS
1889-1906

Harold Faye

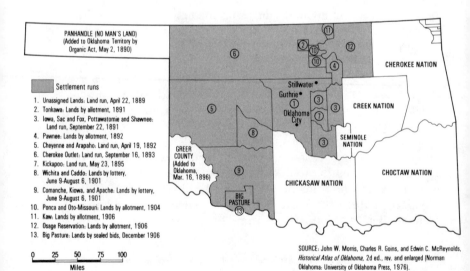

PANHANDLE (NO MAN'S LAND)
(Added to Oklahoma Territory by
Organic Act, May 2, 1890)

Settlement runs

1. Unassigned Lands: Land run, April 22, 1889
2. Tonkawa: Lands by allotment, 1891
3. Iowa, Sac and Fox, Pottawatomie and Shawnee:
   Land run, September 22, 1891
4. Pawnee: Lands by allotment, 1892
5. Cheyenne and Arapaho: Land run, April 19, 1892
6. Cherokee Outlet: Land run, September 16, 1893
7. Kickapoo: Land run, May 23, 1895
8. Wichita and Caddo: Lands by lottery,
   June 9-August 6, 1901
9. Comanche, Kiowa, and Apache: Lands by lottery,
   June 9-August 6, 1901
10. Ponca and Oto-Missouri: Lands by allotment, 1904
11. Kaw: Lands by allotment, 1906
12. Osage Reservation: Lands by allotment, 1906
13. Big Pasture: Lands by sealed bids, December 1906

0   25   50   75   100
Miles

SOURCE: John W. Morris, Charles R. Goins, and Edwin C. McReynolds,
Historical Atlas of Oklahoma, 2d ed., rev. and enlarged (Norman
Oklahoma: University of Oklahoma Press, 1976).

souri accounted for 60 percent of the immigrant whites living among the Five Tribes. Most of them were located in the Choctaw and Chickasaw nations and in the southeastern region of the Creek and Cherokee nations. Fewer whites intruded into Indian Territory from the north, but those who purchased land from the Osages or drifted into the upper Cherokee and Creek nations were primarily from the Midwest.

The results of such settlement patterns were predictable, since ideals, attitudes, and tastes accompanied furniture and provisions in the settlers' wagons. Midwestern wheat farmers settled above the North Canadian River, established churches for Methodist and Disciples of Christ congregations, and voted Republican. Southerners who grew cotton, worshiped in fundamentalist churches, and voted Democratic brought those habits across the Red River. These basic patterns persisted, shaping attitudes toward education, culture, materialism, and a range of other national ideals and problems. The northwestern plains counties retained the name "Jayhawker Country," while the southeastern section of the state became "Little Dixie."

In addition to the thousands of settlers from nearby states, Old World peoples migrated to Oklahoma. The flood tide of immigration that gave national life great variety and richness coincided with the opening of the Indian lands. In the two decades after 1890, about two thousand European immigrants entered the Twin Territories annually. By 1910, almost 8 percent of Oklahoma's population was foreign-born.[17]

Land hunger lured most Europeans to Oklahoma, just as it did most native-born Americans. Thousands of immigrants who came to the Great Plains in the 1880s found the best land already taken. After 1889, they headed for Oklahoma. German-speaking peoples, the largest single group of immigrants nationally, also predominated in Oklahoma. The experience of the Russian-German family of Dietrich Ehrlich was typical of the more than ten thousand Germans who emigrated to the new territory. The Ehrlichs settled first among relatives in Lehigh, Kan-

17. For this interesting and little-known aspect of Oklahoma's history, see Douglas Hale, "European Immigrants in Oklahoma, A Survey," *Chronicles of Oklahoma* 53 (Summer 1975): 179–203.

sas, but fertile land nearby was scarce and expensive. When Congress passed the Free Homes Bill in 1900, the Ehrlichs took the train to Shattuck, a town in western Ellis County near the Texas border. Earlier settlers had avoided the windy, treeless plains, but these lands were attractive to men who knew a similar environment on the steppes of Russia, or in Poland and eastern Germany. Substantial numbers of Russian-German settlers began to concentrate in Oklahoma's northwestern and north central counties.

Mennonite congregations planted the hardy and prolific Turkey Red strain of wheat that proved so well-suited to Oklahoma's soil and climate. After the turn of the century, the immigrant farmers began to prosper. Most increased their holdings, and helped their children settle nearby in an extended family pattern. Eager to preserve their cultural heritage, the immigrants often kept to themselves, worshiped in their own churches, and spoke their native tongue. They published about a dozen German-language newspapers, and more than one enterprising merchant learned to stock pictures of the German kaiser.

In settling and prospering on Oklahoma's unwanted western lands, these immigrants displayed a hardiness and tenacity that sustained them when disaster struck in the 1930s. Most endured the adversities of Dust Bowl days and refused to leave their homes. They were conservative in many ways, yet accepted the new scientific farming. They contour-plowed, planted tree shelters, mulched the topsoil, and waited for rain. Much of Oklahoma's reputation as a conservative state rested in part on the piety, religious convictions, and strong family bonds of these settlers and their descendants.

Not all German-speaking immigrants became farmers, of course. Substantial numbers of Jewish merchants from Austria and Bavaria arrived after 1889. Jewish suppliers and laborers also accompanied the railroad crews building the first lines into Indian Territory after 1865. They settled primarily in cities and towns. The first permanent Jewish congregation in Oklahoma Territory was established at Ardmore in 1899. Jewish merchants quickly assimilated into the fledgling state's civic and commercial life. Along with scores of Syrian peddlers, Jewish traders prospered, especially in the oil towns that boomed after 1900. Max Meyer, a Sapulpa haberdasher, enlivened the town with a colorful array of shirts and ties. His dark complexion and Semitic features were often mistaken for Indian characteristics, and Meyer delighted in telling people who inquired about his lineage that he belonged to the "Lost Tribe." [18]

The infant coal industry also absorbed hundreds of immigrants unable to find work in the crowded mines of Pennsylvania and West Virginia. Large numbers of men from the British Isles, Italy, and eastern Europe mined and processed coal in Indian Territory. By 1910, Italian immigrants were the largest foreign-born element in the three major coal-producing counties—Pittsburg, Coal, and Latimer. Higher wages in the Oklahoma mines caused many men to travel south. By living together and sharing expenses, many frugal Italians saved enough to buy farm land or to establish small businesses, opportunities impossible in Italy.

British miners were widely dispersed and absorbed into the milieu of eastern Oklahoma where there were already scores of Scottish and Irish surnames among the Five Civilized Tribes. But the Italians remained clustered in farming communities near the coal towns of Krebs, McAlester, Wilburton, Coalgate, Lehigh, and Henryetta after mining diminished after 1930. Small groups of Poles, Lithuanians, and Ukrainians drifted from the mines to work in the slaughterhouses and farms around Oklahoma City. The descendants of these immigrants worshiped in Russian Orthodox or Greek Catholic churches in Hartshorne and Jones, and attended fraternal gatherings near Canton, Enid, and Oklahoma City. Their presence testified to the lure of the new land and to the persistence of old beliefs transmitted from one culture to another.

Emigrants from Bohemia also came in the early twentieth century. They formed Czech-speaking farming enclaves in Prague, Yukon, Wheatland, and Mishak, all towns within a fifty-mile radius of Oklahoma City. Excellent farmers, they also owned flour mills and sold agricultural equipment. But like other immigrants, they clung to inherited ways, staging folk fes-

18. See Lewis Meyer, *Preposterous Papa* (Cleveland: World Publishing Co., 1959).

tivals and observing Old World traditions. The lack of concern for the morrow and the expansiveness in American life troubled many older Bohemians. The careless waste of land and timber on the frontier shocked them.

Numerous Negroes, former slaves of the Five Civilized Tribes and their descendants, were present in Oklahoma before the first European immigrants arrived. Despite some efforts to colonize elsewhere, most freedmen remained after 1865. Some farmed, but most worked as laborers for the railroads and coal mines. As blacks attempted to secure their position in post-bellum American society, the experiment of creating separate black towns flourished in the Twin Territories.

In 1905 Booker T. Washington visited Boley, one of the twenty-six all-black towns founded in Oklahoma and Indian Territory between 1865 and 1910. He praised Boley as an attempt "to do something to make the race respected; something which shall demonstrate the right of the Negro, not merely as an individual, but as a race, to have a worthy and permanent place in the civilization that the American people are creating." [19] Despite a lively beginning and some economic success, the black-town experiments in Oklahoma failed. Like their white counterparts, black residents ultimately drifted to larger urban areas or left the state in search of jobs in more industrialized economies. Yet at statehood in 1907, blacks outnumbered both Indians and first- and second-generation Europeans in the Oklahoma population. [20]

In spite of the diversities of ethnic background, social class, and professions in the new population, the hardships of pioneering were a merciless leveler over time. One contemporary observer noted, almost a decade after the first land run, that Oklahoma Territory was still poor, a place where people were drawn together "by the freemasonry of hard times and isolation." [21]

19. William Loren Katz, *The Black West* (New York: Doubleday and Co., 1971), p. 313.

20. First- and second-generation Europeans numbered 130,430 in 1907, with Negroes totaling 137,612 and Indians 74,825. See Hale, "European Immigrants in Oklahoma," p. 179.

21. Helen C. Candee, "Social Conditions in Our Newest Territory," *Forum* 25 (June 1898): 430.

These hardships, as well as rewards, took intensely personal forms in individual lives. The prairies of western Oklahoma were always a subject of lore and expectation. To some they looked as if "the Lord or somebody else has done the best job of clearin' ever seen!" [22] For decades settlers moving west hesitated at the edge of these great expanses of open land. No sane man from the humid east, bent on producing predictable crops that depended on temperate climate and adequate water wanted a home there. It seldom rained, except in torrents. There were no trees for fuel or fencing, and few stones for housing. Water for stock and men was scarce and unpredictable; rivers ran sand one day and torrents of water the next. Railroads were unknown and the human companionship of neighbors uncertain. The very magnitude of space seemed to dwarf even the most ambitious pioneer's projects.

People did not settle the Plains until better land elsewhere disappeared. But extensive settlement in any event was almost impossible without the technology that developed after the Civil War. The railroad, barbed wire, windmills, sod houses, steel plows, and drills all gave the settler fresh ability to fashion a tolerable life in the unpredictable short-grass country.

A venerable frontier anecdote symbolized the clash of old and new thought on the plains. A man from Tennessee traveled to the Southwest to visit nephews who were homesteading. Since it was seventy miles from the railroad stop to the claim, the trio camped overnight at a windmill near a sandy arroyo. One of the nephews began digging at a few mesquite bushes growing in the parched earth. Soon he had enough mesquite roots for a fire. His brother watered the horses at a metal stock tank near the windmill, then tethered them to graze on buffalo grass. Then he hung an iron pail over the pipe leading from the windmill to the tank. Since the wind was not blowing, he climbed atop the machine and turned the blades with his hands until water emerged. He climbed down, filled the coffee pot, and started supper.

The old uncle, watching these proceedings with skeptical interest, suddenly inquired: "Is there ever any water in that

22. Dale, "From Log Cabin to Sod House," p. 403.

creek?'' One of the boys said yes, "when it rains and for a few days or weeks afterward.'' "What's the name of it, anyhow?'' the uncle continued. "Jose Creek,'' answered a nephew, "J-O-S-E, pronounced *Hosay.''* The old man snorted indignantly: "I don't know why you boys want to stay out here. I wouldn't live in any country where you have to climb for water and dig for wood and spell hell with a J!'' [23]

The difficulties of obtaining wood and water confounded every prairie settler. At first, farmers were delighted at not having to remove stumps from the land or cut sprouts and roots in an endless conflict with the forest. But without a steady supply of timber, a family had to find other materials to build a house, to cook and heat, and to make stock enclosures.

The sod house and the dugout became to the prairie pioneer what the log cabin was to his eastern counterpart. In places where the soil was heavy and interlaced with roots, a sod house was usually built completely above ground, from strips or blocks of sod, much like adobe construction in the farther Southwest. If the soil was sandy, the dwelling was built down into the earth, or as part of a burrow into a hillside. Many early houses had weeds and clumps of wildflowers growing in their roofs. But some timber was needed for ridge poles and corner posts, even in the crudest dwellings. And settlers often traveled many miles to a stream or ravine to cut the thin cottonwood or hackberry trees.

Earthen homes, especially dugouts, were cool in summer and warm in winter, but they had drawbacks. Dirt walls were covered with newspapers or plaster, if the family could afford it. But floors were usually bare, hard-packed earth, where fleas abounded even if the family had no dog. One Stillwater pioneer woman described her early years in a dugout: "Rats would burrow into the dirt walls covered by the newspapers, and at night their scratching on the paper would make cold chills run down my spine. When it rained, these tunnels the rats made would bring water into the dugout in steady streams.'' [24]

23. Edward Everett Dale, "Wood and Water: Twin Problems of the Prairie Plains,'' *Nebraska History* 29 (June 1948): 87.

24. Robert E. Cunningham, *Stillwater, Where Oklahoma Began* (Stillwater: Arts and Humanities Council of Stillwater, 1969), p. 214.

Insects, especially mosquitoes and bedbugs, plagued the inhabitants of damp dugouts. The bed, where often an entire family slept at night, doubled as clothes closet and storage area by day. Most dugouts were small, but many were large and overcrowded, while families took in relatives, or awaited the day when crop success would enable them to build a real wooden home.

In good weather, women cooked outside on makeshift stoves or hearths that burned "prairie coal," the dried buffalo chips that littered the landscape. They also used twisted strands of hay, corn cobs, and sunflower stalks for fuel. Most '89ers arrived too late to plant gardens the first year. They lived on stocked provisions of coffee, flour, dried beans, and sugar. But game was plentiful, and wild fruits added some variety to diets that easily became unbalanced and boring.

In 1890 a drought in Oklahoma Territory was so severe that many homesteaders returned to the older states. But most of the settlers had no other place to go and endured hardships that made the original pioneering stage seem easy and pleasant. The situation became so desperate that Congress voted fifty thousand dollars in relief funds. The Rock Island and Santa Fe railroads, eager to retain a developing market, furnished wheat seed at cost. But most settlers rejected any help that smacked of charity and favored self-reliance or the more familiar and less offensive "neighborliness" common to most communities in troubled times. One old nester later boasted that "a man came around offering to help us, but quite a few sand plums were growing along Stillwater creek. They made wonderful jam and jelly, even without sugar, so we refused help." [25] In August, farmers planted the hardy turnip, and fall rains produced such a crop that 1890 became known as the year of the turnip. R. A. Lowry recalled that, in Stillwater, every child found a gift-wrapped turnip in his Christmas stocking that year.

As the population grew, stores were established at strategic points, usually along railroads. At first they carried only staples, but luxuries soon appeared with prosperous crops. Unlike earlier pioneers, Oklahomans with money or things to barter could buy

25. Cunningham, *Stillwater, Where Oklahoma Began,* p. 213.

tinned goods, dried fruits, and an array of drygoods, as soon as the railroad line came through. The technology and transportation system of the new industrial America hastened the end of the worst hardships usually associated with frontier life.

Potable drinking water was also scarce in most prairie areas. Fortunate indeed was the farmer who sank a shallow well and found good water. A dry hole or water at a prohibitive depth was more likely. Most people hauled water in barrels over long distances to supplement the irregular rainfall collected in cisterns and receptacles. Cattle, stray dogs, and wild game also often polluted streams, wallowing in them during hot weather.

When mechanized drilling and the use of windmills for pumping made the supply of water more predictable and plentiful, it was still often impregnated with minerals that had a purgative effect. The public well at Cloudcroft was so full of gypsum that stories of the ignorant stranger caught unawares at its cooling draughts entered local folklore. The windmill was a godsend, helping man harness the wind to store water. The machine's whirring blades and rasping shaft were also some comfort on lonely days and symbolized both action and progress.

Pioneer life was not easy for anyone, but seemed especially hard on women. Husbands were frequently absent to harvest crops or work on railroad or construction crews, leaving women and children alone for weeks at a time. These long periods of loneliness became nightmares if children sickened, an accident happened, or if a baby arrived early.

Some unexpected terror always waited on the half-tamed prairie. One mother told of stopping to rest one afternoon. She lay down on the bed for a nap with her small daughter. As she dozed, the child kept leaning over the side of the bed, then pulling back quickly, convulsed with laughter. The weary mother finally looked to see what was so amusing. To her horror, a huge rattlesnake was coiled on the floor beside the bed. The child pulled back reflexively each time the snake struck, delighted with this strange playmate so eager for a game of tag.

Most women coped with solitude, wind, and isolation. One housewife remembered how dreary everything seemed. Since there was no soap or bluing in these early households, even the cleanest clothes always looked drab. Early photographs showed attempts to alleviate this monotony. Delicate birdcages hung in the windows of soddies where women kept cheerful singing birds as companions. And used coffee cans were filled with blossoming perennials to relieve the earth's brownness.

Hazards to young children were a constant worry for pioneer mothers. Medicine was none too certain at best in nineteenth-century America, and the frontier's was inferior. Fevers of undefined origins and nature killed many infants. Mrs. Thompson B. Ferguson, who lost several children, wrote philosophically that "a part of the richness of this Oklahoma soil must be derived from the sweet bodies of our babies who lie buried there." [26] But many women never adjusted to these harsh emotional demands, hating the life that stole their infants and ruined their own best years. Some deadened their anguish with patent medicines containing alcohol or opium. Others committed suicide or wandered away to die of exposure. Still others sank into depression or madness.

And the quality of neighborliness inevitably varied, even with the best intentions. Where neighbors were close and the friendly frontier spirit prevailed, there were often mutual suspicions between native and foreign-born settlers, Negroes and whites, and whites and Indians. Whether through defensiveness or pride, many European immigrants kept to themselves and rebuffed neighbors' efforts to become friends. Herman Koch, a German immigrant who came from Iowa for the run into the Cherokee Strip, typified that attitude. He obtained a good claim, and his farm prospered with the help of a hardworking family. But the neighbors were indignant that Mrs. Koch plowed and did other field work. The Kochs kept apart from neighbors and the community, spoke little English, and seemed surly. When their baby died of heat suffocation in a tent while its mother plowed nearby, the couple buried the child without notifying anyone in the area. The neighbors then felt bad about their own negligence in not forcing more companionship on the Kochs, yet none had

26. Mrs. Walter Ferguson Manuscript, p. 24, Ferguson Papers, Division of Manuscripts, Western History Collections, Bizzell Memorial Library, University of Oklahoma, Norman, Oklahoma.

known of the tragedy until they noticed the tiny grave mound.[27]

Almost all early Oklahomans continuously tried to alter the landscape in more familiar patterns. They planted trees in places where neither the soil nor the wind was suitable for growing them. They lavished time, water, and money on expensive flowers and shrubs that marked their progress away from frontier rudeness toward the styles of civilization they left behind. Prairie dwellers often insisted on raising fruit trees and other luxury truck crops in the face of wind, cold, and insects, until in most instances fruit trees became ornamental rather than productive. In later years, many wealthy Oklahomans, such as E. W. Marland, the oil tycoon, valiantly insisted that almost every tree or shrub known to man would flourish in the Sooner State. Marland spent large sums to prove his point and to beautify Ponca City. This urge to alter nature and to produce flora and fauna completely unsuited to its climate and terrain was partly nostalgia, but it also reflected a desire to show that Oklahoma was not inferior or unusual.

By the mid-1890s, the five years of residence necessary to retain a claim had passed. Rains produced big harvests, and the land had been arranged for modern farming. Oklahoma Territory produced a bumper wheat crop in 1897. One farmer hauling grain to market met a man on horseback who offered him a dollar a bushel for the load. Thinking the speculator a victim of sunstroke, the farmer politely refused. In town he sold the wheat for $1.10 per bushel and took home a wagonload of both necessities and luxuries to a surprised and gratified family.[28]

Most people used the profits from wheat to buy more land or machinery, or to improve their homesteads. Some purchased pianos and organs, new curtains and carpets, toys for the children, or exotic foods and new clothes, much like modern families. There were soon so many musical instruments in Oklahoma Territory that many educated women turned from farming to teaching music. Books and slates were plentiful in the rural schools. Three literary magazines flourished, and President

---

27. Debo, *Prairie City,* p. 76.

28. E. H. Linzee, "Early History of the Grain Business in Oklahoma," *Chronicles of Oklahoma* 19 (1941): 167.

David Ross Boyd of the Territorial University marveled at the number of Oklahomans who subscribed to *Harper's Magazine*.

The *Harper's* correspondent traveling through Oklahoma City in 1891 believed that "any man who can afford a hall bedroom and a gas-stove in New York City is better off than he would be as the owner of one hundred and sixty acres on the prairie, or in one of these small so-called cities." [29] But people continued to come, even though the frontier was passing rapidly. The early days, however idealized, when people were roughly equal gave way to the predictable society based on money and status. In less than a decade, the thrifty settlers of the first runs became well-to-do. As people depended less on one another for survival or companionship, they became more selective, more critical in choosing associates in leisure activities. Those who endured the unbelievable privations and hardships romanticized the recent past. An attempt to retain or recapture prior ideals, this celebration of the pioneer experience was also an avenue of social respectability and authority in a society without "old families." Revered traditions were simply superimposed on the recent past. "Civilization" had come to Oklahoma in a rush; so must tradition.

The pioneer experience was intensified, as was everything else in Oklahoma, for both Indians and whites. The Indians had been transplanted to a new territory and hoped to continue their old ways while facing mounting pressure from the white man's new civilization. White settlement followed a similar pattern and was firmly established in about a decade, a much speedier process than on earlier American frontiers.

This rapidity of settlement produced a society of exaggerations, especially for the whites in Oklahoma Territory. There was a grim determination among these first settlers to be individuals, as well as to succeed. In rejecting government aid, in stubbornly farming soil unsuited to many crops, in defying terrain and climate to reproduce an inherited ideal of successful life, these pioneers were trying to prove their self-worth. The landless and penniless people who came to Oklahoma were bent on demonstrating that they could win the race of life and that

29. Davis, *The West from a Car-Window*, p. 114.

they could make Oklahoma Territory prosperous and respectable.

Time worked wonders with the pioneer experience in Oklahoma, as it did elsewhere. Failures were forgotten quickly, and successes were magnified until an essentially impersonal process took on vivid life in a thousand individual stories. The great themes of American idealism, hard work, and individualism seemed to dominate the settlement experience. They determined its long-term legacy in the retellings that transformed legends into traditions.

The pioneers deserved praise for stamina and courage. The raw new frontier doubtless allowed scope for the basic American optimism, experimentation, and hard work that developed the nation's economy. That legacy persisted well into the twentieth century and seemed to pervade the air that Oklahomans breathed. The black writer Ralph Ellison, an Oklahoma City native, recalled its general power in his formative years: "One thing is certain, ours was a chaotic community, still characterized by frontier attitudes and by that strange mixture of the naive and sophisticated, the benign and malignant, which makes the American past so puzzling and its present so confusing," he recalled. The total was a "mixture which often affords the minds of the young who grow up in far provinces such wide and unstructured latitude, and which encourages the individual's imagination—up to the moment 'reality' closes in upon him—to range widely and, sometimes, even to soar." [30] The qualities of the land and the human legends thus encouraged a sense of scope, a desire for freedom, and a fear of control that had positive effects on the emerging state's life.

Yet that same open, pioneer experience had other, inhibitory effects. The pioneer and his immediate descendants were often content to waste precious resources without planning for future needs. The future was somewhere else, or resulted from an automatic system he had now conquered. Many pioneers were content to make an immediate living, waiting for the railroad or some other agent to inflate values. And though the pioneer tradi-

---

30. Ralph Ellison, *Shadow and Act* (New York: Random House, 1964), p. xiii.

tion embraced technological innovation and some new ideas, the social system it produced resisted alteration.

The pioneer experience that inculcated a desire for scope and success in economic affairs did not carry over into less tangible intellectual or cultural pursuits. The stark contrasts of life on this last frontier, the ever-present reality of boom or bust, reinforced a circumscribed emotional life that often made people wary of cultural experiences. Wheat and cotton inevitably became more important than books and music. The arts needed money and emotion that the frontier experience channeled into seeking a secure livelihood. Only with industrialization and the discovery of oil in the twentieth century would Oklahomans turn toward what culture represented.

The age of settlement in Oklahoma's history was all the more vivid for being so sudden and intense. And whatever the mixture of its blessings, the heirs of the '89ers recalled only the giants in the land.

4

Statehood

*O*KLAHOMA's politics seemed destined to resemble her weather, sometimes violent, often confusing, yet occurring within a certain logic. As Edna Ferber remarked in *Cimarron,* "Anything can have happened in Oklahoma. Practically everything has." [1] The state's political parties and attitudes were born in the turbulent land runs. The people who came began their lives as Oklahomans dissatisfied with the existing order that had frustrated them elsewhere. Farmers especially disliked the cattlemen, who, in their view profited handsomely from grazing the Indian lands that they wished to make into family farms. During early territorial days, nesters carried rifles to warn off cowboys determined to run cattle over their crops. The animus between cattlemen and homesteaders involved more than differing economic activities. By the beginning of the twentieth century, this historic tension had matured into a suspicion of big or complex business enterprise and a corollary bias toward the small farmer that became the core of political attitudes as Oklahomans looked toward statehood.

The early pioneers represented all the elements of older states. Newcomers confronted settled Indian civilizations. The settler with lengthy lineage in another area confronted recent European immigrants. Whites faced blacks. Former Union soldiers resided near former Confederates, and Harrison Republicans collided

---

1. Ferber, *Cimarron,* p. x.

with Cleveland Democrats. People who favored the gold standard and the predictable economic order it represented argued
against proponents of free silver and the reckless experimentation it symbolized. Oklahoma's politics were formed in
the twilight of the great party battles of the Gilded Age, further
intensified in a turbulent frontier milieu.

Political orientations in the Twin Territories reflected history
and the patterns of original settlement. Though administered
from Republican-dominated Washington, Indian Territory had a
southern and Democratic tone. Among the Five Civilized
Tribes, political attitudes that were shaped in the Civil War
remained strong into the twentieth century. The Democratic
party was confident of victory among the Chickasaws, Choctaws, and Stand Watie Cherokees. But Republican influence
prevailed among "loyal" Creeks, Seminoles, and Cherokees.

Oklahoma Territory was predominantly Republican, since the
first lands opened were closer to Kansas and the upper plains
states than to Texas. But as more lands in the south opened,
Democratic strength increased. A Republican administration in
Washington for all except four years from 1890 to 1907 meant
that only one territorial governor was a Democrat. Yet many
Democrats in Oklahoma Territory voted for Republican congressional delegates to promote statehood among national Republican leaders.

To the casual observer, the GOP seemed dominant, but its
hold on territorial politics was shaky. The Republican Central
Committee boasted on the eve of statehood that the party's total
vote had increased in every election since 1890. They neglected
to note, however, that the Republican percentage of the total
vote cast declined between 1890 and 1906, except for a small
increase in 1898. Democratic migration was eroding Republican
power.

With the election of the first legislature for Oklahoma Territory in 1890, three parties actually contended for the voters'
allegiance. Many settlers were quickly disillusioned at seeing
the outlines of a new life fade into the familiar patterns they had
fled. High local freight rates, a crop-lien system, mortgages,
scarce investment funds, and tenancy became all too familiar.
Frustrated homesteaders soon joined the Populist crusade that

shook national politics in the turbulent 1890s. The People's party became the dominant voice of agrarian protest in Oklahoma Territory during that decade, and neither older party was secure enough to ignore it. But feuds among Democrats and the return of good times with the wheat harvest of 1897 dissipated the movement. "Populism as a living force or entity and as a political organization in this Territory is dead," the editor of the *Noble County Patriot* declared in 1896.[2]

The editor was partly correct. The People's party as an organization was spent, but the conditions and uncertainties that produced Oklahoma's element of discontent were merely dormant. And many Oklahomans were Populists without having heard the word or joined the party. When hard times returned, after World War I, men who had struggled for agrarian rights under the Populist banners of the 1890s regrouped under a socialist flag.

Because of the way the new lands were opened and the scarcity of immediate resources, territorial politics was primarily concerned with the necessary division of spoils in administering the new territory. Politicians tended to ignore labels and ideologies as they sought offices and public institutions for their fledgling towns. George Gardenhire, a Payne County Populist who was elected president of the first Territorial Senate, for instance, backed Oklahoma City Republicans in their struggle to outbid Guthrie Republicans for the territorial capital. Although Guthrie prevailed, the Oklahoma City delegates kept their promise, and Gardenhire secured the agricultural and mechanical college for Stillwater.

Resentment against "carpetbag governors," strife over patronage, and the turmoil of periodic investigations to embarrass unpopular officials set the tone of political life. Politics mirrored the turbulent society of small landholders desperate to succeed on this last frontier and resentful of the inhibitions and regulations of older societies. Quarrels in Oklahoma Territory were usually open, however fierce, and alliances were more casual, in sharp contrast to the politics of Indian Territory. Among the influential landowners and leaseholders of the Five Civilized

2. *Noble County Patriot*, November 26, 1896.

Tribes, politics grew from a different tradition. There the focus was on tribal matters, rather than on controversial policies designed to develop the external domain. Such discussions among the Tribes developed a more covert and subdued tone than in Oklahoma Territory.

Political differences sharpened and focused on the emerging question of statehood at the beginning of the new century. Admission to the Union might take several forms. Oklahoma Territory could enter as a single state, with Indian Territory remaining separate or free to seek admission as an Indian commonwealth. The two territories might also merge and enter as a single state.

The drive for admission began immediately after the run of 1889 in Oklahoma Territory, though without much support from national politicians. Between 1865 and 1900, statehood was a popular solution to the political and economic problems of territories beyond the Mississippi. In those years, nine new states appeared on the national map. But in due course, national leaders of both parties questioned the wisdom of early admission for western territories. Their populations seemed turbulent, their narrowly based economies were unsound, and they tended to send radical or unusual spokesmen to Congress. To those in older states, the small territorial populations also seemed over-represented in both Congress and presidential contests.

By the 1890s, that skepticism combined with several special circumstances in Oklahoma to make national leaders cautious about statehood. Financing state and local government in the new territory was especially troublesome. Much of the land was exempt from taxation because it was being homesteaded or because of the terms governing allotments to western tribes. Until land could be taxed adequately and predictably, public finances seemed insufficient to support a new state.

Geography and the distribution of natural resources also inhibited early efforts at statehood. Oklahoma Territory consisted of only about forty thousand square miles, about half the land area of most states west of the Mississippi. There was good farm and range land in the west, but the timber and minerals necessary for a balanced economy were in Indian Territory. Leaders of the Five Civilized Tribes, however, had no interest in uniting with Oklahoma Territory. Until the turn of the century, they successfully resisted every effort to interfere with the remaining treaty arrangements preserving Indian Territory.

Party politics also worked against immediate statehood. National Republican leaders, working tirelessly to secure a new national majority, were skeptical of the GOP's future strength in Oklahoma Territory. They knew it would take time and skill to build a lasting Republican party in the Democratic Southwest. But local Republicans believed that obtaining statehood would rebound to their enduring credit with future voters. Territorial Governor Thompson Ferguson urged his Republican friends to use any means to persuade Republican congressmen to admit Oklahoma Territory as a state. If they failed, he warned, Democrats from Indian Territory would dominate the new state. "It is now a matter of politics with us," he wrote a friend, "as it has always been a matter of politics with Congress." [3] But most Republican leaders agreed with Speaker of the House Joseph G. Cannon, who favored single statehood for Oklahoma because he feared the Democrats would control a dual arrangement and thus elect as many as four senators. That strategy had two advantages. It permitted the Republican party to retain patronage for Oklahoma Territory. And when the Twin Territories were admitted as one state, the Democrats would have a maximum of two new senators, with the chance of a divided House delegation.

The national Democrats were more united on statehood. Their congressional leaders worked to admit Oklahoma Territory alone, confident that Republican strength was waning. Although the process of allotting western Indian lands was just beginning, in 1893 the Territorial Democratic Central Committee petitioned Congress to admit Oklahoma Territory without delay. The plan provided for the new state to annex former Indian reservations as they were opened, and then Indian Territory when the Five Civilized Tribes sought statehood. When Congress rejected that plan for piecemeal absorption and refused to delegate the task of

3. Thompson Ferguson to H. I. Wasson, November 26, 1902, Ferguson Papers, Western History Collections, Bizzell Memorial Library, University of Oklahoma, Norman, Oklahoma.

allotment to a state, most Democrats in the Twin Territories turned to single statehood as a sure way of obtaining political supremacy in the new state.

By 1900 the combined population of the Twin Territories was about 790,000, eight times that of California when that state was admitted in 1850. While most whites were sure that Congress would create a single state, certain leaders among the Five Civilized Tribes worked to avoid union with Oklahoma Territory. They were fearful of being discriminated against in offices, education, and public institutions in any state that whites dominated. The Indian aristocracy that governed the Five Tribes did not wish to be a minority in a white man's democracy.

Pleasant Porter, principal chief of the Creeks, joined W. C. Rogers of the Cherokees and Green McCurtain of the Choctaws in calling for delegates to attend a statehood convention in Muskogee in August 1905. The Indian leaders knew the importance of gaining the support of whites who lived among them if the plan for an Indian state were to succeed with Congress and the President. So Porter sought the backing of one of Indian Territory's most influential whites, Charles N. Haskell, a railroad promoter from Muskogee. Haskell knew that a separate Indian state was politically unacceptable and economically unsound, but he had lived among the Indians long enough to respect their sincere belief, voiced through Porter that "from time immemorial the Indians, as a heritage of the original inhabitants, have been promised a state, an empire of their own." [4]

In 1898, in exchange for the surrender of certain tribal assets, the Indians believed that the national government had reaffirmed the promise to create a state from the Five Civilized Tribes' domains when conditions warranted. Shortly before the Indian statehood convention opened, Porter admitted to Haskell that he doubted that the federal government would ever honor this "Atoka Agreement." But he believed the tribal leaders duty bound to submit their claim. If Congress refused their petition, the Indians would accept the creation of a single state from the

4. Oscar Presley Fowler, *The Haskell Regime, The Intimate Life of Charles Nathaniel Haskell* (Oklahoma City: The Boles Publishing Co., 1933), p. 53.

Twin Territories. Convinced of the Indians' good faith, Haskell agreed to support the plan and help pay for the convention. Years later, recalling his role in that "Sequoyah Convention," Haskell believed that his actions had helped ease the pain as the old dream of an Indian state was put to rest. "When that effort had been made by some of the leading citizens of Indian Territory whose friendship [the Indians] could not doubt, they were willing to submit to the inevitable," he noted.[5]

The 182 men who gathered in Muskogee on August 21, 1905, represented the most distinguished and influential citizens of Indian Territory. They elected Porter president of the convention, with 5 vice-presidents representing the Tribes. The vice-presidents included Haskell, representing the Creeks, and William H. Murray, an intermarried Chickasaw citizen and tribal attorney for that nation. These two men formed an alliance at Muskogee that affected the new state of Oklahoma's politics for some three decades.

Murray came to Tishomingo, capitol of the Chickasaw Nation, in 1898, wearing a Prince Albert coat and a derby hat and carrying a carpetbag that contained a frayed copy of the United States Constitution. The son of a poor Texas farmer, Murray had been a schoolteacher and sometime journalist before entering the Lone Star State's political battles as a supporter of the Farmers' Alliance-Democratic insurgents who rallied around James S. Hogg in the 1890s. Defeated twice for office, Murray turned to the law, then decided to seek fame and fortune in Indian Territory.

Murray immediately adapted to circumstances. He exchanged his elegant suit for one of white cotton. He also took a wife, Mary Alice Hearrell, the niece of Douglas Johnston, governor of the Chickasaw tribe. Through marriage, Murray became a legal member of the tribe. As an Indian citizen with significant family and political ties, Murray soon became a tribal attorney. And successful law practice gave him the funds to develop extensive tribal acreage. Because of his experiments at growing alfalfa, he was later widely known as "Alfalfa Bill." Within a

5. Paul Nesbitt, editor, "Governor Haskell Tells of Two Conventions," *Chronicles of Oklahoma* 14 (June 1936): 205.

short time, this failure from Texas was part of the small circle of men who dominated Indian Territory.

Murray quickly realized that within a few years Indian Territory would become part of a state. Determined to hold a prominent position in the coming new order, he studied constitutional law and participated enthusiastically in Democratic politics and farmers' organizations. Murray was ready when Pleasant Porter called the constitutional convention. Most of the Chickasaws opposed the statehood movement, but with Haskell's backing, Murray almost singlehandedly organized the elections for delegates. Although he preferred to postpone the whole question of statehood until Indian land problems were settled, Murray actively promoted the Sequoyah movement. The chances for a separate Indian state seemed remote, but he agreed with Haskell that the Sequoyah Convention "would convince Congress that the Indian was quite capable of drafting instruments of law for a modern state." [6] A dignified, productive convention would enhance the Indian image, whether the tribes became part of a new state or remained separate. It might also increase their authority.

The heat of August in Muskogee may have expedited the convention's business. The delegates divided into eleven subcommittees, and in only two weeks formulated a complex set of proposals for a redrafting committee. Murray, Haskell, and three others in this crucial group transformed the reports into a 35,000-word document ready for the full convention's consideration on September 6, 1905.

That document was a tribute to the Murray-Haskell alliance. In addition to sitting on the redrafting committee, Murray was a member of the subcommittee to determine county boundaries. Virtually every small town wanted the honor and benefits that came with being a county seat. Haskell and Murray freely indicated that the delegates who co-operated with the redrafting committee enhanced their town's chances of being named county seats. When delegates balked at certain ideas, Murray's mere suggestion that a county line might pass through a town or isolate it usually ensured acquiescence, if not enthusiasm.

6. William H. Murray, "The Constitutional Convention," *Chronicles of Oklahoma* 9 (June 1931): 133.

The Sequoyah Constitution that emerged from these debates and machinations was a remarkable document. Its clear, concise language was the work of Alexander Posey, Creek poet, editor, and essayist who was secretary of the convention. It followed the national Constitution with a Bill of Rights and three separate, but equal, branches of government. It also embodied many advanced social ideas. While suffrage was restricted to men, provisions regulated the labor of women and children, the purity of food and drugs, and safety requirements for mining. Sections governing corporations, landownership, and education reflected the strength of agrarian ideals in Indian Territory. The document created a corporation commission with extensive regulatory powers. It prohibited aliens or corporations from owning farm land. At Murray's insistence, it also provided for the teaching of agricultural and domestic science in the public schools. And it prohibited the use of alcoholic beverages, an extension of federal policy in Indian Territory and a bow to an emerging national progressive issue.

The election to ratify the Sequoyah Constitution was the first referendum ever held in Indian Territory. Mindful of voter apathy and ignorance about complex constitutional questions, Haskell knew that, to produce a heavy vote, "we would have to put some element of personal interest in it." His solution was the county-seat question. "Not all of the voters cared about the constitution but in case it should be successful—and the success of the convention had exceeded all expectations—no one wanted to fall down on the matter of county seats." [7]

The strategy worked, and the Sequoyah Constitution was ratified, despite the overwhelming opposition of Indian Territory's press and a turnout of about half the qualified voters. But the victory was ephemeral. Less than two weeks later, President Theodore Roosevelt declared: "There is no obligation upon us to treat territorial subdivisions, which are matters of convenience only, as binding us on the question of admission to statehood." [8] Although humiliated and disappointed, the Indians

---

7. Nesbitt, "Governor Haskell Tells of Two Conventions," p. 203.

8. James D. Richardson, compiler, *A Compilation of the Messages and Papers of the Presidents,* 11 vols. (Washington, D.C.: Bureau of National Literature, 1913), 10: 7400.

were loyal to their pledge to accept joint statehood. The long hope of an Indian commonwealth was extinguished forever.

Despite its brief life, the Sequoyah Constitution helped prepare the Indians to accept statehood and a new social and political order. Out of the Muskogee meeting emerged the nucleus of a skilled coalition that dominated the next constitutional convention called for both territories. And many of the progressive aspects of the Sequoyah document influenced the later state constitution; some provisions were adopted word for word. In no other state was the Indian contribution to the governing of their white neighbors so direct.

Though deaf to pleas for a State of Sequoyah, Congress finally passed the Oklahoma Enabling Act with the formula for statehood in June 1906. The Twin Territories would enter the Union as one state. The act authorized a constitutional convention with fifty-five delegates from each territory. Two more would come from the Osage Nation, where allotment was still in progress and no county governments were functioning. The act contained numerous guidelines to ensure that the new state document conformed to the national Constitution. It also had two unique mandates that caused Texas Senator Joseph W. Bailey to complain that "Congress has put upon [Oklahoma] the bane of incompetency by refusing to let her select her own capitol and denying her the right to regulate her own affairs by forcing prohibition." [9]

The provision retaining Guthrie as the state capital until 1913, abrogated in 1910, was the work of Henry Asp, prominent Republican and chief attorney for the Santa Fe Railroad in Oklahoma. And it was a serious tactical error for the Republican party. Designated a land office in 1889, Guthrie had served as territorial capital. In 1906 it was a city of twelve thousand people, with nine railroads and forty-two daily passenger trains. This "progress" and vitality ironically played into the Democrats' hands. Resentful of the federal administration and the railroad influence that Guthrie symbolized, Democrats now charged that a conspiracy of railroad and business interests act-

9. Irving Hurst, *The 46th Star: A History of Oklahoma's Constitutional Convention and Early Statehood* (Oklahoma City: Semco Press, 1957), p. 2.

ing through Asp and the GOP would dictate the constitution.

To avoid any doubt about the direction they thought state government should take, Democratic candidates for the constitutional convention campaigned on William Jennings Bryan's interpretation of democracy. They promised racial segregation in education and transportation, free school books, municipal ownership of utilities, direct democracy, and regulation of corporations. Many Democrats also endorsed the "Shawnee Demands," which the Twin Territories Federation of Labor and Farmers' Union had advocated that summer.

Many Republicans preferred the assurances of national party patronage to the uncertainties of local electoral politics, and they were handicapped from the beginning. As territorial officials, their best men were disqualified from serving at the convention. Depicted as the party against statehood, despite efforts of Republican Territorial Delegate Dennis Flynn to foster the movement, it was predictable that the GOP would lose. Oklahomans chose one hundred Democrats and twelve Republicans.

These "Twelve Apostles" chose to obstruct ideas they disliked and thus fostered charges of irresponsibility from the Democrats. The resulting original negativist image persisted. The Democrats drew on a strong southern heritage and support from labor and farm groups to forge a party that ruled the state for fifty years.

The delegates who gathered in Guthrie on November 20, 1906, to write Oklahoma's constitution were relatively young founding fathers. They represented a variety of occupations, but a group of farm-and-labor spokesmen dominated the proceedings. There were also bankers, merchants, teachers, and cattlemen. And as C. V. Rogers remarked, "it would be a Godsend to this convention if there wasn't so damned many lawyers here." [10] Thirty-four of the fifty-five delegates from Indian Territory had been at the Sequoyah Convention. William Murray, an active participant in the Farmers' Union as well as a Sequoyah veteran, saw his years of joining now pay off. Surveying the roster of delegates, he later remarked: "I saw at once

10. Ketchum, *Will Rogers: His Life and Times,* p. 57.

I would be President. . . . I was the only man who could poll both elements." [11]

The campaign furor over railroad influence prevented Haskell from seeking a convention post. But he disliked the constraints of parliamentary duties in any event, preferring the freedom and excitement of activity behind the scenes. In that capacity he engineered Murray's election as convention president.

The Oklahoma constitutional convention convened during a period of intense social and political change. The great depression of the 1890s dramatized in human terms the unequal distribution of wealth that accompanied the progress and sophistication identified with industrial growth. A strong desire for the modernization that sustained that growth warred with a yearning for the older virtues of liberty and individual effort that seemed ill-suited to the new economic order.

Urbanization, ethnic tensions, fear of bigness, and impersonality were all fuel for the reform movements that dominated national politics. Influential national magazines and newspapers were filled with articles decrying every kind of injustice and imbalance in society. This intense new kind of communication drew the fledgling state of Oklahoma into contact with both national problems and advanced solutions. Most of her residents had witnessed or experienced the prevailing issues in former homes. Many sought a new life in the Twin Territories, only to confront the same poor public facilities, political corruption, and economic disadvantages they thought they had left behind.

Oklahoma's new spokesmen were also conscious of the state's rawness in the rest of the nation's eyes. They wished to preserve both the tone and the content of their much-vaunted pioneer heritage. But they also intended to make the new state and its governmental forms modern and respectable to the rest of the country. Whatever their accommodations to the realities of the moment, these leaders meant to enter the Union with as much pride and modernity as any predecessor.

Eager to avoid the apparent errors of other states, while devoted to preserving an agrarian way of life, the delegates at

11. William H. Murray, "The Constitutional Convention," p. 133.

Guthrie were imbued with the reform sentiments sweeping the national political scene. More than local issues and ideals dominated the constitution-making spirit in Soonerland. The desire for modernism that reform typified joined with the optimism of a new century, when men seemed to believe anything possible. As the *Nation* said later: "As a matter of fact, [the Oklahoma constitution] undoubtedly comes nearer than any other document in existence to expressing the ideas and aspirations of the day." [12]

The constitutional convention delegates alternated between the serious work necessary to produce a new state and the colorful vulgarity common to American political events. Journalists from major national newspapers and magazines covered the convention, and they left few unusual or bizarre details to the imagination, even while outlining the framers' serious purposes and convictions.

The thirty-seven-year-old presiding officer, "Alfalfa Bill" Murray, gaveled the convention to order with a brusque command: "Delegates will take their seats, loafers and lobbyists will get out!" He then led the assembly in singing "Nearer, My God, to Thee," an appropriate anthem for either ambitious or uncertain men. [13]

As presiding officer, Murray had great power and influence with committees. He also delivered a long opening address encompassing the attitudes and aims of the Sequoyah veterans, labor groups, and the farm element. He called for a constitution to protect the rights of Indians and whites equally, though that tolerance did not extend to black Oklahomans. Racial segregation was a major issue in the selection of delegates. Most of them shared Murray's oft-stated view that "it is an equally false notion that the Negro can rise to the equal of the white man in the professions, or become an equal citizen to grapple with public questions." [14] There was to be no progressivism on that issue and no departure from the southern racial attitudes com-

12. "A New State's Ideas," *Nation* 84 (April 4, 1907): 304.

13. Frederick U. Adams, "A Twentieth-Century State Constitution," *Saturday Evening Post* 180 (November 16, 1907): 3–4, 25.

14. Hurst, *The 46th Star*, p. 7.

mon in much of the new state. Murray's closing remarks to the delegates at the first session perfectly encapsulated this paternalism: "I appreciate the old time ex-slave, the old darkey, (and they are the salt of the race), who comes to me talking softly in that humble spirit which should characterize their actions and dealings with the white man, and when they come thus they can get any favor from me." [15]

This racism soon filtered into every phase of constitution-making and profoundly affected the new state's political system. It also affected red men, as well as whites. Leaders of the Indian nations, proud of their heritage and conscious of their political ability and social rank, did not intend to accept an inferior status in the new state. And men like Murray, who were tribal citizens through marriage, intended to shield their children from any future discrimination based on color. As a result, the Oklahoma constitution reserved the terms *colored* and *colored race* for persons of African descent. "The term 'white race' shall include all other persons," the document provided. [16]

Even that definition did not go far enough for the seventy-five delegates born in the South. Almost all of them had campaigned on a promise to write rigid "Jim Crow" restrictions into the state's organic law. Although sympathetic, Haskell and Murray warned against including those provisions in the constitution. They feared, correctly, that President Theodore Roosevelt and the national Republican party would reject a constitution that was blatantly discriminatory. The Jim Crow laws were removed, with the tacit understanding that the first legislature would enact them. This racism was also strong enough to prevent the adoption, by one vote, of women's suffrage, one of the few advanced ideas of the day that did not enter the constitution in some form. The new state's founding fathers shared a widespread belief that voting was unladylike; but they also feared that allowing women to vote would increase the Negro vote. [17]

15. *Dallas Morning News,* November 22, 1906.
16. Article XXIII, Section II.
17. See Hurst, *The 46th Star,* 14–15; Albert H. Ellis, *A History of the Constitutional Convention of the State of Oklahoma* (Muskogee: Economy Printing Co., 1923), p. 162; and James Ralph Scales, "Political History of Oklahoma, 1907–1949" (Ph.D. diss., University of Oklahoma, 1949), p. 46.

On other questions, the delegates seemed committed to placing most power in the hands of the masses. Lacking faith in legislative wisdom, mistrustful of executive officials, and skeptical of the power of uncontrolled courts, their constitution became essentially antigovernmental. These "cornfield lawyers," as William Jennings Bryan described them, believed fervently that governments were to serve people; citizens were not to serve authority.

Because the delegates wished to avoid loose ends and elastic clauses open to later interpretation, they spent much time on such questions as the form of the state seal. Some wanted it shaped like the hatchet the state's borders formed. Others opted for a more traditional and dignified five-pointed star, which finally won. The final draft also spelled out in great detail the boundaries of counties and townships and the nature of the flash test for kerosene. The *Nation* reported that the constitution was so long that "the newspapers seem to have no idea of printing its full text until they are paid for it out of public funds." [18]

To thwart machine-style politics, a reflection of the bitterness over appointive territorial officials, gubernatorial elections were scheduled for nonpresidential years. The executive was limited to one four-year term. All statewide offices, from that of justice of the supreme court to that of commissioner of charities, were elective rather than appointive. The legislature, whom the delegates regarded as closest to popular opinion, received the greatest power. And the voter shared that power through a system of initiative and referendum procedures. These political reforms all implied that governmental power, with longevity, tended toward inefficiency and absolutism; that politics could still perfect or improve men; and that written rules were necessary to legitimize the process.

Most of the fashionable social provisions concerning child labor, the eight-hour day, and mine safety were copied from the Sequoyah Constitution. But prohibition, one of the most popular reforms of the Progressive Era, had a more circuitous history. A statewide ban on Demon Rum was not included, although the Enabling Act required a twenty-one-year prohibition clause for

18. "A New State's Ideas," p. 304.

Indian Territory and the Osage Nation. Haskell, now flirting with prohibitionist sentiment that he would need in any later race for governor, advocated going further. He opposed any "Calico Constitution," with different laws for various parts of the state, but he feared that statewide prohibition in the constitution might endanger ratification. He and Murray again devised a strategy to circumvent the controversy. A statewide prohibition amendment on a separate ballot would be offered to voters at the election to approve the constitution.

The question loomed large enough in Haskell's mind to ensure that he leave nothing to chance. Engineering a position on the committee dealing with county boundaries, he won votes for his strategy in return for attention to boundaries and county seat sites. He remarked wryly that "the little towns will trade prohibition or the Saviour to gratify their ambitions to become a county seat." [19] The final names of counties, and of many towns across the state, said much of Oklahoma's political divisions. Northwestern counties were usually named for national Republican leaders such as James G. Blaine, James Garfield, Abraham Lincoln, George Dewey. Those in the southern and eastern parts of the state bore the names of famous Indians or southerners. These symbolized the state's political complexion for a surprisingly long time.

Outside of Oklahoma, the most controversial parts of the new constitution affected economic power and land tenure. President Roosevelt declared his thoughts on them unprintable and dispatched his Secretary of War, William H. Taft, to oppose such radicalism. Roosevelt and Taft especially objected to the statutory nature of the constitution, which had become "a code of laws," to its definition of race, and to a provision for the popular election of judges. But the system of economic regulation that Taft predicted would result in a "bourbonism and despotism flavored by socialism" genuinely bothered both men. [20]

Yet these measures were not the work of a "zoological garden of cranks," as Taft later said. [21] The apparently radical

19. Nesbitt, "Governor Haskell Tells of Two Conventions," p. 214.

20. *Kansas City Star,* August 25, 1907.

21. L. J. Abbott, "The Zoological Garden of Cranks," *Independent* 69 (October 20, 1910): 870.

provisions were a logical result of Oklahoma's unusual historical development and economic situation as of 1907. Protecting
individual ownership of resources, and, especially, preserving
the family farm and agrarian ideals were the motives for economic regulation in the constitution. Thus aliens could not own
land, nor could corporations buy, sell, or speculate in land as
their sole endeavor. And the state could not engage in the business of agriculture. The men who had transformed "cow country" into small homesteads thus opposed British syndicates that
owned vast tracts of land in Texas and the far Northwest. And
delegates from Indian Territory wanted to protect tribal allotments from speculators and grafters. These restrictions were
designed to preserve the system of landownership and philosophy of land usage in vogue at the time of statehood. Murray,
chief advocate of reinforcing the state's agrarian basis, also
shrewdly saw the landownership provisions as the most effective antidote to socialist radicalism among potentially turbulent
farmers and tenants.

The constitution's controversial provisions regulating business were not designed to destroy corporations, but to prevent
or control monopolies. Railroad activity in promoting townsite
development and in exploiting mineral and timber resources had
long angered the Five Tribes. Settlers in western Oklahoma
were also hostile to railroads because of discriminatory freight
rates and schedules. After the turn of the century, eastern oil
companies seeking to control local production seemed, to many
people in the state, another major villain. Reflecting a thorough
knowledge of the weaknesses in the Sherman Antitrust Act, the
framers established a state corporation commission to control
freight rates, stock and bond issues, and utility charges. It also
had the power to levy fines for violations of its rules. Monopoly
was formally prohibited, and corporate records were subject to
state examination.

The delegates' reverence for rural ways prompted them to
adopt the Sequoyah Constitution's plan requiring agricultural
and mechanical courses in public schools. Murray explained
that that kind of education would enable boys and girls "to protect themselves in a vocation rather than to burden them with a
false education which leads exclusively to professions and office

holdings, the breeder of the vagabonds of society.'' [22] That was one more statement of the agrarian pioneer's desire for practicality rather than theory. The state would develop a truly remarkable system of agricultural education and teacher training. But the reigning strain of anti-intellectualism summarized in Murray's remarks also starved and retarded the development of excellence in general education.

The constitutional convention recessed in mid-March so that the political parties could nominate candidates for the fall elections. As soon as the Democrats gathered, there were rumblings that the ''Constitutional Cabal,'' Murray, Haskell, and Robert L. Williams, would try to divide the new state's offices among themselves. Haskell made no secret of gubernatorial ambitions. His adroit handling of the volatile prohibition question and the county-seat boundaries had made him the most effective political broker in the Twin Territories. Williams had written many of the constitution's economic provisions. He wanted to represent the forty-sixth state in the United States Senate, as did Murray. Realizing that neither could be elected, they both opted for other posts, Murray choosing the legislature and Williams the Supreme Court.

In spite of any differences, this triumvirate and the ideas they represented had consolidated their influence in the new state. In leaving the Senate seats open to men who had not served at the constitutional convention, they disarmed critics' accusations of conspiracy. Born of the Sequoyah movement and refined at the Guthrie deliberations, the alliance of Haskell, Williams and Murray survived many tensions. As governor, chief justice, and speaker of the house, they would control all three branches of government in the new state.

Throughout the late spring and summer of 1907, members of the constitutional convention campaigned for ratification. In July, the delegates reassembled briefly to make forty-three changes in the document to overcome President Roosevelt's objections, then scattered again to resume campaigning. Confident of their basic strength, the Democrats ran in favor of the consti-

22. William H. Murray, ''The Constitution of Oklahoma,'' *Strum's Oklahoma Magazine* 55 (March–April 1907): 8–9.

tution without much qualification. But the Republicans wanted statehood, while criticizing the constitution, apparently to placate Roosevelt and national leaders. That was a poor beginning for the GOP in Oklahoma. As the *Kansas City Star* noted: "The spectacle of that party of Roosevelt and Taft being used merely for an obstruction to defeat the progressive sentiment of the new state is a situation so anomalous as to excite sympathy for such near-sighted generalship." [23]

When the balloting was over, the prohibition amendment passed and the Democrats won an unqualified mandate to govern. They carried sixty-two counties, Republicans won ten, and three divided evenly. For the next half-century, Democratic control of the courthouses in Oklahoma was the party's power base in both state and national campaigns.

Seeing where the future of political power lay, ambitious men flocked to the Democratic party. With little hope of attracting strong leaders or numbers of voters, the Republicans virtually abandoned competitive politics. They could not overcome the state's southern heritage that favored the opposition. Nor did social changes or economic growth increase their appeal to urban and nonagrarian voters until well into the twentieth century. The sectional nature of Oklahoma politics was confirmed in that early contest: the northwest tended to be Republican, with the southeast strongly Democratic. And the Democrats profited greatly in seeming to favor progressive ideas and statehood. Even the traditionally strong Republicans among the Five Tribes found it difficult to remain loyal during the early years of statehood, when the national administration stood by, as much of their landed estate was despoiled.

Except for a few government clerks from the Twin Territories, no officials from the new state were on hand when President Theodore Roosevelt signed the statehood proclamation. But the lack of ceremony in Washington did not dampen the holiday mood in Guthrie. Early on the morning of November 16, 1907, crowds began to form near the steps of the Carnegie Library, where the ceremonies took place. The sight of people arriving by train, in farm wagons, and on foot or horseback

23. *Kansas City Star*, June 20, 1907.

recalled the great runs. Many in the crowd were original settlers, come to rejoice at the end of carpetbag government. Whites from Indian Territory had come to celebrate their new full citizenship in the new state. Many spectators came to see the symbolic marriage of a Cherokee bride in a beaded-buckskin, Plains Indian wedding outfit to a young man from Oklahoma Territory. Hundreds more simply came for the outing, or to sample an array of barbecue and picnic dinners.

Virtually every community observed the day with rallies and festivities. Country people swarmed into town, and merchants closed their stores for the day. Brass bands, fireworks, and mischievous boys all punctuated the proceedings. Oklahomans were naturally euphoric. As the *Muskogee Phoenix* proclaimed: "Today we have entered into our inheritance . . . and taken our place in Columbia's household as the most favored of all the nation's children . . . with confidence in the future, proud of the record of yesterday, masterful in the strength of today, and [we] meet the future, secure in the belief that tomorrow will bring to us but additional triumphs." [24]

But the mood was different in the oldest settlements of Indian Territory. The celebrants who gathered were primarily whites and young mixed-bloods. The old Indians, especially full-bloods, were absent and silent. Having witnessed the slow but inexorable dissolution of their way of life, most conservative Indians viewed statehood with sadness and fear. They saw the irony of the situation: the government that wanted to teach the Indian the white man's laws and political forms in the nineteenth century, denied him his own territory at the beginning of the twentieth.

Statehood in 1907 ended the Indians' dream of a Sequoyah commonwealth, though its memory lingered. Thirty years later, a Cherokee woman married to a white man recalled her husband's asking her to attend statehood festivities with him. She had refused. He went alone and returned later to say: "Well, Mary, we no longer live in the Cherokee Nation. All of us are now citizens of the State of Oklahoma." There were tears in her eyes on remembering. "It broke my heart. I went to bed and

24. *Muskogee Phoenix*, November 16, 1907.

cried all night long. It seemed more than I could bear that the Cherokee Nation, my country and my people's country, was no more." [25]

25. Edward Everett Dale, "Two Mississippi Valley Frontiers," *Chronicles of Okla-homa* 26 (Winter 1948–1949)· 382

5

Tides of Social Change: Socialism, the Klan, and Prohibition

WHEN John Gunther traveled through Oklahoma in the early 1940s gathering material for his book *Inside U.S.A.*, he noted that "no state has more explosive politics than Oklahoma . . . its political behavior can be positively Balkanesque. 'Knock 'em, sock 'em, rock 'em,' is the rule." [1] During the decades following statehood, political and social radicalism warred for dominance with the conservative ethics of pioneer individualism. Like oil and water, these compounds did not blend, but made an interesting mixture.

Tensions and anxieties originated in the contradictory aspirations of the statehood generation. Imbued with the new century's idealism, they tried to fashion a system of government that retained the virtues of a simple pioneer past, one that would also somehow ameliorate the conflicts that accompanied change and modernization. Weary of the upheaval and uncertainty that characterized pioneer life, that generation longed for order and security that would not sacrifice the individualism that had made settlement in Oklahoma possible. They believed that government should enlarge individual freedom and correct imbalances

1. Gunther, *Inside U.S.A.*, p. 970.

93

in opportunities to succeed. In the end, they created a system with authority so dispersed that constructive government was difficult and often impossible. Like many reformers, they lived to see their handiwork grow into a system they did not recognize.

Drawing on the experience of other states, Oklahoma's founding fathers believed they had foreseen the great social and political problems of the day. But as early as 1907, Oklahoma was already passing from the agrarian state they knew into a modern industrial society they did not recognize. The very speed of this change made every alteration larger than life and every response exaggerated. The problems confronting the new state were doubly disturbing: not only were they unanticipated, they also seldom responded to the prescribed rules.

Although Oklahomans were committed to a system that preserved and protected the agrarian way of life, the fledgling state had a large landless population. Land had attracted thousands to the borders of Indian Territory in the late nineteenth century, and the continuing desire to own land was the catalyst of radical political movements in the twentieth.

There was never enough land for the thousands who came in each land run—there were only so many good homesteads. People lucky enough to stake and retain a farm site often had no capital for livestock, implements, or improvements. The penniless homesteader struggling merely to hold his 160 acres faced the hardships of both nature and a mature economic system. The hapless farmer was often forced into a debt cycle from which foreclosure was the only escape. The Oklahoma farmer was at a disadvantage in depending on distant markets and in competing with growers of staple products like wheat and cotton, for which production costs were lower elsewhere. Freight rates were high, and the farmer had no alternative means of shipping his products. The steep tariffs that protected eastern business and labor from European competition also raised prices for farm machinery. As the pioneer Oklahoma socialist Oscar Ameringer noted: "Instead of escaping industrialism and finance capitalism, as they had hoped, the last frontiersmen had brought it with them, sticking like cockleburrs to their blue-jean breeches and flowing Mother Hubbards.'' [2] This last agrarian society was born into a mature industrial order that offered it few compensations for upholding frontier values.

Farmers were also vulnerable to low rainfall, hail, insects, or fluctuations in market prices that they could neither foresee nor control. In hard times, in the best American tradition, they blamed society and especially the government for their problems. In the 1890s, hot winds, grasshoppers, and falling prices converted thousands of farmers into Populists who supported William Jennings Bryan and free silver. By the time Oklahoma achieved statehood, the Populist party had vanished, but lingering similar circumstances caused many discontented farmers then to join the Socialist party.

Like biblical tares, the Socialist party flourished on the thin soils of eastern Oklahoma. Men born in Dixie and reared in the tradition of reflexive allegiance to the Democratic party had settled the southeastern cotton-producing counties. They had hoped to escape the tenantry that forced small farmers out of the Old South's Cotton Kingdom after 1865. Many were also congenital movers who believed that the existing system had counted them out. They were "the stragglers of routed armies. Always hoping that somewhere in their America there would be a piece of dirt for them." [3]

But the tenant system, illiteracy, poor nutrition, and bad times came in their baggage. Oscar Ameringer, who came to the Twin Territories just before statehood to enlist coal miners and building tradesmen in the Socialist party, dismissed these farmers as poor fuel for any Socialist bonfire. His earlier experience among midwestern farmers had convinced him that they were minor capitalists and unlikely revolutionaries. He told Otto Branstetter, the Socialist party secretary in Oklahoma, that people of that sort would fight before joining any co-operative commonwealth. Branstetter agreed with the general view, but shrewdly suggested that Ameringer go and see for himself.

Though hardened to the sights and smells of urban poverty,

2. Oscar Ameringer, *If You Don't Weaken* (New York: Henry Holt, 1940), p. 261.
3. Ameringer, *If You Don't Weaken*, p. 234.

Ameringer was unprepared for eastern and southern Oklahoma. On his first stop, at Harrah, a farming village of two hundred people east of Oklahoma City, dozens of people braved a spring flood to hear his speech. These were not the sturdy, prosperous farmers of the Midwest, but "an indescribable aggregation of moisture, steam, dirt, rags, unshaven men, slatternly women and fretting children. . . . [Yet] they were farmers! I had come upon another America." [4] Farther south, he saw women prematurely aged from malnutrition and overwork and men too worn down to be desperate at their plight.

Convinced that Oklahoma tenant farmers lived more poorly than New York sweatshop workers, Ameringer began to talk socialism wherever people would listen. To draw a crowd, he often played his clarinet. After a few bars of "Turkey in the Straw" or "The Arkansas Traveller," an audience assembled, and music gave way to politics. He once teamed up with one Jim Mooney, hypnotist, phrenologist, mind reader. That worthy humbugged the crowd while Ameringer taught the principles of socialism.

Ameringer soon adopted the techniques of religious evangelism, whose procedures were as natural as breathing to the crowds. Grateful for anything that relieved their monotony, thousands of isolated farm families attended Socialist encampments. Some 205 of these popular events were held in 1915 alone. They were usually sited near small towns, whose leaders, in the spirit of the times, saw their hamlets becoming mighty cities. Local chambers of commerce competed frantically to attract encampments. On one occasion, merchants in Elk City decorated all the lampposts and telephone poles between the campground and downtown with red flags, and storekeepers displayed the red flag of brotherhood. Local sponsors provided water, firewood, and toilet facilities, and each family brought food and bedding. Extra expenses were met from a general collection at the encampment's end.

These gatherings usually lasted a week, and there was always a good deal of music mixed with the oratory. Soloists and members of the chorus were deputized on the spot, and

4. Ameringer, *If You Don't Weaken,* p. 229.

Ameringer and his three sons often played classical music. Starved for some beauty and refinement in their lives, these people recognized familiar folk music ennobled in the works of Bach, Mendelssohn, and Wagner. Ameringer recalled how they especially responded to the Hungarian rhapsodies of Liszt, "selections as quick and devilish as the reels and jigs of the hearers' forgotten Scotland and Ireland." [5]

Besides the music, there were study sessions three times a day. Borrowing from the techniques of country preachers, socialist speakers sprinkled their talks with appropriate examples from the Bible concerning landlords, labor, and money. Prominent national Socialists often appeared, including Eugene V. Debs, the greatest American Socialist.

Socialists were successful at mobilizing some exploited people, but socialism was more than a political movement. It appealed to the Oklahoma tenant farmer because it offered a solution to specific human grievances. Its doctrine seemed to fit local circumstances, if its abstractions were disregarded. Socialism was also an emotional outlet for the shared misery and frustration of embittered elements of society. As religion had done, earlier, socialism now helped to fill the lonely lives of landless tenants while promising them a better material life.

The presence of socialism was a great irony in Oklahoma's early history. Of all political doctrines, it was the least suitable to a society reared on the virtues of individual competition, in which everyone wanted to be a landholder and to achieve wealth. Lifelong conditioning led farmers, even tenants, to believe that they could succeed on their own. Despite the number of people superficially attracted to its goals, socialism in Oklahoma could not overcome the weight of history that preached the merits and possibility of success within the existing order.

But socialist spokesmen made the doctrine fit and, like other politicians, focused on the land question that underlay Oklahomans' ambitions. Sooner socialism emphasized the disappearance of free land, tenantry, and declining farm prices, all of which made it unlikely that many tenants would ever become landowners. The party platform for 1914 proposed a "Renters

5. Ameringer, *If You Don't Weaken*, p. 266.

and Farmers Program'' to enlarge the state's public domain. A tenant under that ideal arrangement would rent land until he had paid its equivalent value. He and his children would have the right of occupancy and use, but title remained with the commonwealth. That proposal resembled the system of landholding among the Five Civilized Tribes. Though difficult if not impossible to reconcile with Marxist dogma, the proposal was an effective appeal in Oklahoma and Texas, where similar conditions prevailed for cotton farmers.

Despite much talk of the brotherhood of man, the practical Sooner Socialists avoided the race question. Like the Populists, the Socialists flinched whenever their national spokesmen or platforms proposed racial equality. Local candidates played that down, assuring potential supporters that they would not have to worry about *that*.[6]

Socialism in Oklahoma was the logical successor to Populism, the weapon at hand for discontented farmers. The party's modified doctrines did not depart much from the average Sooner's inherited thinking about what was necessary to achieve farm prosperity. Any belief in ideology was superficial. Most Oklahomans who voted for Socialist candidates between 1910 and 1914 were unaware of the movement's international goals or theoretical underpinnings. The existing order was at fault, and they simply attacked it with a Socialist vote, hoping to make it work in their favor. Recognizing that the Democratic party was unresponsive and being pathologically suspicious of the Republicans, these desperate farmers espoused the only alternative at hand, socialism.

The Socialists never won any statewide race, but their vote total increased from 1907 to 1914 in the southern cotton-producing counties. When Eugene Debs captured 6 percent of the national vote for president in 1912, he won 16 percent of Oklahoma's ballots. At the outbreak of the European war in 1914, Oklahoma socialism was at its peak. The party's gubernatorial candidate received 21 percent of the total vote, and the Social-

6. See Howard L. Meredith, ''A History of the Socialist Party in Oklahoma'' (Ph.D. diss., University of Oklahoma, 1969), p. 97.

ists elected five state representatives, one state senator, several county officials, and numerous township officers.

Local and state Democrats sought to blunt socialism's apparent appeal. Hoping to pacify their disgruntled constituents, Democratic legislators tried to adopt a strong antiusury law. State leaders praised the Wilson administration's new farm credit programs and other measures designed to bolster, if not save, the small farmer. But fearful that such laws and gestures alone would not kill socialism, Oklahoma Democrats passed a registration law that required all voters to give their place of residence and party affiliation. This was intended to discourage Negro voters and to identify Socialists. Critics also bitterly attacked the Socialists as atheists, a threat to family, church, and patriotism.

When the United States entered the war in 1917, the Socialists tried to capitalize on the rural areas' widespread opposition to U.S. participation. That seemed logical, since Oklahoma's Democratic Senator Thomas P. Gore was a vocal critic of Wilsonian interventionism. There were also several demonstrations against military conscription within the state. But antiwar sentiment and Socialist appeal both faded rapidly under the assault of inflamed patriotism. In rural areas and small towns, resistance to the draft, refusal to buy bonds, or overt criticism of the war were highly visible individual acts that made socialism seem unpatriotic and un-American and reinforced the notion that socialism was a foreign creed, unsuited to real Americans. Officially sanctioned repression, usually the work of local Councils of Defense, weakened the Socialist organizations as the war progressed. By 1918, because of the wartime economy's insatiable demands, farm prices rose dramatically and revealed Oklahoma socialism's shallow roots. Men who once suffered intimidation for the Socialist party were busy clearing new fields to supply the expanding agricultural market. Old dreams of affluence, landownership, and status revived with the bugle calls of patriotism that seemed as appealing as the grand ideas of socialism.

Basically, the Oklahoma farmer's flirtation with socialism was just that. The extreme, often desperate, hopes and ambitions of these last frontiersmen fortified a normal American tendency to develop strong rhetorical answers to economic distress. That gave a deceptively violent tone to Socialist talk. In many ways, Oklahoma socialism was a gun without bullets.

The war temporarily distracted Oklahomans from local grievances, but there was some opposition in rural areas to embroilment in European affairs. Men struggling to feed their own families were not overexcited about the war in Belgium and France. And just as the price of cotton rose and the tenant farmer might be able to save toward buying his own farm, the government wanted to send his sons to Europe.

Before 1917, many debt-ridden sharecroppers living in the tangled blackjack and post oak near the South Canadian River had joined local radical groups known as Working Class Unions. These fraternal groups, ostensibly formed to discuss ways to improve the farmer's lot, were actually secret orders with elaborate rituals involving six-shooters and Bible quotations. Leaders of the Industrial Workers of the World saw these groups as easy converts to their plans for sabotage and unrest. They encouraged the discontented farmers to resist the draft as a protest against economic inequities.

Because of their isolation and a long tradition of individual action, these farmers believed that direct action was necessary and justified. A ragtag group of poor whites and Negroes, with some Seminoles, began burning railroad bridges, dynamiting oil pipelines and water mains, and tearing down public fences to protest the draft. That guerrilla activity became known as "the Green Corn Rebellion," because Oklahomans believed the rebels planned to live on green roasting ears foraged from fields as they marched on Washington. The march was soon curtailed, as authorities arrested leaders, and the local press demanded the scaffold or life imprisonment for the rebels.

Since most of the disturbances had occurred in counties with Socialist strength, local Democratic leaders saw the chance to eradicate the troublesome "reds." Scores of Socialists and sympathizers fled to the rough backcountry or slipped into neighboring states. Although no Socialist party leader was connected to the Green Corn Rebellion, the party's pacifist leanings were equated with subversion.

The thoroughness of local authorities in snuffing out the Green Corn Rebellion helped subdue radical politics for the time being. Soon the state throbbed with wartime activity. Lagging farm prices soared, oil wells spouted higher profits, and Oklahoma communities vied with each other in buying bonds. The propaganda activities of the local councils of defense sometimes amounted to intimidation. In describing plans for the first Liberty Loan, the Oklahoma City *Daily Oklahoman* headlined: "Buy Bonds Lest Slacker Wagon Get You." The subhead warned: "Employees Must Buy or Quit Their Jobs." [7] The city surpassed its quota.

Other areas used similar tactics to ensure patriotism. In Cleveland County, the Defense Council erected a "slacker pen" and threatened to detain those who failed "to do their duty" in the drive to buy war stamps. [8] In Alfalfa County, the draft board decreed that young men exempted from military service to grow crops could either "Buy a Bond or Fight." That county oversubscribed its goal by $300,000. [9]

As young men left for Europe, reactions to the war became personal. Supporting the war effort meant backing up a son, brother, husband. But personalizing the conflict also exaggerated fears of sedition. Oklahoma had a small foreign-born population and few major terminals or depots, but the authorities were watchful, especially in the oil fields.

Such an atmosphere of suspicion eventually led to some violence. A dentist in Oklahoma City suspected of disloyalty found his office wrecked. At Shattuck, the Defense Council compelled a man to kiss the flag and swear allegiance in public. At Bessie, a local citizen who defended a Farmers' Union official's right to speak was dragged from his bed in the early morning, coated with tar, and warned to keep quiet. And at Elk City a mob of patriotic citizens abducted a Socialist lecturer from police protection, tarred and feathered him, and ran him out of the county.

Immigrants were sometimes treated harshly and forced to demonstrate their patriotism in public. Most Germans suspected

7. *Daily Oklahoman*, June 8, 1917.
8. *Daily Oklahoman*, September 22, 1918.
9. *Daily Oklahoman*, April 15, 1918.

of disloyalty were of Mennonite or Brethren congregations with pacifist or Socialist leanings. Some families emigrated to Canada rather than alter their religious feelings. Yet other Mennonite communities weathered the storm, and their members returned after the conflict. But at the war's end, the German-Russian-Mennonite settlement of Korn, west of Oklahoma City, changed its name to Corn to forestall any further suspicions of disloyalty.[10]

Despite the atmosphere of anxiety, there was relatively little sympathy for the enemy in Oklahoma. Differences in political, social, and economic aspirations actually underlay the violence and suspicion. The public made little distinction between acts that seemed to further the enemy's cause and those that merely continued unpopular prewar views. As in other states, the experience of people working together created a real sense of unity. Just as it glossed over fundamental problems in the national society, the war effort produced a dangerous tendency to equate conformity with patriotism and to punish dissent of any kind.

As the temporary prosperity and unity of the war years receded, Oklahoma entered a period of turbulence that rivaled that of territorial days. Social tensions shaped politics to an unusual degree in the confused 1920s. Oklahomans joined the rest of the country in voting for "normalcy" in 1920, out of weariness with moralistic reform, governmental wartime regimentation, and suspicion of foreign entanglements.

Servicemen returned home in search of jobs just as a general price decline began. Cotton and corn prices plummeted first, then wheat. With grain prices down, the livestock market fell. Then a more serious problem appeared. During the war, much marginal land had been plowed to raise more foodstuff and fiber. To acquire and cultivate that additional land, farmers often went heavily into debt. Only high prices could service the resulting debt level. As the postwar slump became a full-scale depression, there were extensive foreclosures and the added anguish of bank failures.

The price decline also affected Oklahoma's mineral produc-

10. Debo, *Prairie City,* p. 157; O. A. Hilton, "The Oklahoma Council of Defense and the First World War," *Chronicles of Oklahoma* 20 (1942): 18–42.

tion. Oil dropped from $3.50 per barrel to $1.75 in less than a year. Coal production revived strongly during the war, when miners earned $6.00 per day. But as the paychecks of coal miners and oil-field workers now dwindled or disappeared, labor unrest grew, reviving the specter of radicalism. At one point, some eight thousand miners in eastern Oklahoma were on strike. Business leaders and politicians quickly blamed IWW agitators. Governor James B. Robertson estimated that 40 percent of the miners were foreign-born and asked United States Attorney General A. Mitchell Palmer to deport aliens who interfered with mining. Failing federal action, Robertson promised to jail foreign agitators, or escort them to the state line.[11] As the state's "red scare" grew, in concert with one on the national scale, Robertson finally declared martial law in the troubled coal counties. But strikes and protests spread rapidly to other segments of the economy in the throes of postwar readjustments. Mines closed, factories slowed, and many farmers lapsed back into tenancy or disappeared under debt. Angry people were ripe for new forms of action, whether radical or traditional, to solve problems.

But the war years had changed more than economics for Oklahomans. Increasing industrialization, urbanization, and prosperity had undermined the moral *status quo*. The new generation communicated with a wider world of values and tastes. Personal fulfillment, or amusement, soon triumphed over concern for inherited values or social stability. People committed to the unquestioned rural values of home, family, church, and school found their world topsy-turvy.

The war-generated urbanization developed rapidly in the greater Southwest. Between 1910 and 1920, the nation's urban population increased some 29 percent. In Oklahoma, the growth was almost 69 percent. The state's population was still predominantly rural, but the growth of cities and towns was accelerating before men's eyes. And urban growth meant urban problems, based on detachment from the hallowed ethics that defined Oklahomans' lives.

Oil was the catalyst for many of the new urban troubles. Dis-

11. *Harlow's Weekly,* November 5, 1919.

coveries of enormous gas and oil deposits transformed Cushing, Seminole, Okmulgee, and Oklahoma City, much as gold and silver strikes had transformed California and Nevada towns two generations earlier. Farmers left their land, rootless people converged on the strike areas, and the resulting towns were caricatures of everything wrong with American life. They fairly celebrated disorder, greed, violence, and indifference to the earth itself.

Crime rapidly became the most sensational and widely noted aspect of life in these boomtowns. Concern became intense as brutal, random attacks on the general public increased, and crimes of passion outpaced the usual crimes against property. These widely reported stories inevitably made citizens of every town feel unsafe, fearful of a spreading change they hoped to stop at their city's limits.

The automobile, movie theater, and public dance hall seemed suddenly to supplant the church, schoolhouse, and fair grounds. Bootleg whiskey flowed freely, and flouting the law gained a certain respect in many circles. Law enforcement agencies seemed corrupt, and politicians could no longer arrest—let alone control—social change. Many Oklahomans turned, as did citizens in other states, to a revived Ku Klux Klan to enforce both laws and moral behavior.

The KKK in the Southwest after World War I differed from its predecessor of Reconstruction days. Although its codes were still secret, and violence was a major weapon, its national following in the 1920s supported nativist as well as racist goals. In the nation at large, the Klan became the enemy of Jews, Catholics, and modernists of all kinds, as well as Negroes. But in Oklahoma, as in other southwestern states with small foreign-born populations, the Klan became a device for the ruthless dictation of community-approved morals.

Socialism had appealed to the rootless in Oklahoma; the Klan attracted those with a stake in society. The citizen concerned with the old social values listened receptively when white-robed men told him that the KKK "stands pre-eminently against night auto-riding and roadside parking," the "salacious literature and modern dress," the "jazz dance" and "the seducer of girls or the rape-fiend,'' that symbolized sudden social change.[12] The KKK quickly became an effort to restore the old virtues of sobriety, chastity, and the family as a social ideal. The force and intimidation that accompanied this restoration did not seem ironic to men accustomed to frontier ways or to the extreme experiences of the World War. Ironically, the Klan appeared progressive, reformist, something larger than materialism to those inclined to approve its avowed goals.

People from every walk of life entered the Klan. Ministers, lawyers, businessmen, and college professors joined, along with mechanics, farmers, and oil-field workers. Because the Klan's primary role seemed at first the restoration of moral authority, the membership even included some non-Protestants and non-whites.

The Klan's elaborate rituals gave members a sense of drama and respectability, while assuring anonymity. Klansmen usually announced their mission in a town on a dark night. A lone horseman clad in ghostlike regalia galloped through the streets, holding high a burning cross and warning gamblers, bootleggers and hijackers to beware. The local chapter soon punished car thieves, unfaithful husbands, rumrunners, prostitutes, and public officials who overlooked crime. By 1922, some seventy thousand Oklahomans had joined the KKK crusade to renovate society and restore the old virtues.

In its first days, the Klan had virtually no opposition from the respectable elements of society. What frustrated Muskogeean, for instance, could criticize an organization that whipped a man who had kidnaped a boy able to identify him as a burglar? A sense of helplessness coupled with the pioneer ethic of direct action helped explain why the Klan at first escaped public censure. An Oklahoma judge summed it up well: ''In actual results, the thing [Klan coercion] worked pretty well. I don't defend it, of course, but from what I've seen I should say that the night-riders averaged nearer justice than the courts do.'' [13]

12. *Colonel Mayfield's Weekly,* November 21 and December 3, 1921; January 7, 1922.

13. Stanley Frost, ''Night-Riding Reformers: The Regeneration of Oklahoma,'' *Outlook* 135 (November 14, 1923): 439.

Ethnic and religious minorities were careful not to attract Klan attention in the early 1920s. Yet there were instances when people had to deny their heritage to prove their patriotism, as in the ugly days of war scare. In 1920 an incident involving a prominent Jewish haberdasher, whose family came to Oklahoma in the 1890s and established clothing stores in Tulsa, Muskogee, Bartlesville, and Oklahoma City, illustrated the latent anti-Semitism in the state. Ben Madansky traveled to Mexico City as a member of an Oklahoma City Chamber of Commerce delegation. On returning, he was forced to prove his American citizenship at the Mexican border. Given the growing power of the Klan and other signs of prejudice, Ben Madansky and his brothers decided to change their name. Ben put an ad in the *Daily Oklahoman,* announcing that *Madansky Brothers* would become *May Brothers.* The family wished "to prove ourselves wholly American in every sense of the word," as they had always been.[14]

But approval of the Klan and what it represented was never unanimous. Many critics obviously adopted a wait-and-see attitude, assuming that in due course the organization's methods would alienate many potential supporters. Gusts of reaction to social change, like bad weather, often simply had to pass through a society. As Klan-inspired violence increased in 1922, many Oklahomans began to fear that the organization was too powerful. Whatever its intentions, virtue armed had become arrogance enthroned. The irony of trying to restore law and order with extralegal means dawned on many people. The political situation also deteriorated daily. With control of the legislature divided between the two parties for the first time in the state's history, partisan conflict, investigations aimed at embarrassing the governor, and attempts to impeach officials precluded any serious legislative work.

Racial troubles compounded the confusion, when a major riot broke out in Tulsa in 1921. Martial law and the national guard were required to suppress the disturbance, in which eighty persons died and two square miles of property were destroyed. But

14. *Daily Oklahoman,* March 27, 1921.

the political parties and people involved in the legislative process seemed oblivious to underlying causes. The political civil war was so engrossing to those involved that in 1922 the sixty-day legislative session expired without the necessary appropriations to run state government.

As political paralysis complemented social disorder, a coalition of farmers and workers, similar to the group that had dominated the constitutional convention, met in Shawnee in the fall of 1921. The resulting Farmer-Labor Reconstruction League resembled similar organizations in the Dakotas. Its platform was designed to satisfy discontented elements throughout the state. The group advocated public ownership or regulation of utilities, flour mills, grain elevators, coal mines, stockyards, packing plants, and cotton gins. Farm implements and improvements were exempted from taxation. There were to be free schoolbooks, subsidies for tenants and homebuilders, and bonuses for the doughboys.

This "Christmas tree" approach, clothed in the rhetoric of old values, was designed to win the Democratic nomination for governor in 1922. The league's candidate was John C. Walton, a civil engineer turned politician. Elected mayor of Oklahoma City in 1919, Walton had refused to intervene when infuriated strikers turned against scabs. A member of a railroad brotherhood, "Our Jack" seemed the perfect standard-bearer for the embattled farmers and workers.

Walton triumphed in the three-man primary contest, chiefly because the Klan divided its support between his two opponents. And mounting Klan violence frightened many voters into supporting Walton because of his alleged antipathy to the secret order. Walton's general election campaign featured a jazz band to draw voters and demagoguery to hold them. Money was scarce, and Walton assured audiences that his campaign funds had not come from the hated "still-faced boys," the banking community. His most effective fund-raising speech ended with the story of the three dimes, the gift of "a hardpressed widow with seven children." Holding aloft this widow's mite, he thundered: "May my right hand wither and may my tongue cleave to the roof of my mouth if I ever desert the honest farmers and laborers who so loyally support my candidacy with their dimes!'' [15]

In the fall election, conservative Democrats joined the Republicans, but Walton and most of the league slate won. The regular Democrats captured the congressional delegation and the legislature, where many members were Klansmen hostile to the league. ''Our Jack's'' campaign attracted national attention, and his inaugural ceremonies were a Jacksonian substitute for the usual rites. The celebration lasted two days and nights for most visitors to the capital, and longer for some enthusiasts. The food served included beef, buffalo, reindeer, antelope, chicken, turkey, opossum, rabbit, and wildfowl, all cooked in a mile of smoking trenches.

Representatives of various Indian tribes encamped around Oklahoma City, and in due course mingled with a wide variety of Sooners come to celebrate the new day. On inauguration morning, a ten-mile-long procession including one hundred bands wound from downtown to the fairgrounds, where Walton spoke to 100,000 people after taking the oath. Afterwards, there were fiddling contests, hoedowns, cakewalks, and clog dances, culminating in a boisterous square dance spread through the four stories of the state capitol. In those solemn surroundings, people dressed in furs and jewels jostled with cowboys, Indians, farmers in overalls, and other examples of the state's population. The groups performed every known dance, and some that were unknown. Nor were the proceedings uniformly dry. The *New York Times* saw the spectacle as a microcosm of the state's history, and viewed the promised new era with genial tolerance. Many a new broom had promised to sweep Oklahoma clean, and Walton's attack on corruption might produce much or little action. ''It is not necessary to take a strictly moral view of these things,'' the *Times* said, of past and impending scandals. ''The oil and gas in the Oklahoma nature easily takes fire.'' [16]

Quite soon, these descriptions fitted the new administration's prospects. The alliance that made Walton's election possible ensured a brief and chaotic tenure. Patronage was the root of the

15. Ameringer, *If You Don't Weaken,* pp. 375–376.
16. *New York Times,* January 10, January 11, 1923.

problem. At first, attempting to solidify his base, Walton distributed the spoils of victory in the traditional manner. But the state government was split between league members and regular Democrats, many of whom were Klansmen. Efforts to appease or win the two sides alienated both. When the supply of regular loaves and fishes failed, Walton turned to the educational system. His search for offices there touched off a chain of events that forced him from office. Prior to the election, the Reconstruction League had expressed concern over the small number of graduates of Oklahoma Agricultural and Mechanical College at Stillwater who actually returned to the state's small farms and shops. In their view, "this institution of learning had been turning out, to the vast disgust of our farmers and miners, a pedigreed collection of potential life-insurance, lightning-rod, patent-fence-gate, and oil-burner salesmen, prepared to bite the paternal hands that fed them." [17]

Imbued with the reigning American notion that education could cure anything, the league leaders wished to remake Oklahoma through educating the farmers. Walton acquiesced with a somewhat idealistic intervention into A & M College affairs, which resulted in dismissal of the president and resignation of several faculty members in favor of politically more amenable appointees. These events convinced Walton that the educational system was a rich vein of spoils and influence.

Within a few months of taking office, Walton had also interfered at the University of Oklahoma at Norman. He replaced five members of its board of regents, and a sixth resigned in protest. The university's president finally resigned, to avoid a confrontation. The alumni of both the Stillwater and Norman institutions gradually became alarmed at the governor's tampering. Such angry demonstrations occurred at Stillwater that a military escort was required to help install the new president, George Wilson. But public opposition finally forced Walton to name yet another board to cancel Wilson's appointment. The governor's patronage game might have seemed merely shoddy had the results been less destructive and embarrassing to concerned Oklahomans.

17. Ameringer, *If You Don't Weaken,* p. 379.

Walton's political ineptitude angered both the league and regular Democrats. His policy of commuting all death sentences to life imprisonment alarmed citizens already concerned about crime and lawlessness. Walton also alternated between supporting and criticizing the Klan as its fortunes rose and fell. As his league support dwindled, Walton increasingly became anti-Klan in a last-ditch effort to refurbish his image.

The general confusion pervading the state in 1923 heightened the kind of atmosphere in which Klan violence flourished. That summer, after the brutal whipping of a man in Okmulgee and similar Klan-inspired violence in Tulsa, Walton declared martial law throughout southern Tulsa County. He also suspended the privilege of the writ of habeas corpus, a clearly unconstitutional act. Despite the presence of troops in Tulsa, the governor was unable to control press criticism. The *Tulsa Daily World* continued to uncover corruption and expose his unconstitutional use of authority, and the *Tulsa Tribune* led in calling for his impeachment. When a grand jury was formed in Oklahoma City to investigate charges of misconduct among state officials, including the governor, Walton placed the entire state under martial law. He ordered machine guns trained on the Oklahoma County courthouse to prevent the grand jury from assembling, all in the name of defeating the deadly Klan.

To rid the state of Walton, the anti-Klan forces joined with the Klan. With more than three years left in his term, Walton was impeached on twenty-two counts and convicted of eleven, the least of which was general incompetence. In one sense, Walton was a victim, however willing, of the politics of default. He lacked both the experience and the intelligence to govern the state during the postwar period. In their haste to reshape the state, the Farm Labor Reconstruction League had not asked whether he had the ability or the desire to resist the temptations of power and profit. The whole Walton episode tragically forced people who did not condone the KKK to choose between the Klan and the despotic governor. The Klan was actually on the wane when Walton set out to crush it in 1923. The alliance necessary to oust him then fortified the Klan within the Democratic party. As a result, the KKK continued to be influential in state politics after most Oklahomans had abandoned its professed ideals.

The Klan typified the major transition of values and attitudes that characterized the 1920s everywhere and that seemed to be occurring with especial intensity in Oklahoma. By the mid-1920s, most Oklahomans probably realized the irony of trying to enforce morality with extralegal methods. Yet, on an equally important and fundamental social question, prohibition, they remained hypocritical. The state was legally dry; yet, no one seeking liquor had difficulty finding it. When the Eighteenth Amendment was ratified, in 1919, Oklahoma had lived with the "noble experiment" of prohibition for twelve years. And it was a failure from the first.

Despite the long-standing congressional ban on alcoholic beverages in Indian Territory, when Oklahoma Territory organized in 1890, the licensed sale of intoxicants was legalized. Like every other frontier society, the Territory sustained a certain amount of lawlessness and violence. Drunkenness, brawling, and prostitution, usually centered on the local saloon, dramatized the problem. People who opposed legal liquor found the saloon synonymous with crime. Saloons were frequently the most prominent businesses in frontier towns. The tiny northwestern community of Woodward had twenty-three in 1901. These "resorts" dispensed liquor from walnut and mahogany bars, complete with lewd paintings and female faro dealers. Oklahoma City, the center of Territorial liquor trade, was also considered wicked. One devout dry held that the whole city was given over to "revelry, debauchery, throatcutting, robbery, and all the usual industries accompanying the saloon system." [18] Whatever its moral implications, prohibition also divided the population according to values, aspirations, and conceptions of freedom and respectability.

The problems of disorderliness and drunkenness associated with the liquor traffic were not unique to Oklahoma Territory; in spite of the congressional ban on selling alcohol to Indians, whiskey consumption was so widespread in the 1840s that the Choctaw and Cherokee Temperance Societies were formed. Prohibitionists in the Twin Territories skillfully used the Indian to gain support for their cause in early territorial days. Speaking

18. William E. Johnson, *Ten Years of Prohibition in Oklahoma* (Westerville, Ohio: American Issues Publishing Co., 1917), p. 7.

to southerners, who understood the rationale for keeping liquor from blacks, the drys argued that liquor must be kept from the Indian for his own and society's protection.

As plans for statehood matured in the late 1890s, the Women's Christian Temperance Union and the Anti-Saloon League, allied with Protestant churches, began to organize and agitate for constitutional prohibition. Carrie Nation visited Guthrie without her hatchet in 1905 and founded a branch of the Prohibition Federation. She also purchased a press that printed tracts, the *Smasher's Mail* and the *Hatchet*. Prohibition developed a strong base through such efforts of both local and national figures.

The proliquor forces, usually businessmen, opposed the drift toward prohibition. They argued a direct correlation between prosperity and the saloon's fellowship. Disorderliness and violence in this view were the fault of individuals, not of institutions. Temperance rather than prohibition became their option, since a certain amount of disorderliness and struggle were necessary to progress. To the wets, the drys were sour fanatics, intent on destroying prosperity, curtailing good cheer, and curbing individual freedom and responsibility.

The struggle over formal prohibition at the constitutional convention in 1906 was an integral part of the progressive reformism then dominating the country. Prohibition was an attempt at individual perfection and social stability admirably suited to the delegates at Guthrie wishing to construct a model modern state. A generation intent on rectifying corporate power and cleaning up politics could not fail to distrust the saloon and all it represented.

However fiercely debated across the country, the drive for prohibition made a certain sense in the progressive era. Its economic, moral, and social appeals were obvious. But a law-abiding generation also saw few problems of enforcement. People in that era debated ends and means on every great social question and tended to obey any laws that resulted. Obedience to law was as reflexive as loyalty to the flag. The greatest irony in the long crusade for national prohibition was its triumph at just the moment in American history, the 1920s, when society was no longer disposed to obey moralistic laws.

There was added force to the prohibitionist argument in Oklahoma. Liquor came to represent the violence and turmoil that many Oklahomans associated with their adolescent, territorial past. It was one part of the fabled frontier heritage they wished to forget. At statehood, Oklahomans had a chance to leave behind the crudeness and vulgarity that liquor symbolized and be born again, both sober and modern. This triumphant sobriety and the moralistic industry it represented would then radiate out and maintain the best values in the new state's society.

The Enabling Act of 1906 that contained guidelines for Oklahoma's admission to the Union required prohibition for twenty-one more years in the former Indian Territory and the Osage Nation. With that edge, the antiliquor forces sought statewide prohibition. But the dry forces ultimately agreed to present statewide prohibition as a separate amendment to the state constitution. Citizens opposed to prohibition could thus vote against the amendment without jeopardizing the constitution.

On the eve of the constitutional election in 1907, the *Tulsa World* wryly predicted that the prohibition amendment would carry if only because "Indian Territory wanted to play a joke on Oklahoma [Territory] by making that end dry." [19] The amendment passed, but fourteen counties in Indian Territory and the Osage Nation opposed it.

Charles Haskell, the state's first governor, reminded Oklahomans that the prohibition law was "not placed in our constitution as a political requirement nor for mere sentimental purposes, but because a majority of the people believe that humanity will be better by having such a law and by having it enforced." [20] As the inaugural crowds drifted away that November evening in 1907, thousands who had voted dry drank as if they considered it their personal duty to exhaust the remaining liquor stock before the law went into effect. Some saloon keepers offered "Alfalfa Bill Bourbon" and "Old Crow" at cut-rate prices. Others, such as Anheuser-Busch, flushed 27,000 gallons of beer down Oklahoma City's sewers. Still others planned to convert from saloon-keeping to tending drugstores,

19. *Tulsa World,* April 13, 1907.
20. *Daily Oklahoman,* November 16, November 17, 1907.

with ice cream sodas replacing the red-eye on the ornate bars.

On that last night before statewide prohibition, the uplifted glasses of thousands of Oklahomans who had supported prohibition symbolized the dichotomy that plagued the state for the foreseeable future. Prohibition expressed Sooner society's duality, a struggle between idealism and reality, between what people aspired to be and what they were willing to be.

From the outset, prohibition was difficult to enforce. The first legislature passed an enforcement statute known as the "Billups Booze Bill." It placed enforcement in the hands of an agency responsible to the governor. It also provided a state dispensary to make spirits available for medical purposes. The first prohibition enforcement officer was deemed incompetent, and "Old Sunnybrook," the official whiskey for the dispensary system, soon became a term that provoked knowing smiles. The "Billups Booze Bill" and many subsequent laws were repealed, modified, or ignored.

The public's growing resentment at arbitrary "star chamber" methods underlay the failure to enforce the law. Many a law-abiding citizen who voted dry believed that rationality would make men refrain from drinking. But he stoutly resisted enforcement statutes that interfered with personal liberty or required much tax money to implement.

Despite the contradictory public attitudes about enforcement and the enormous expense and effort required for even a token policing of the state's seventy thousand square miles, Governor Haskell persisted in his pledge to make Oklahoma dry. The number of arrests for liquor violations rose dramatically. Between 1908 and 1910, in fifteen counties around the state, there were more than nine thousand cases involving bootleggers. Unable to admit that public hostility made enforcement impossible, Haskell blamed the federal government: as long as Washington allowed interstate shipment of liquor, Oklahoma would be wet, or at least damp. By 1910, it was clear that the "Noble Experiment" was not working. Thousands of bootleggers imported liquor from other states to satisfy Sooner thirsts. The illegal traffic's most notable result was simply to corrupt law enforcement officials and politicians.

The hypocrisy of the situation persuaded many former prohibitionists to join wet forces in calling for repeal and substituting a local-option measure better suited to the state's various areas. In attacking prohibition, the prorepeal forces stressed the loss of tax revenue, continuing drunkenness, and official corruption. But the voters were not persuaded. Compared to the original 1907 election, in 1910 the prohibitionists actually increased their tally. The defeat of repeal in 1910 confirmed the situation's ironies. Oklahomans supported a law they would not obey, all in the best tradition of gestural liberalism. They had adopted ideals impossible to attain, although a majority of people believed those concepts to be correct. The churches and respectable elements in nearly every community argued that repeal would be a symbolic abandonment of ideals necessary to progress. Voters seemed to prefer the dualism of the status quo, where "the Wets have their liquor and the Drys have their law." [21]

National prohibition went into effect in 1920, and the dry forces in Oklahoma welcomed federal enforcement. But Sooners were shocked at the effects of the Eighteenth Amendment. Stills appeared all over the state, drawing customers from every social level. And the oil finds of the 1920s raised a new series of boomtowns where illicit and often dangerous liquor fueled crime and violence. No part of the state was immune. Scores of upstanding citizens perished in drunken brawls. People of good families died from drinking bathtub gin. And for the first time since territorial days, drunkenness was a problem among high school students and other young people.

While many dedicated law enforcement officers gave their lives to uphold prohibition, there was also widespread corruption. Public attitudes toward enforcement penalties also undermined the efforts of the most dedicated officials. Many a prosecuting attorney emulated the Tulsa County prosecutor who dismissed fifteen liquor cases in 1922 with the observation: "I am not going to force anything down their [Tulsa residents'] throats that they don't want." [22] By the 1930s, after a decade of

---

21. Gibson, *Oklahoma: A History of Five Centuries,* p. 420.

22. Jimmie Franklin, *Born Sober: Prohibition in Oklahoma, 1907–1959* (Norman: University of Oklahoma Press, 1971), p. 80.

national prohibition, Oklahoma was still a notorious haven for bootlegging.

The state's liquor laws were not liberalized until 1933, after the repeal of national prohibition. And then the change merely authorized the sale of 3.2 beer, arbitrarily defined as nonintoxicating. But the vote favoring that minor relaxation of the law revealed an important change in Oklahoma society. The referendum was overwhelmingly successful in urban centers. Only twenty of the state's seventy-seven counties turned in antibeer majorities, and these were primarily the sparsely settled western counties. Although many of these new urban voters had just left the farm, the varied appeals of urban life and the loosening ties of religion and tradition that characterized postwar America were clear in Oklahoma.

Between the legalization of 3.2 beer in 1933 and repeal in 1959, Oklahomans continued to stagger to the polls and vote dry, as Will Rogers allegedly remarked. But at each election, the margin of dry victory declined. That gradual drift toward repeal revealed the state's urbanization and industrial development, which promoted a more permissive view of public morality. After World War II, prohibition was clearly a vestige of the state's rural past. But the rural counties continued to dominate state politics. They controlled the legislature and could destroy any governor who threatened repeal. Yet repeal required a dynamic and fearless executive, unafraid to challenge inherited ways.

In 1958, Oklahomans elected Democrat J. Howard Edmondson governor with the largest majority in any gubernatorial election to date. The thirty-three-year-old former Tulsa County attorney had pledged to give the state's voters a chance to judge repeal. Winning in spite of Old Guard opposition, Edmondson announced that his administration would enforce prohibition ruthlessly. Officials in Oklahoma City and Tulsa immediately began raiding illegal clubs, arresting both producers and sellers of liquor. By January 1959, there was so much statewide furor over prohibition that one legislator quipped that the traditionally wet inaugural festivities would be "a buttermilk ball, and you can bring your own cow." [23]

23. *Oklahoma City Times,* January 8, 1959.

Joe Cannon, the commissioner of Public Safety whom the wets dubbed "the crew-cut commando," enforced the law ferociously. Working with the highway patrol, he organized roadblocks, searched cars, examined ladies' purses when necessary, and raided private clubs. Bootleggers installed radios tuned to the police frequency, but the police used secret codes and imposed radio silence. With the highway patrol often appearing from everywhere at once, frantic bootleggers used buses and airplanes to deliver their goods. "Pint Pitchers," bootleggers who delivered to the door, adopted disguises as repairmen and salesmen.

The predictable panic, irritation, and confusion grew with each new level of enforcement. Hotel and restaurant owners complained of reduced business. As more and more citizens were inconvenienced or embarrassed, the legislators' mail became abusive and wet. The debate on passing a repeal referendum was tense and often angry. Tempers flared, and the House speaker kept order at one point only by reminding colleagues that they were on public view through television.

Oklahomans voted on the referendum on April 7, 1959. Earlier warnings that strict enforcement would turn the state wet came true. The electorate would not tolerate the cost of either expensive illegal liquor or even more expensive and embarrassing enforcement of a hypocritical law.

Repeal carried, but the curious dualism surrounding prohibition's history survived—for, while legalizing the sale of beer in licensed bars, Oklahoma voters turned down local option and mixed drinks. One could "brown bag" with a personal bottle or have mixed drinks in a private club, but mixed drinks were not available in public bars. The open saloon awaited yet another round of agitation, enforcement, and referenda.

But the passing of prohibition marked an end to a major phase of the state's history. Socialism, the Klan, and now prohibition passed into history. The old tensions and aspirations that they represented yielded to new problems and responses. The waning of these social movements revealed how much change had come to the forty-sixth state in only two generations.

6

The Politics of Modernization:
From the 1920s to the 1960s

*T*HE record of the first fifteen years of statehood disappointed those who thought that they were establishing truly democratic government in 1907. In spite of Oklahomans' persistent idealistic belief in man's goodness, old injustices remained. From the first, the combination of an unwieldy constitution and an exploitative political system rooted in the frontier ethic of grab-and-run shaped the merry-go-round quality of Sooner party politics and state government.

The basic constitutional provision forbidding the governor and other elected officials from succeeding themselves was designed to prevent the courthouse gangs so familiar in American political history. In practice, it promoted a spoils system. Ambitious men learned to exchange offices and support each other's campaigns. "Swapping keys," as the practice was called, gave the state some honest and experienced administrators, but it also left a large number of corrupt or incompetent officials undisturbed.

The number of candidates the system generated thwarted the progressive idea that elected rather than appointed officials best represented the voters' wishes. Confronted with a bedsheet ballot, most people voted "by guess or by God," ignorant of the candidates' abilities. In the 1930s, numerous candidates with famous names compounded the problem of voter recognition. In

1932 a public school teacher from Moore named Will Rogers capitalized on his namesake's popularity and won election to Congress. Illustrious names appeared regularly on Oklahoma ballots after that. Mae West, a telephone switchboard operator from Oklahoma City, received more than 65,000 votes for Commissioner of Charities and Corrections in 1938. Oliver Cromwell, Daniel Boone, Brigham Young, Joe E. Brown, and Patrick Henry vied for other offices.

The cynical held that anyone who ran for office was probably a scoundrel, anyway; voting him in and then driving him out of office might warn others of like mind. Incessant bickering over patronage within state government and pressures from without prevented many conscientious officials from doing their jobs. Oklahomans were not unique in their disenchantment with politics after World War I, but wide swings of public mood made any real political stability difficult.

Just as national attention focused on the president, so local voters looked to the governor for leadership. After the near-civil war of the Walton episode in the 1920s, Oklahomans were ready for the respite of Martin E. Trapp's interim administration. Lieutenant governor under three different chief executives, Trapp was the epitome of the professional politician. An able administrator, accustomed to working with a touchy legislature, he provided peaceful leadership. It seemed ironic that more or less by chance the state had acquired an able man as governor during a critical period of transition.

To many, it looked as if the querulous politics of the statehood era were over. And as the 1926 election approached, many Democrats hoped that Trapp could be a candidate, since, technically, he had thus far served only as "acting governor." Popular with the voters and acceptable to the faction-ridden Democratic party, Trapp probably would have won election. But the state supreme court upheld the constitutional provision of one term per governor, and the prospect of a stable administration faded.

Henry S. Johnston, a frail, bookish, country lawyer succeeded Trapp when the hue and cry of electioneering abated. A prohibitionist, veteran of the constitutional convention, and first president *pro tempore* of the state senate, Johnston posed as a founding father and an Old Testament prophet. His moralistic speeches were somewhat attractive to an electorate weary of biting personalism.

Soon after his inauguration, however, it became clear that Johnston had as many old-time faults as he had old-time virtues. Intolerant of opponents, he seemed blind to weak friends. He ignored party leaders and legislators in favor of a strange coterie of private advisers. He procrastinated in making decisions and spent hours meditating over Rosicrucian philosophy or consulting with his private astrologer. On one occasion, he told a startled press conference that he chose the specific hour to sign a bill because of favorable zodiac signs. He also offended old-fashioned callers in appointing Mrs. Mayme Hammonds his personal secretary. Her prim screening of Johnston's visitors offended many sensibilities. Soon there were rumors of another "Mrs. Woodrow Wilson," then the inevitable charges that the governor was neglecting his duties.

Despite these personal and personnel matters, Johnston might have avoided a break with the legislature had he not tampered with highway department patronage and become embroiled in a controversy over the merits of asphalt versus cement for paving state roads. But Johnston, like Walton, seemed out of touch with political reality, almost bent on destruction. The growing revolt among legislators might have simmered without exploding, except for the 1928 presidential election. President Calvin Coolidge was never popular among Sooners. The Democrats had recaptured the United States Senate seat lost in the Republican landslide of 1920 and were entrenched on the state level. Yet, overnight, the nomination of Al Smith changed everything. Hundreds of state and local Democratic candidates were allied now with a cocky city slicker who was wet—and a Catholic, to boot.

Johnston the procrastinator acted with uncharacteristic decisiveness. He announced that while he personally disliked Smith, as titular head of the Democratic party in Oklahoma, he would actively support the national ticket. As a militant dry, a Protestant, and a Klan sympathizer, Johnston was talking when he should have been meditating.

Smith did not help matters. In Oklahoma City, he bitterly denounced former Senator Robert Owen, leader of the Democratic insurgents who would not support the national ticket. The New Yorker held that Owen, who charged that wicked Tammany Hall was subverting the Democratic party, had avidly sought the Hall's support in his presidential bid of 1920. Smith blasted the KKK, the Anti-Saloon League, and religious bigotry. When Johnston tried to repair some of the damage, arguing that "prohibition is not an issue in this campaign," he only inflamed the insurgents further.[1]

The state GOP barely stirred during the fall campaign, confident that anti-Smith Democrats would push Herbert Hoover over the top. Yet even they underestimated the effects of rum and Romanism on the rebellion. Hoover carried all but eight of Oklahoma's seventy-seven counties, and those were in the Democratic stronghold of Little Dixie. Many Democrats rationalized their bolt as antiliquor rather than pro-Republican. To everyone's surprise, Republican candidates were elected to nearly every seat in Oklahoma's lower house and made substantial inroads into the state senate, while capturing several state offices and three seats in Congress.

Yet, despite Hoover's decisive victory, to which thousands of rebellious Democrats contributed, the local party leaders blamed Johnston for devastating losses at home. Impeaching him was the first order of business when the legislature convened in 1929. After six weeks of testimony, by turns spectacular and pathetic, the Oklahoma Senate finally convicted him of general incompetence.

The constitutional validity of these grounds for impeachment were debated long after Johnston left office. But many thoughtful Oklahomans were ashamed of the embarrassing national publicity the trial engendered. Johnston seemed as competent when impeached as when elected. William H. Murray typically remained true to his grass-roots populism and offered the hapless Johnston a certain sympathy. "We must remember that the

1. *Chickasha Daily Express,* October 11, 1928. See also *Daily Oklahoman,* July 27–29, 1928.

people have a right to elect a fool," the Sage of Tishomingo noted, "and the best way to cure them of that habit is to let him stay in office." [2]

Johnston's impeachment and the term of his successor, W. J. Holloway, finally signaled the decline of Oklahoma's fascination with impeachment as a solution to party ills. The KKK was also in decline, and the public served notice that it expected more from the political system than personal feuds. Uncertain economic conditions, sharpened after the stock market crash of 1929, foretold the onset of a new kind of political action. Government must now face a new set of challenges involving public finance and benefits.

Movement toward any new style or purpose in state politics was neither easy nor smooth. As the 1930 elections approached, the effect of the national depression settled on Oklahoma. Farmers who had experienced price slumps, surpluses, and high mortgage rates since the end of World War I now saw natural disaster developing. Drought threatened to destroy not only their shrunken income, but also the soil itself. In the wake of financial collapse after 1929, other sectors of the state economy began to suffer in what seemed a general disaster. Industrial activity slowed, mines closed, oil prices plummeted. Oklahomans continued to believe that hard work and expansion would overcome any temporary handicaps. They were first bewildered, then frightened, as nothing seemed to offset the deepening crisis. Unable to understand what was happening, Sooners, like most other Americans, sought answers in political leadership.

In the spring of 1930, before the GOP was identified with the depression, it seemed that Republicans might consolidate their 1928 gains into a viable state party and elect a governor. After a decade of impeachments, Klan violence, and fratricidal politics, the Democrats were disintegrating. Almost every Democratic leader was tainted with scandal or identified with disorder. The Republican party had always remained associated with respectability and order. Its time now seemed at hand in Oklahoma.

The prospects of Republican resurgence foundered on the unpredicted depression, and the even more unlikely figure that hard times revived, William H. Murray. Alfalfa Bill was the only significant Democrat to escape the frays that divided the party.

A prominent figure since before Oklahoma attained statehood, Murray always desired to govern the state that he had helped to create. Logically, he should have been the first governor, but his loyalty to Charles Haskell caused him to wait. And by the end of the first legislative session in 1908, Oklahoma House Speaker Murray's highhanded tactics had generated widespread animosity among politicians. He served two terms in Congress, from 1913 to 1917. Then, as Oklahoma matured and her voters grew more sophisticated, Alfalfa Bill became a reminder of a vulgar frontier past. Careless of his appearance, a man who strained coffee through a wad of tobacco and a scraggly mustache and vilified enemies in purple prose, he remained a familiar figure in state affairs. Yet he had never won over "the best people," even while remaining attractive to voters in the countryside and small towns. Many a denizen of the hitching post and cow lot would vote for Murray, no matter how much the state changed. And Murray's dogged determination seemed a nice balance of acceptable ambition and genuine concern for the downtrodden. "I have never been over-elated by success," he claimed, "nor unduly depressed by defeat." [3] But losing a second try for the gubernatorial nomination in 1918 left him exhausted and apparently embittered.

Denied the chance to govern the state he loved so well, Murray became restless. He sensed at some level that the rural values he revered were disappearing. Unable to accept an industrialized world, he decided to start again elsewhere. From 1924 to 1929, Murray tried to establish a utopian agrarian colony in Bolivia.

While Murray was still in South America, Oklahoma's rural press began calling for his return. By 1929, the Bolivian colony was clearly a failure. Few families were willing to risk that country's isolation, chaotic politics, and hardships. The prospect of some new success in Oklahoma beckoned the restless

---

3. Keith L. Bryant, Jr., *Alfalfa Bill Murray* (Norman: University of Oklahoma Press, 1968), p. 98.

Murray home. The family returned in August 1929, and within a few weeks the Sage of Tishomingo was touring the state. Under the guise of lecturing about Bolivia, Murray was testing the political waters. There were reunions. Veterans of the constitutional convention and the first legislature gathered to praise their old leader. Rural papers reported every step of the tour, but the big city dailies ignored the hubbub. When several metropolitan dailies failed to print Murray's announcement of candidacy, he warned them that he would be nominated because the country voters were aroused.

When other candidates began to buy expensive radio time, the frugal Murray purchased *The Blue Valley Farmer,* a former socialist weekly printed at Roff. Published when funds permitted and hand-delivered to the places where Murray was scheduled to speak, the paper became Alfalfa Bill's official voice and a legend in Oklahoma politics.

Murray's principal opponent in the Democratic primary was Oklahoma City oil millionaire Frank M. Buttram, who promised an efficient and orderly administration. Buttram's billboards, radio spots, and newspaper advertisements all told of his Horatio Alger-like rise to fortune and provided perfect foils for Murray's underdog campaign. In a "cheese and crackers" canvass, allegedly financed with a forty-two-dollar loan from the First National Bank of Tishomingo, Murray concentrated on issues that appealed to financially troubled Sooners.

In a state with dramatic differences between rich and poor, Murray's rhetoric was designed to stir up class animosity. To farmers without markets and homeowners with unpayable mortgages, Murray decried the state's tax inequities. He held that Buttram was typical of the rich who paid few taxes while living luxuriously. He promised to lower the rates on farms, ranches, small businesses, and homes. There would be free seed for penniless farmers and a state road-building program to create jobs.

As the campaign gained momentum, first Murray, then even his critics predicted his victory. In the primary, he received twice as many votes as Buttram, carrying fifty-four counties across the state. The largest margins came from rural areas, and the Sage clearly reaped the political benefits of hard times. For once, Murray was in the right place at the right time.

Murray did not receive a majority, however, and faced a runoff with Buttram. More frightened by Murray's eccentricities than any ideology, E. K. Gaylord, powerful publisher of the *Daily Oklahoman* and *Oklahoma City Times,* launched a vigorous personal attack on Alfalfa Bill. Gaylord wrote a series of front-page editorials and printed the special articles on Murray of one Miss Edith Johnson. She claimed that the Sage was incompetent and reprehensible. He never bathed, he lived in a house with a dirt floor and outside plumbing, he sopped his bread with syrup, and he allowed long underwear to show below his trouser cuffs. For once, Murray failed to respond in kind, asking, instead, rather wryly, on what authority the lady knew these things. The numerous Oklahomans who shared that alleged life-style saw a winner in Murray. The newspaper attack backfired, and Murray emerged, stronger than ever, as the underdog arrayed against the rich and smug.

Murray easily won the runoff and in the general election contest displayed the old political skill that had made him influential in the state's early history. He continued to win support from farmers and other victims of the depression, but shrewdly balanced his appeal for other voters. He continued to spurn socialism, and he softened the radical tone of his earlier days. "I'm not an extremist," he assured businessmen. "I believe firmly in our capitalistic plan, if capitalism can be forced to restrain its ungodly greed and to serve the needs of humanity." [4]

Murray soundly defeated his Republican opponent, and the Democratic slate won, with one exception. But the results were not so sweeping as they seemed. Despite Murray's margin of victory, many unfriendly or skeptical fellow Democrats went to the legislature. Still, it was a personal triumph. In her hour of greatest need, Oklahoma turned to one of her oldest favorite sons.

Murray soon dispelled any doubts about his administration's tone. His inaugural address retained the shrewd, though perhaps subconscious, combination of self-interest and concern for the common people, the desire for progress without disturbing old

---

4. Edwin C. McReynolds, *Oklahoma: A History of the Sooner State* (Norman: University of Oklahoma Press, 1954), p. 363.

values that informed his entire career. "I shall honestly and honorably represent those who choose to call themselves the 'better element,' " he promised, "but this is one time when Oklahoma Indians, niggers and po' white folks are going to have a fair-minded Governor too." [5]

Emergency relief was the new administration's most obvious problem. Still the agrarian philosopher, Murray told the inaugural crowd that running the state resembled managing a good farm. Like more orthodox thinkers, he remained a fiscal conservative in matters of spending, though not of taxation. The emerging Keynesian doctrines involving debt and inflation were a book as firmly closed to him as to Herbert Hoover. Murray believed that the state could distribute free seeds and commodities, but must reduce other expenditures wherever possible. When angry politicians kept from the pork barrel talked of impeachment, Murray warned that process would "be like a bunch of jack-rabbits tryin' to get a wild cat out of a hole." [6]

In spite of his insistence on emergency relief measures, Murray believed that charity was basically a private matter. It began at home; and, to prove it, he contributed some six thousand dollars of his own money to feed the hungry. He tapped state employees for relief funds and stopped cities from arresting drifters seeking work. He also allotted half-acre plots between the state capitol and executive mansion for hungry Oklahoma City residents to plant vegetables. But at no time did popular clamor for relief programs overshadow strong public demands for governmental frugality. Oklahomans consistently defeated initiative petitions to increase state funds for relief.

As the depression deepened, Murray joined other governors in seeking federal funds. An ardent states'-rights champion, he saw no conflict of theory so long as he administered federal aid. Murray's highhanded tactics in distributing these funds ultimately caused the national administrator Harry Hopkins to intervene. Murray dismissed a few incompetent local officials under pressure, but he replaced most with cronies. These tensions and

5. Gordon Hines, *Alfalfa Bill: An Intimate Biography* (Oklahoma City: Oklahoma Press, 1932), p. 277.

6. Hines, *Alfalfa Bill,* p. 285.

charges that Murray made relief recipients subscribe to *The Blue Valley Farmer* finally forced Hopkins to make all Federal Emergency Relief Administration workers federal employees. Oklahoma was the only state denied the right to administer federal relief programs, though Murray's record was probably better than that of Huey Long in Louisiana.

When tough talk, personal charity, and implied threats failed to exorcise the devils of depression, Murray sometimes turned to force. He used the national guard to enforce a moratorium order aimed at stopping bank runs and bank failures. He employed state troops to stabilize the price of oil. The economic collapse of the 1930s and the flood of oil from huge fields in Seminole, Oklahoma City, and east Texas caused the price of Oklahoma crude to drop to fifteen cents a barrel in 1931. State revenues largely derived from a gross production tax on petroleum declined sharply. When Corporation Commission efforts to regulate production failed, three thousand men meeting in Tulsa called for closing all oil fields until prices rose. Murray agreed, and put state troops around 3,106 oil wells, while assessing nonco-operating companies for the cost of guarding the wells. He then appointed a distant cousin, Cicero Murray, "proration umpire" to enforce a production limit when the fields reopened. State troops remained at the wellheads for 618 days to prevent excess pumping. Largely through Murray's efforts, Texas, Kansas, and New Mexico adopted a uniform allowable policy with Oklahoma. That co-operative action stabilized oil prices, which reached one dollar a barrel at the end of Murray's term.

Murray then began to use state troops casually to enforce his wishes or court orders. Declaring that no one would be imprisoned for debt, he had guardsmen rescue Colonel "Zach" Miller of the famed 101 Ranch, jailed for failure to pay alimony. Troops collected tickets at University of Oklahoma football games while the athletic department was being investigated. They also enforced segregation laws in Oklahoma City.

Murray's most spectacular use of troops was in the famous "bridge war" between Texas and Oklahoma. When owners of toll bridges spanning the Red River secured a federal injunction to close three free bridges that the two states had built, Murray decided to take personal charge. Arguing that federal courts favored toll-bridge operators at public expense, he sent the national guard to the scene. Murray held that the Louisiana Purchase Treaty gave Oklahoma title to both banks of the Red River. National magazines carried pictures of the governor clad in a khaki uniform, directing traffic across the bridge between Durant and Denison, Texas, in cool defiance of the federal courts, Texas Rangers, and Governor Ross Sterling of the Lone Star State. A court ruling finally upheld Murray's views of Oklahoma's southern boundary, and Murray had the added satisfaction of gloating over Texans. In four years, Murray called the national guard into action twenty-seven times and proclaimed martial law thirty-four times to enforce executive orders. Some Oklahomans naturally criticized such use of executive power, but most voters saw Murray as championing the rights of little people.

By 1932, he was the country's best-known governor except for New York's Franklin D. Roosevelt. National magazines vied for the latest "Alfalfa Bill" stories. He addressed the legislature with one leg propped on a desk. He demanded dormitories for lawmakers, to keep them away from the temptations of women, booze, and lobbyists. He attacked the state universities for turning nice boys and girls into "high-toned bums." And he chained his office chairs to the wall so that no sinister or persuasive caller could edge too close. Most writers saw that Murray's idiosyncracies were designed to attract attention and to reinforce his rustic image.

Oklahomans probably applauded anyway. Frustrated and beaten people saw Murray getting the job done, no matter how, and they liked his sound. He said things many others normally were afraid even to think, a refreshing habit in any politician. He was sometimes embarrassing, but he seemed to be a frontiersman gone to ample seed, still an honorable category of human endeavor. Voters who retained any ideals applauded his definition of a public servant as one "too honest to be bought; too wise to be deceived; too brave to be intimidated." [7]

7. William G. Shepherd, "King of the Prairie," Collier's 88 (November 28, 1931): 45.

Events and his habit of mind inevitably made Murray think of national office. In 1932 he hoped to parlay his activist-underdog role into the Democratic presidential nomination. But his "Bread, Butter, Bacon, and Beans" campaign never had a chance. In the balloting at Chicago, he received a mere twenty-three votes, twenty-two from Oklahoma and one from his brother, a member of the North Dakota delegation. The "Alfalfa Statesman" won some curiosity seekers, but few votes.

After that fiasco, Murray began to encounter resistance to his legislative proposals and dissension within his official family. He soon lapsed into personal invective, as other politicians frustrated his ambitions and programs. Too late, Murray realized the perils of the decentralized government he had helped to construct in 1907. He also replaced many people in state boards and offices with "deserving" relatives and friends. His actions finally alienated the Oklahoma League of Young Democrats so much that they denounced his administration as the "reign of old men" left over from the constitutional convention.[8] Out of both disappointment and genuine fear of federal power, Murray also began to attack the New Deal and innovative social legislation. The agrarian radical of the 1890s had become a reactionary of the 1930s.

Whatever his failures or achievements, Murray remained a central figure in Oklahoma life. Opponents saw him as the past they hoped to overcome; supporters viewed him as the past they hoped to restore. But he was a bridge between the old, inherited freedoms and exaggerations and the new restraints necessary in a complex industrial society. Despite the first waves of modernization in the 1920s and the beginnings of a sophisticated oil economy, Oklahoma values remained rural. The great crisis of the 1930s made Murray attractive as a man dedicated to restoring older values in a present that did not seem to work.

Murray continued to typify a great deal of Oklahoma's tone. Maturing amid the farmers' revolts of the 1890s, he yet remained a Democrat, spurning third parties and bolters. He was never a dedicated progressive, though he favored some economic and political reforms. Like many others, he balked at the

8. See *Muskogee Daily Phoenix*, February 22, February 23, 1931.

social implications of progressivism. Murray also often sought reforms out of revenge, as in favoring an income tax for the well-to-do, while exempting farm property. He saw no conflict in advocating low tariffs on farm machinery and supplies and high tariffs on farm products. A confirmed agrarian, he spent a lifetime trying to arrest the forces changing America from a nation of small farms to an urban industrialized society.

Murray summed up his administration as "one damn thing after another," but there were some accomplishments.[9] His program of shifting taxes to the rich and assisting the needy was in order. His success at halting the slide of oil prices also helped preserve the basis of the state's economy for future growth. But by 1934, his public career was clearly over, and he had created no logical successor.

As the 1934 elections approached, Oklahomans generally agreed that temporary relief measures could never halt economic distress, especially as bad weather began to compound the farmers' troubles. An increasing number of people looked for some kind of government planning to end the depression. "Elect me and bring the New Deal to Oklahoma" was the slogan that put E. W. Marland in the governor's mansion.

Marland's career was another Oklahoma fable. A Pennsylvanian, Marland arrived at statehood broke, then amassed a fortune of $85 million in oil by 1920. But in 1930 his petroleum empire collapsed and, like thousands of fellow Sooners, Marland was poor. In prosperity, he was an indulgent and generous philanthropist to his adopted state. When he lost his fortune, Marland turned to politics and saw in the New Deal an outlet for his expansive humanitarianism. After a term in Congress, 1933–1934, he entered the Democratic gubernatorial primary in 1934, along with fifteen other candidates. As a newcomer to politics, he was virtually free of the old controversies. He also appeared to be a pioneer on a grand scale, both in success and adversity. As he told of losing his interests to eastern bankers, he struck a responsive chord in many voters who lost a good deal less, but in the same process.

Marland ultimately won the race and viewed his success in

9. *Tulsa Tribune,* January 1, 1935.

hard times as a compelling mandate. Genuinely devoted to the principles of the New Deal, he clearly intended to carry out a reformist mission. "I am going through with it," he said firmly, "and those who object must be saved in spite of themselves." [10]

Controversy over the New Deal dominated the remainder of the 1930s, as thousands of people eager for relief from their immediate plight balked at any fundamental social reforms. In 1934 many frightened or destitute Oklahomans voted for Marland as they had voted for Roosevelt in 1932. They believed in the New Deal's general ambition of recovering the economy and preventing future depressions. In practice, however, the national program's general philosophy clashed directly with Oklahoma's historical development. Pioneer tradition always allowed for both individual and communal efforts, but individualism was the font of progress. Communal actions were acceptable in emergencies or to help sustain individual achievement through public schools, free textbooks, or public roads. But the New Deal involved regulation and planning of some kind and proposed to curb the exploitative pioneer ethic. It also seemed to threaten states' rights, skirted the dangerous problem of the Negro, and frightened many with the prospect of good intentions hardened into bureaucracy.

Marland moved against this stubborn attitude and introduced some New Deal concepts into state government. A Planning and Resources Board was set up to inventory the state's natural resources. The state complied with the Social Security Act; but the legislature stubbornly refused to appropriate funds for welfare and educational projects, nor would it raise taxes on gas and oil to support growing expenses. It grudgingly increased appropriations for roads, partly to increase jobs, but chiefly for patronage purposes.

Eager for federal largess, Oklahoma co-operated with the New Deal's alphabetical agencies throughout the depression. And although farmers accepted restraints like crop reduction as a desperate remedy for a desperate situation, they did not generally agree with the principles involved. Opening new lands was

10. *Oklahoma News*, November 7, 1934.

the goal of most American farmers near a frontier. Mining the soil was synonymous with progress, but retiring good land was disgraceful. And to be paid for not growing products seemed dishonest. "When you come right down to it," one farmer noted, "it's not right for a man to be paid for not working." [11] Oklahomans who said they wanted larger relief appropriations continued to elect representatives committed to budget balancing and frugality. A frustrated and disappointed Marland presided over a state like most others, still unwilling to abandon old ideals rooted in fear of government for alleged benefits to be derived from governmental action.

By the end of Marland's term in 1938, the state and nation alike were beginning to react against the New Deal, as the new governor Leon C. ("Red") Phillips exemplified. An attorney with modest service in the legislature, Phillips was committed to making the state solvent and to adopting modern business practices in state government.

A tall, heavy, red-faced man who kept a black cigar clamped between his teeth, Phillips was a political cartoonist's delight. *Time* reported that the new governor was "as typical of Oklahoma as the oil derricks that stood on the Capitol plaza—not pretty, but useful." [12] As a legislator, Phillips had learned the details of state finance. As governor, that knowledge allowed him to intimidate or control any ill-informed department head or politican. He introduced modern controls over expenditures and won public approval for a budget-balancing constitutional amendment. His rigid economies produced a balanced budget in 1941, but mobilization for World War II really pulled the state, and the nation, out of economic crises.

As the European war widened and the presidential election of 1940 approached, a serious rift occurred in the state Democratic party. With the Oklahoma GOP virtually dormant, growing anti-New Deal sentiment naturally erupted in the Democratic party. Governor Phillips disliked the growing federal power and intrusions into state affairs, and he refused to support Franklin Roosevelt's third-term bid. Determined to control the Oklahoma

11. Debo, *Prairie City,* p. 217.
12. "Oklahoma: Sooner Strong Boy," *Time* 35 (January 22, 1940): 21.

delegation to the national convention as he had run state government, Phillips threatened Oklahoma National Committeeman Robert S. Kerr: "If you support Roosevelt, I'll break your back." [13]

Kerr, an Oklahoma City oilman who was a major fund-raiser in Phillips's 1938 campaign, was not intimidated. While canvassing the state prior to the 1940 convention, he found that Roosevelt remained personally popular, whatever the grumblings about the New Deal or state socialism. He decided to seek a delegation pledged to the president's re-election. A pragmatic appraisal of his own future, rather than any basic enthusiasm for Roosevelt or the New Deal, dictated Kerr's break with Phillips. When Roosevelt was renominated, Kerr stumped the state for the ticket. His split with Phillips in 1940 laid the ground for his own campaign for the governorship in 1942.

The Oklahoma of 1942 bore little real resemblance, whatever the rhetoric, to the state of a generation earlier. Dugouts, Indian teepees, prairie schooners, and land runs were all memories of a distant past. The boisterous oil boomtowns of the 1920s were now settled communities where men held steady jobs and raised God-fearing families. Munitions factories and military airfields dotted the prairies. Royal Air Force fliers trained near Ponca City for the attack on Berlin. And columns of heavy army vehicles thundered along highways once crowded with Okies in pursuit of the California dream. About half of all Oklahomans still farmed in 1942, but machinery, the radio, electrification, and news of the world all had changed their lives. The exodus to urban centers such as Oklahoma City, Tulsa, Muskogee, Lawton, Enid, and Bartlesville continued and would clearly change the state. The era of clashing titans seemed over, though Oklahomans would always reward the historic virtues. But now voters sought brains and a broad national viewpoint, as well as sentiment and concern for purely local questions.

Entering public life at this crucial moment of transition to regional and national questions, Robert S. Kerr developed a political style that savored of Oklahoma's past while he worked for her future. The eldest son of a tenant farmer, Kerr began life

13. Ray Parr, in *Daily Oklahoman,* July 27, 1942.

with all the trappings of an American folk hero. Born in 1896 in a fourteen-foot-square, windowless log cabin in the Chickasaw Nation, he grew up in rural poverty. His parents sacrificed to give their children an education, religious heritage, and a strong sense of civic pride.

As a young boy, Kerr told his father that he wanted three things in life: a family, a million dollars, and the governorship, in that order. He had fulfilled the first two ambitions by the mid-1930s, and he was elected governor in 1942. The tall, impressive millionaire with an attractive family and a ready wit was popular. Oklahomans shared his pride at rising to wealth. He was also a realist with a streak of romance in the soul. "I'm just like you," he often told crowds, "only I struck oil." That view appealed to the old ideal that, with hard work and luck, anyone could make it big.

Kerr was also an impressive campaigner, enjoying speech-making, flavoring dull facts with humor. During the 1942 primary, his opponent, Gomer Smith, said that Kerr had a drinking problem and campaigned with a pair of blondes. Teetotaler Kerr responded good-naturedly that he would visit Seminole with the blondes. At the appointed time, he arrived with his wife and his ten-year-old daughter, both suitably blonde.[14]

Hatless in the blistering summer heat, with the sleeves of his blue shirt rolled up, tugging at red suspenders, Kerr was reminiscent of Alfalfa Bill Murray at his best. Both men were visionaries of sorts, identified with Oklahoma in different ways. Murray, the cantankerous politican who wrote off "the electric-light towns," remained a classic rustic. But Kerr was a curious combination of tycoon and common man, and he symbolized the state's future direction. He sensed the need for a new frontier and realized that the old individualism was chaotic and dangerous. Under Kerr's leadership as governor and then as United States senator for fourteen years, Oklahoma moved from parochial to regional, then to national concerns. Free land was gone, and the possibility of major mineral strikes remote. Kerr wanted to develop a modern frontier based on industry and connections to the national economy.

14. Marquis Childs, "The Big Boom From Oklahoma," *Saturday Evening Post* 221 (April 9, 1949): 118.

The Kerr administration of 1943–1947 marked the beginning of a new epoch in Oklahoma history. The lush prosperity of the war years gave Kerr a politician's dream, the ability to spend lavishly while retiring debts. The governor retained unusually good relationships with legislators. He also knew that any administration friendly to the White House would get roads, dams, military installations, and government contracts. He continued to raise funds for the national party, and in 1944 he keynoted the national convention with a ringing endorsement of the New Deal.

Anticipating the need for diversified industry if the state were to avoid repeating her post-World War I experience, Governor Kerr traveled over 400,000 miles outside Oklahoma extolling Sooner products and blessings. He wrote a comprehensive plan for developing water resources that became the foundation for Oklahoma's industrial development and continued agricultural prosperity. The idea involved numerous conservation projects, but centered on developing the Arkansas, White, and Red river basins. Once completed, this elaborate project would check soil erosion, trap water for electricity and recreation, and provide an alternative to railroad transportation of heavy goods. The plan was designed to develop the entire state economy; it also combined rural and urban support for Kerr's political career. Elected to the United States Senate in 1948, Kerr attained an impressive legislative career.

Unlike other Oklahoma leaders, Kerr was neither an eccentric personality nor the champion of a single interest. Though endowed with ample flair, he presided over the end of Wild West politics. He brought a sense of maturity to state government and steadily educated the public in the complexities of modern living. He secured federal largess during the war and prepared the state for postwar development. He consciously helped restore Oklahomans' sense of pride and place, and he gave them a feeling of involvement in large national affairs.

When World War II ended, Oklahoma's leaders were anxious to lay a broad basis for future growth. The state had a good climate, abundant fuel, geographic proximity to other growing areas, and a diligent congressional delegation. It ranked eighteenth among the states in war contracts and facilities. Tulsa and Oklahoma City were third and sixth, respectively, among the nation's cities in terms of expanding job rates. Total income in the state rose some 132 percent as a result of the wartime expansion. Receipts from agriculture surpassed even those of industry because of the voracious demand for food and fiber. Wheat soon surpassed cotton, however, and the war marked the decline of large-scale, competitive cotton culture in Oklahoma.

The war also emphasized the same rural-to-urban shift in population that marked national changes. That meant accelerated demands for housing, schooling, highways, and health care. And while thousands moved from the farm to nearby small towns, or from towns to big cities, many Sooners continued the exodus of the 1930s to other states. Of the approximately one million people who left Oklahoma between 1930 and 1960, a third were productive people in their twenties. Within the state, the proportion of people aged over sixty-five more than doubled, and the age group ranging from forty-five to sixty-four increased some 40 percent during the same period.[15] Until the postwar period, the state had relied on welfare checks rather than realism in dealing with the social and economic problems that these unhappy statistics symbolized. Oklahoma was first among the states in the ratio of welfare expenditures to population, chiefly for old age assistance, but ranked almost last in expenditures for education. By the mid-1960s, welfare checks would be the largest form of payroll in many rural counties, especially in the depopulated southeastern quadrant.

For the first time in her turbulent history, Oklahoma was becoming a state of old people. Drastic measures were necessary to provide jobs for displaced farm workers and skilled workers from war industries as the economy shifted to peace-

15. The net out-migration for the thirty-year period was about one million people, some 300,000 between 1930 and 1940, some 400,000 between 1940 and 1950, and about 200,000 between 1950 and 1960. The number of residents aged sixty-five and over rose 157 percent from 1930 to 1960, and in 1960 the state had a larger proportionate number of people over sixty-five than had the nation as a whole. Only ten states had more elderly people than Oklahoma. See Richard W. Poole and James D. Tarver, *Oklahoma Population Trends,* Economic Research Series Number 4 (Stillwater: Oklahoma State University Press, 1968), pp. 53–55. For an interesting contemporary view of these general changes, from a national viewpoint, see "The New American Market— The Southwest," *Business Week* (July 26, 1947), pp. 39–46.

time production. And the youthful population of the state must remain, if Oklahoma were to avoid supporting a stagnant population drawing from a declining economy.

A new kind of economy was clearly the answer, and the wartime experience showed how it could be attained. Like so many other events in the state's history, the war effectively telescoped several stages of change. Prior to 1940, Oklahomans seemed content to remain in a colonial economic situation, exporting food, fiber, and fuel to be refined, processed, and marketed elsewhere. They lived in response to economic conditions they barely influenced. But the war years dramatically illustrated the state's potential for a sophisticated economy built on more than one stage of production.

Developing leadership and taking political action were clearly the first steps in realizing these rather vaguely felt ambitions. Building on Kerr's efforts to attract eastern investment, subsequent chief executives advertised the state's industrial and recreational potential. Every postwar governor especially emphasized Oklahoma's fiscal conservatism and solvency in trying to lure industry. Legislatures in the 1950s and 1960s voted increasing sums for highway construction and offered tax incentives to attract new factories. The growing power and longevity of the congressional delegation was highly important in winning major federal facilities, especially in Tulsa and Oklahoma City.

Many of the state's leaders sought or sensed the social changes that inevitably accompanied such new kinds of economic growth. Learning to live in a complex, interdependent society was not easy. Boosterism and individual achievement characterized the first four decades of statehood. Oklahoma's history was a series of confrontations that produced change. White faced Indian; cattleman opposed farmer; agriculture competed with oil; Tulsa challenged Oklahoma City; and governors warred against legislatures. Such a series of exaggerated frontier rivalries was colorful, but exhausting. After World War II, men and communities seemed to sense that co-operation was the only way to retain, in peacetime, the expanding prosperity of wartime.

In their first concerted effort at statewide co-operation, business leaders in 1947 financed a fifteen-car train that exhibited

Oklahoma products in eastern cities. Some 162 volunteers told potential investors how Oklahoma communities had raised up to $500,000 each to help firms willing to locate in Oklahoma. The response was dramatic. The state's total industrial development jumped some 36 percent in 1948, compared to a national increase of 10 percent.

In the 1950s and 1960s, other co-operative efforts helped broaden and enrich the state's economic base. Leaders in business, education, and politics in 1954 formed the Frontiers of Science, to determine how recent technological and scientific developments could be applied in Oklahoma. In the mid-1950s Oklahoma City agreed to co-operate with her rival, Tulsa, in aiding the congressional delegation in securing federal funds for the Arkansas waterway project. Co-operation also increased in politics, as new interest groups such as veterans, teachers, and public employees joined the traditional pressure groups of farmers, welfare recipients, and businessmen to seek more services from government.

A fresh sense of economic progress touched most of Oklahoma in the postwar decades, but fundamental social attitudes predictably resisted change. Of predominantly southern origin and attitudes, most Oklahomans shared the racial prejudices of the day. Although a substantial number of freedmen had lived among the Five Civilized Tribes, and some blacks had succeeded in the early land runs, Indians and whites alike considered blacks inferior. Many frontier towns discouraged black settlers, both out of bigotry and to inhibit the hated Republican party. Reflecting the racial bigotry of the 1890s, the editor of the *El Reno Democrat* proclaimed: "With a big crop of corn, wheat and cotton and a small crop of niggers, thus diminishing the chances of the GOP, we expect to thrive in this neck of the woods." [16]

Formal segregation was not included in the constitution, but the first legislature promptly enacted a set of segregation codes for schools, public facilities, and transportation reminiscent of those of the Deep South. These acts reflected the state's basic southern heritage and soon filtered into politics. Fearful that

16. *El Reno Democrat*, February 16, 1892.

Oklahoma would become a Republican state during the progressive era, Democrats quickly disenfranchised blacks. New statutes required a stringent literacy test based on the state's tortuous constitution. Known as the "grandfather clause" because it exempted the direct descendants of all persons eligible to vote prior to January 1, 1866, the law effectively kept blacks from the polls.

In 1915, the United States Supreme Court invalidated the Oklahoma "grandfather clause" as a violation of the Fifteenth Amendment. But Sooners were neither impressed nor repentant. The editor of the *Daily Oklahoman* doubtless spoke for most of them: "This is a white man's state . . . and must forever remain a white man's state." [17] Like other black Americans, Oklahoma blacks awaited the civil rights legislation of the 1960s to exercise the full rights of citizenship.

The state's statutes were discriminatory enough by any standard and conformed with social attitudes in general, with those of Little Dixie, in particular. Yet the human relationships involved seemed more open than in the Deep South. The distinguished black novelist Ralph Ellison grew up in Oklahoma City in the 1920s, where his family moved in search of greater opportunities than there were in the older South. He was aware of segregation and discrimination, but he also understood that Oklahoma City was "the capital of the state where Negroes were often charged by exasperated white Texans with not knowing their 'place!' " [18] Smaller towns were less tolerant, however. Unwritten "sundown laws," meaning that no black could stay in town after dark, existed even in the university town of Norman. Formal segregation was especially rigid in the public schools and seemed unsuited to the social changes so clearly transforming the state after 1945. Shortly after World War II, Ada Sipuel, a graduate of Langston University, the state-supported Negro college, sought admission to the University of Oklahoma Law School in Norman. Langston offered only a bachelor's degree, and blacks desiring professional education

17. *Daily Oklahoman,* June 23, 1915. See also Scales, "Political History of Oklahoma, 1907–1949," p. 128.

18. Ellison, *Shadow and Act,* p. xiii.

had to go out of the state. Like many other southern and western states, Oklahoma gave tuition grants to blacks to attend out-of-state universities. President George Lynn Cross of the University of Oklahoma had to refuse Miss Sipuel admission to the Law School under a 1941 statute that made it a misdemeanor for any university official to admit a Negro to a white school.

With the aid of the National Association for the Advancement of Colored People, Miss Sipuel asked the courts to instruct university officials to admit her, but the judge ruled that they could not be forced to disobey the law. When the state supreme court upheld that ruling, Miss Sipuel's attorney, Thurgood Marshall, appealed to the United States Supreme Court. The case became nationally famous and developed into a legal landmark.

The high court swiftly reversed the Oklahoma decision and ordered the state to provide a legal education for Miss Sipuel and other blacks. The court did not definitely strike down segregated facilities, however. The situation developed from drama to farce, en route to possible tragedy, as state officials swiftly established a separate law school for blacks. With three rooms in the state capitol, the state's collection of law books, and a faculty of two former attorneys, the Langston University School of Law was open for business. But its only student refused to attend. Miss Sipuel renewed her fight to cross the barriers of segregation and attend the University of Oklahoma.

While Miss Sipuel awaited the outcome of the legal process, the situation grew more confused and gained in scope. In late January 1948, six more blacks sought admission to the University of Oklahoma Graduate College. University officials denied the applications, as the law required. But Governor Roy Turner instructed the state regents to devise a plan for suitable "separate-but-equal" graduate studies in architecture, engineering, education, social work, and zoology at the Langston campus by that summer.

Although there was some anti-Negro bias at the university campus and among the citizens of Norman, most students and townspeople showed little interest in the question. As the litigation continued and the empty Langston University Law School became more ludicrous, many Oklahomans reflected on the hypocrisy as well as the injustice of the situation. Laurence H.

Snyder, dean of the University of Oklahoma Graduate College, accurately expressed the thought that troubled the conscience of many faculty and civic leaders: "If universities, which are supposedly the epitome of culture and learning in our society, cannot practice the principles of democracy and illustrate them by example, where in the world will they be illustrated and practiced?" [19]

Meanwhile, the so-called "Deans Committee" charged with solving the problem of equal-dual education recommended that qualified applicants be admitted for graduate work to both the University of Oklahoma and to Oklahoma A & M College at Stillwater. Their study showed that creating equal educational facilities for blacks at Langston would require fifty to sixty new departments and a physical plant costing at least twelve million dollars and taking some five years to construct. The report did not recommend integration, but it vividly illustrated the cost of providing the law's fabled separate-but-equal facilities.

Miss Sipuel's attorneys followed the path of law and challenged the quality of education at Langston's fictitious law school. They demonstrated through expert testimony that, despite the spacious physical plant, rich library, and low student-teacher ratio, legal education at the Langston school was not equal to that of the University of Oklahoma. The most remarkable testimony against the Langston experiment came from the University of Oklahoma law faculty. Dean Page Keeton remarked dryly that he favored larger classes than seemed possible at Langston. Law professor Henry H. Foster, Jr., shocked the court when he charged state officials with "cheap political chicanery" and dismissed the putative Langston school as "a fake, fraud and deception." [20] The court finally denied Miss Sipuel's contentions, but the decision was a gesture, since events were taking Oklahoma colleges beyond segregation.

In June 1948, George McLaurin, one of the six applicants rejected in January, sued in federal court for admission to the

19. "Where Else?," *Time* 51 (March 8, 1945): 84. The story of desegregating the University of Oklahoma is well told in *Blacks in White Colleges: Oklahoma's Landmark Cases,* by George Lynn Cross (Norman: University of Oklahoma Press, 1975).

20. *Oklahoma City Times,* May 25, 1948.

University of Oklahoma Graduate College. In late September, without voiding the state's segregation laws, the court ordered McLaurin admitted. The farce continued. Seated in a separate-but-equal anteroom that Thurgood Marshall termed a broom closet, McLaurin began graduate work. The university provided separate-but-equal toilet facilities, a separate-but-equal table in the Student Union, and a separate-but-equal study area in the Library.

Oklahoma lawmakers continued to resist, though the trend of federal court decisions was clearly against segregation. Faced with additional requests from black graduate students and with the possibility of finally having to construct a duplicate graduate school, the state legislature capitulated in May 1949. The lawmakers agreed to admit blacks to the Norman campus, but opposed integration. They insisted that instruction to blacks and whites be given at different times, in separate places.

The legislation failed to spell out details, and university officials were left to improvise. They simply roped off sections of existing classrooms for black students. When Miss Sipuel entered the law school at Norman that summer, her seat was identified with a sign "For Colored Only." John B. Cheadle, professor of law and legal adviser to the regents, likened the absurdity of the 1949 law to a situation saying that "Negroes may not be eaten by lions or tigers which heretofore have eaten only white people." [21]

The absurd irony of segregation in places of learning proved impossible to maintain. White students occasionally cut the rope barriers for souvenirs or in protest. They ostentatiously sat at tables with blacks. And the "For Colored Only" signs disappeared after Miss Sipuel's first day in law school.

Even more important, adverse national publicity hastened the end of segregation. Although the legislature was responsible for the laws, President Cross inevitably became the focus of criticism. Several letters to him from Oklahomans betrayed the old fears of miscegenation. One woman from a rural area assured Cross that segregation gained respect for blacks in white communities. But most letters criticized Oklahomans for being

21. Cross, *Blacks in White Colleges,* p. 112.

backward. A Californian thought that the desegregation problem reinforced the unfortunate Okie image. And a distressed alumna feared that such publicity would help the Russians demonstrate that there were inequality and hypocrisy in American life.[22]

In June 1950, the United States Supreme Court invalidated Oklahoma's evasions, and the McLaurin case entered the train of what became a general assault on segregated schools. In 1954, when the high court struck down the separate-but-equal doctrine, Oklahoma was one of seventeen states still maintaining segregated schools. Governor Raymond Gary assisted in ending segregation, accepted court rulings, and urged voters to abandon dual taxation for dual school systems. The NAACP praised Gary's realistic stand, a happy contrast to events in neighboring states, especially Arkansas. Gary quietly informed school district officials that failure to obey the law meant loss of state funds. The governor later explained that "no organized opposition ever developed anywhere in Oklahoma, because we didn't allow it." [23] Newspaper editors and reporters, though often disliking the changes, generally co-operated in urging public acceptance of segregation.

Public school integration without violence testified to the state's growing modernization. Officials simply pointed to the policy as inevitable, liked or not, as a way of calming public fears. But people rather readily accepted that inevitability. Politicians also shrewdly noted the excessive cost of maintaining dual school systems, always an effective appeal to an electorate that never spent much on education of any kind. But on the whole, the acceptance of the inevitability of desegregation was evidence of how much both the power structure and the people of the state had changed in less than a generation.

As Oklahomans approached their semicentennial celebration in 1957, many still smarted from the criticisms that Governor Johnston Murray had made on leaving office two years earlier. In a *Saturday Evening Post* article entitled "Oklahoma Is in a

22. Examples of this correspondence appear in Cross, *Blacks in White Colleges,* pp. 118–122.

23. Raymond Gary, "The South Can Integrate Its Schools," *Look* 23 (March 31, 1959): 119–121.

Mess," Alfalfa Bill's son declared that his native state was "at least a generation behind the times." Murray blamed his father's generation for creating an unresponsive political system. He denounced the legislative apportionment that allowed rural politicians to govern an urban state now undergoing industrialization. He believed that too much power resided in the hands of county commissioners, who inevitably retained narrow views. Their vision was especially narrow when it came to building roads that ultimately served the whole state and even extended regionally. The tax system, especially earmarked revenues, was backward and inhibitory. The whole approach fostered haphazard and wasteful government, in which local voters sent representatives to Oklahoma City "with instructions to 'chop down a Christmas tree and drag it home.' " Murray acknowledged some improvements in the state's economy and clearly saw the social changes that accompanied it. But he noted that Texas attracted forty-four hundred new industries in 1953, while Oklahoma gained five hundred. Nearby Arkansas, Kansas, and Missouri still outstripped Sooners in income, production, and growth. But Murray worried most over the exodus of young people. The state press usually dismissed these emigrants with the rationalization that "we're losing in quantity, but gaining in quality." But Murray was impatient with rhetoric of that sort: "No such snobbishness can alter the fact that Oklahoma has diminished for lack of individual opportunity." [24]

The metropolitan press generally agreed with Murray's sharp article, while deploring his airing of dirty linen. Raymond Gary, Murray's successor, hinted that the former governor was angry because his wife had not succeeded him in office and suggested the slogan "Oklahoma is O.K.," which ultimately appeared and was retained on the state's license plates for years. A lively debate followed, and despite much wounded vanity and posturing on both sides, almost 75 percent of the Oklahomans responding to the *Post* article agreed with Murray. [25]

Murray's hotly debated article was shrewdly designed to shock Oklahomans into some kind of action. He maintained that

24. Johnston Murray, "Oklahoma Is in a Mess," *Saturday Evening Post* 227 (April 30, 1955): 20.

25. "Letters to the Editor," *Saturday Evening Post* 227 (June 4, 1955): 4.

"we get bad government because we hold still to be skinned." He challenged fellow citizens to "acquire the fiery patriotism which so marvellously serves our neighbor to the South [Texas]." Adverse comparison with the hated Texans usually galvanized even the most complacent or provincial Sooner.

Murray's views, and perhaps his article, helped spur many changes in Oklahoma during the 1950s and 1960s. Numerous spokesmen worked to restore the Sooner sense of pride and vitality, which two decades of adverse national publicity had worn down. Oklahomans began to seek a new image, based on new frontiers, dealing with science and technology. Slogans advertising the state's changed life, "From Arrows to Atoms," or "From Tipis to Towers," appeared in national publications. Astronauts Thomas P. Stafford and L. Gordon Cooper joined the traditional state heroes Sequoyah, Jim Thorpe, and Will Rogers. Wealthy philanthropists began endowing art museums, symphony orchestras, and private colleges, as their predecessors had done in the 1920s. And slowly the national concept of Oklahoma as the home of refugees in broken-down jalopies covered with mattresses and washtubs began to fade.

In the mid-1960s, Governor Dewey Bartlett sent 58,000 letters to former Sooners telling them of renewed opportunities at home, and some 11,000 responded favorably. Oklahoma leaders wished to avoid the worst aspects of urban congestion through locating plants in smaller towns, as well as in the two large cities, Tulsa and Oklahoma City. The hope was to expand opportunities with a minimum of dislocation and inflation. The state also financed a lavish system of parks and recreational areas, deliberately trying to maintain the best parts of rural life and leisure while the economy changed. In the 1960s, the net outflow of people ceased, then reversed. More new people came with the growing industrial boom, and numerous former Sooners returned. "Every time they have an earthquake or a hippie rebellion in California, another handful of Okies comes back home," one resident noted wryly.[26]

Johnston Murray's agenda of political reforms, legislative reapportionment, a merit system for state employees, tax revi-

---

26. "Oklahoma 1970: The Dust Bowl of the '30's Revisited," *Time* 95 (January 26, 1970): 17.

sion, and modern accounting methods in expenditures were all reflected in his successors' campaigns and performances. The movement toward modernization affected party politics, as the Republicans became beneficiaries of demands for change. In 1962 they successfully challenged the old, rural-dominated Democratic party and elected Henry Bellmon the first GOP governor since statehood. Dewey Bartlett succeeded him, and both men went on to the United States Senate, before the pendulum swung back to a recovered Democratic party.

But the rise of a viable Republican opposition illustrated how much the state had changed and the scope of fresh demands on government. The era of one-party politics, that so easily degenerated into factionalism and drift, appeared over. The spirit of competition that Sooners praised in economics seemed at hand in politics. Oklahomans tended to vote for Republican presidential candidates, while retaining powerful Democrats like Carl Albert and Tom Steed in Congress.

Fortunately for Oklahoma, changes such as desegregation and urbanization occurred in prosperous times. The Sooner public generally saw social dislocation as part of an actively sought modernization. It thus seemed logical, if not always desired, rather than forced. It was part of long-term beneficent growth, rather than a threat to private beliefs, as it had appeared in the 1920s. Politicians also were fortunate in being able to give rather than deny favors during these expansive times, thus helping to blunt the effects of social change in people's lives.

As a society, Oklahoma digested these events rather well, whether from desire, indifference, or a sense of the inevitable. Yet the state remains an object of affection for politicians of the right in both parties. That testifies to the tenacity of frontier myths and to a society still rooted in regard for the family, the land, religion, and personal liberty. The state's conservative electorate likes a government and a society that justifies change in terms of enhancing rather than regulating individual conduct. It will respond to modernization couched in terms of efficiency and economic growth. To date, it has accepted rather well the inevitable human and social changes that follow in the wake of growth and new ideas. That, too, may testify to the frontier expansiveness that made the state what it was and will become.

7

Economics and a Modern Society

IKE so much else in the state, Oklahoma's economy, it seemed, was born grown. Within a few years of the early land runs, the stereotype of the typical Oklahoma farmer as a plowman with a wife and children, cows, chickens, and pigs, a garden, and some cotton or corn to sell for cash was a thing of the past. The combination of technological advances, railroads connected to eastern and world markets, good soil and climate rapidly changed subsistence farming into an intensive agricultural system.

Cotton production dominated the pioneer era in Oklahoma Territory, as it had in Indian Territory. Although the Civil War destroyed the extensive Choctaw and Chickasaw plantations, southern farmers working as tenants on Indian lands after 1866 revived cotton-growing. And with the opening of the southwestern and central portions of Oklahoma in the 1880s and 1890s, thousands of new acres were planted in cotton. When the Twin Territories merged in 1907, cotton farming was the new state's economic mainstay.

Other staples of national and international consumption dominated other parts of the state. The Kansans who settled in the northern and western parts of the territory planted wheat, which soon surpassed corn as the leading grain crop. Ranching suffered a temporary decline as land-hungry farmers swarmed onto former grazing areas; but it revived somewhat, as people gave up claims that were unsuitable for farming or went bankrupt through lack of developmental capital. In all these endeavors, the long-term trends extending into the twentieth century emphasized scope and complexity, though Oklahoma was glorified as the last haven for the small family farm.

The years between 1898 and 1920 were a high point of prosperity for the American farmer. Industry spread rapidly from the Northeast around the Great Lakes. As some fifteen million immigrants entered the country, the nation's cities burgeoned. Oklahoma's raw materials found good markets, as cotton became clothing, cattle became food and leather, and wheat became bread. International demands for these basics were also strong throughout the first generation of statehood. The Oklahoma farmer who started well and planned carefully seemed bound to succeed.

Recognizing the enormous potential of their agricultural wealth, many early Oklahomans followed developments in scientific farming. An agricultural experiment station was opened in territorial days at the Oklahoma Agricultural and Mechanical College in Stillwater. After statehood, additional agricultural schools and experimental farms opened; and Langston College for Negroes, established in 1897, was designed chiefly to train black farmers. The state constitution required agricultural courses in the public schools. And the farmer benefited from advice and direction generated from federal agencies.

Yet that advice had a double edge. Most farmers were interested in increasing yields and conveniently overlooked warnings against soil depletion. Settlers kept coming, and the best lands disappeared rapidly. Homesteaders arriving later had to farm the unfamiliar and often marginal lands of the dry plains. Yet they could take heart from the widely held theory that crops increased an area's humidity and the likelihood of rain. Most of these farmers merely repeated the optimism that they had seen or heard of elsewhere. Like many generations of Americans before them, they cleared and overplanted wherever they could.

The wet cycle of the late 1890s continued into the new century. Cotton, corn, and wheat led the production lists, but a variety of other grain crops were grown to feed livestock. Technology enhanced yields, as steam, then gasoline engines replaced mules and horses. The farther west these techniques and crops traveled, the greater the danger to the soil. But amid the era's agricultural bonanza, it was easy to overlook the eroded gullies and leached soils that foretold disaster.

The boll weevil that plagued southern cotton farmers was slow to appear in Oklahoma, and cotton acreage expanded rapidly. Before World War I, Oklahoma outranked the states of the old Cotton Kingdom in bales produced, and in 1925 was second to Texas. Wheat acreage expanded on as great a scale, and the sudden boom of 1914–1918 pushed up production of almost every kind of agricultural raw material. While high prices and good weather held, these gamblers in overalls were safe. But drought, insects, or a drop in demand would spell severe retrenchment or ruin for many.

When the war ended in 1918, Oklahoma agriculture was clearly overextended. Cotton, a ruthless consumer of soil fertility, was planted in every county. Wheat grew well beyond both its natural and economical boundaries. And the state depended on exports of fuel, food, and fiber to the rest of the country. The postwar national recession thus became a major event in Soonerland. Farmers who had counted on paying debts with inflated dollars faced foreclosure when prices dropped. Banks failed, and the price of oil declined from $3.50 per barrel to $1.75 in a year. Labor troubles inevitably erupted in the coal fields, in railroading, in the building trades, and in manufacturing. Every wage-earner felt the pains of adjusting to harder times, but the change was sharpest for the farmers who composed most of the population.

Other sectors of the economy gradually improved after 1919. But while the oil industry roared during the 1920s, agriculture remained depressed in Oklahoma and the nation. Farm tenancy, always high in the state, rose dramatically, as many marginal farmers lost their land. In 1920, more than half the state's farmers were tenants. Some of the farmers so classified actually owned land and rented additional acreages, but most tenants were transients who owned no property. It was customary for many such "to break loose like the tumbleweed every year and go rolling across the prairie until they [lodged] against a barbwire fence, only to break loose . . . and go tumbling on again.'' [1]

With no personal stake in the lands they farmed, these tenants seldom practiced crop rotation or soil conservation. Mismanagement continued until depression and drought in the 1930s finally forced Oklahoma farmers to change the wasteful practices of their youth. There was simply no new land to plant. If agriculture were to survive, prodigal pioneer farmers would have to learn the Indian lesson of stewardship of the soil.

The farmer remained the state's symbol, but there was even more spectacular development in mineral resources. Long before oil riches transformed Tulsa from a muddy Creek village to the world's petroleum capital and tales of rich Osages distorted the nation's concept of Oklahoma Indians, commercial mining was well established.

The fabulous tales of golden kingdoms that drew Coronado across the plains in the 1540s persisted into the twentieth century. There were legends of a buried Spanish hoard of gold bars stacked like cordwood in a cave in the Wichitas. One mining company hoping to find this treasure spent ten thousand dollars on a smelting plant that eventually produced two pennyweights of gold, one bar of silver, and two bars of copper. Prospectors' camps and gold towns flourished like mirages on former Kiowa, Apache, and Comanche lands. Thousands of worthless mining shares changed hands. And the dream of hidden El Dorados persisted among local folk well into the twentieth century.

Despite the absence of the gold so common in other western territories, Oklahoma did possess valuable minerals. Lead ore, found in lumps above ground and used for bullets in the frontier era, was common in northeastern Oklahoma. Repeated rich strikes near Miami, along with the discovery of zinc, created boomtowns that rivaled the gold camps of Colorado and California. In about fifty years, a billion dollars' worth of minerals was

1. John Caulfield, "Humanity's Tumbleweed—The Tenant Farmer of the Southwest," speech to the Southwestern Social Science Association, Oklahoma City, Oklahoma, April 16, 1939. In Lyle H. Boren Papers, Division of Manuscripts, Western History Collections, Bizzell Memorial Library, Oklahoma University, Norman, Oklahoma.

extracted from the Tri-State District where Oklahoma joined Kansas and Missouri.

Coal was also abundant in eastern Indian Territory, where it was strip-mined for domestic uses and blacksmithing in early days. But there was no market to stimulate commercial coal mining until the coming of railroads in the 1870s. At the end of the Civil War, an Arkansas Confederate colonel, J. J. McAlester of Fort Smith, happened to see a geologist friend's notebook containing an account of a government party that explored Indian Territory before the war. The notes indicated high-quality coal deposits near the juncture of the Texas Road and the California Trail in the Choctaw Nation. McAlester decided to seek his fortune in Indian Territory. Without divulging any information about the coal discovery, he moved to Bucklucksy in the Choctaw Nation. With some lumber and a small amount of canned goods, he opened a typical frontier store. Marriage to a Chickasaw girl entitled him to dual citizenship in the Choctaw and Chickasaw tribes. Under Choctaw law, any citizen had the exclusive right to own and work mines within a radius of one mile of his discoveries. McAlester formed a company with several other intermarried Indians and began to plan mines. But he needed a secure market. In the early 1870s, he hauled wagon loads of coal to Kansas for officials of the MKT Railroad to inspect. Congress had offered a right of way to the first railroad to operate in Indian Territory, but the MKT was uncertain of which route to take out of Parsons, Kansas. McAlester's coal helped persuade its officials to route a southern line through the Choctaw coal fields.

When the tracks reached Bucklucksy in 1872, the MKT graciously renamed the town McAlester. Although Colonel McAlester owned and operated the first shaft mines at nearby Krebs, Jay Gould's Missouri Pacific Railroad and the MKT quickly dominated Oklahoma coal production, opening shafts at Lehigh, Coalgate, Dow, Bache, Hartshorne, and Henryetta.

Unemployment in eastern coal fields in the 1870s caused numerous miners to accept the railroad's offer of free transportation to Indian Territory. And scores of skilled immigrants from the British Isles came to the Oklahoma mines. A generation later, Irish, Scottish, and Welsh surnames were common in the southeastern part of the state.

Indians were reluctant to work underground mines, but many Choctaw and Chickasaw freedmen abandoned subsistence farming to dig for coal. The pick and shovel fit their hands as easily as the plow handle or mule reins and held a prospect of success that farming could not match. During the long, bitter strikes over union recognition between 1898 and 1903, hundreds of Alabama blacks were imported as strike-breakers.

Other immigrants—Lithuanians, Slovaks, Poles, Magyars, Russians, and many Italians—also came to the Oklahoma mines. They were willing to work for low wages and long hours in the hope of ultimately buying farms. The Italians predominated, and by the turn of the century there was a colony of more than a thousand at Krebs, with hundreds more scattered in nearby communities. They were generally penniless southern Italians, filled with the hope of saving money to buy land. And even the harsh conditions in the mines were an improvement over their lot at home. Most were single men, living in groups to cut costs. They had such a reputation for frugality that in 1905 an estimated $50,000 lay buried under the town of Krebs. Mutual-aid societies were common among the Italians, but they were seldom, if ever, political. They were conservative, family-oriented, church-centered people who had no taste for the radical politics that appealed to so many western miners.

The Oklahoma miner's basic wage of $2.45 per day in 1903 was higher than that in the east, but Oklahoma mines were more dangerous. Little machinery was used because of the surfeit of willing labor. Operators accepted only lump coal, and in some mines men worked knee-deep in water or crawled on all fours for twelve-hour shifts. After 1894, as the shafts deepened, fatal explosions and cave-ins were common. In 1906, one man died for every 73,000 tons of coal mined in Indian Territory.

Labor unions developed slowly in the Oklahoma fields. But in 1903, after a five-year strike, Peter Hanraty, a United Mine Worker organizer, negotiated a settlement on behalf of the Oklahoma miners. The landmark agreement specified an eight-hour day, established grievance committees, and allowed a check-off system for union dues. The operators agreed to accept sack as well as lump coal. Through Hanraty, the UMW became influential in early state politics. As vice-president of the constitutional convention of 1906, Hanraty secured many enlightened labor provisions in the new constitution.

The coal industry declined temporarily with the development of oil and gas, but production soared during World War I. Between 1917 and 1920, there was a serious shortage of miners, and Oklahoma operators paid six dollars a day to likely prospects. Coal production peaked in 1920 at five million tons, but mining was a sick industry. Wartime demand had caused too many mines to open. There were strikes, closures, and bank failures as prices and wages declined after 1918. Rather than refurbish decrepit mines, many operators simply went bankrupt. Oklahoma's then known best-grade coal was also exhausted by the 1920s. With the discovery of the rich oil and gas fields in the mid-1920s, coal was no longer a competitive power source. As one operator prophesied, Oklahoma's "future belongs to oil." [2]

That remark was true. In 1859, when the first commercial oil wells were drilled at Titusville, Pennsylvania, petroleum was accidentally discovered in the Cherokee Nation. While drilling a water well to boost salt production at Grand Saline, Lewis Ross found oil. Petroleum seepages, which Indians called "oil springs" and used for medicinal purposes, were fairly common, but commercial drilling was unknown. Indian Territory was too remote from refining and marketing facilities to prompt much more than curiosity or wonder.

Cudahy Oil Company drilled the first commercial well at Bartlesville in 1897. But because of the distance to market, the well was capped until the Santa Fe Railroad reached the area. Yet the excitement and frenzy that that brief boom generated was repeated over the next four decades, as Oklahoma produced one bonanza oil field after another. The local editor vividly described the invasion of adventurers:

---

2. Frederick Lynne Ryan, *The Rehabilitation of Oklahoma Coal-Mining Communities* (Norman: University of Oklahoma Press, 1935), p. 73.

Here the representatives of nearly every civilized nation on the globe are to be found—the sturdy Norseman from the "Land of the Midnight Sun," the industrious German, the Englishman who has had his eye-teeth cut, the excitable Frenchman, the "Wild Irishman," the carefree son of Italy, the polite scion of the Montezumas, and the patient laborer from the Isles of Greece. All are here animated by a common desire—to capture and sequester the Great American Dollar.[3]

Exploration declined in the late 1890s, as oil men waited for the Dawes Commission to complete allotment and to establish a more favorable leasing policy for Indian lands. The Curtis Act of 1898 required that mineral lands be leased for the benefit of each tribe, but companies of Cherokees and Creeks continued to negotiate individual leases with outside investors and drillers. The technicalities yielded. On June 25, 1901, when the message "Oil is spouting over the derrick" crackled along the telegraph wires, a new era of Oklahoma rushes began.[4] Promoters from Kansas and Texas crossed the border, and others from New York, Chicago, and Pennsylvania scrambled for leases in the area. The Interior Department delayed another year before approving individual lease contracts for citizens of the Five Tribes, but wildcat drilling and speculative madness were in full swing. Just as the relentless Boomer agitation for land in western Oklahoma triumphed in 1889, so men's hunger for the new wealth beneath the land hastened the fall of those barriers that had kept Indian Territory a refuge.

Discovery followed discovery, and each new well seemed more productive than the ones before it. By the summer of 1905, there were 255 producing wells in Indian Territory. The Prairie Oil and Gas Company was laying a pipeline to refineries in the north. In November, shallow oil sands rich in kerosene were discovered ten miles south of Tulsa on the Ida Glenn farm. Almost overnight, the Glenn Pool flow of from one thousand to three thousand barrels a day was the most sensational small field in the world.

3. Carl Coke Rister, *Oil! Titan of the Southwest* (Norman: University of Oklahoma Press, 1949), p. 24.
4. Fred S. Clinton, "First Oil and Gas Well in Tulsa County," *Chronicles of Oklahoma* 30 (1952): 313.

By the end of 1906, Oklahoma oil wells had produced more than twenty-seven million barrels of oil, worth about fourteen million dollars. Oklahoma proudly entered the Union as the Southwest's leading producer of crude oil, a lead she maintained until 1928, when Texas passed her. The atmosphere of oil development in the 1920s was charged with hyperbole and superlative. Each discovery broke old records and added another layer of legend to the history of Oklahoma.

Oil men, whether workers or owners, were a special breed, as the career of Thomas B. Slick typified. A lease promoter for a Chicago financier, Slick paid one dollar per acre for leases within a ten-mile radius of a discovery well at Cushing in 1912. To keep the strike secret while he obtained a monopoly, he hired all the livery rigs in Cushing and paid the town's notaries to take a day off, so that no one else could file. Although the secrecy of the Cushing strike was never duplicated, Slick's ingenuity characterized the men who made it big in Oklahoma oil. Harry Sinclair, J. Paul Getty, E. W. Marland, Frank Phillips, and scores of others were a peculiar type of frontiersman. An aura of recklessness and extravagance distinguished them from the more sober pioneer in search of land. They talked easily of millions of dollars. The gambling and uncertainty, the scope of operations and risk, obviously enamored them as much as either money or oil. Slick realized two million dollars from the sale of his Cushing properties and retired at twenty-six. A few years later, he returned to the oil business to make another thirty-five million dollars. His inability to quit was common among early oil men. "I'm not working simply for the money. I've got enough. I keep at it because of the love of the game," he said. "I get a kick out of it, even when I don't win. It thrills me to know that I'm doing a man's work, producing something, and as long as I can win at it I'll keep going." [5]

A year after the Cushing discovery, the Healdton field near Ardmore came in. The enormous production of these two fields made Oklahoma the nation's major oil producer. Cushing's peak was 310,000 barrels a day in 1915, and the Healdton

---

5. Ruth Sheldon Knowles, *The Greatest Gamblers: The Epic of American Oil Exploration* (New York: McGraw-Hill, 1959), p. 123.

field's was 95,000 a day in 1916. The flood of crude drove down prices from $1.05 to $0.35 a barrel in 1915, and thousands of barrels sold below the market price. The situation was so bleak that wits suggested barbers raise the price of a shave because oil men's faces were so long.

But the outbreak of war in Europe and rising sales of automobiles in the United States soon caused oil prices to climb. Farmers anxious to take advantage of wartime prices purchased gasoline-driven equipment. Between 1912 and 1915, the nation's oil consumption doubled. The state's oil- and gas-producing fields increased from 39 in 1908 to 110 in 1915, and refining capacity more than tripled.

As the country prepared to enter the war, the search for new oil intensified. Operators who had dismissed geologists as witch doctors, a few years earlier, now employed them to direct explorations. New fields were discovered throughout the state, and old wells were redrilled to tap deeper pools. During the war years, Oklahoma wells produced nearly a hundred million barrels per year, as the price soared to $3.50 a barrel. New methods of exploration, the use of special scientific techniques, and improved drilling all expedited the location of ten more major finds in the 1920s. The prolific Burbank and Tonkawa fields appeared in the early 1920s. Oklahoma kept the national lead in oil production, with the California basin second and Texas third.

By the mid-1920s, the Greater Seminole Field, which encompassed five counties and seven major pools, pumped 10 percent of all the oil produced in the country. Despite an ominous downward trend in the price of Oklahoma crude, oil continued to flood the market. Attempts to limit drilling and pumping failed. Big companies proposed to store excess oil. The small operator feared that his pool would be drained through other wells if he did not pump. Production advanced, and prices retreated, and excess oil often fouled the land.

Natural gas, nature's means of pushing oil to the surface, was also dissipated as wells were drilled too close together or allowed to flow wide open. As gas pressure diminished, the oil "dried up" and had to be pumped. In many fields, the natural gas was simply burned off in dramatic flares. At Cushing alone, the yearly waste of gas was equal to the heating capacity of five million tons of coal.

As the petroleum market deteriorated, the Oklahoma City field, with wells a mile deep, roared into existence in December 1928. Gas pressure was so strong that many wells gushed for days before being controlled. The "Wild Mary Sudick," drilled in 1930, rampaged for eleven days, spraying two thousand barrels of oil and ten million cubic feet of gas *every hour*. With high winds, the threat of fire was so great that residents could not even strike a match to cook meals.

The oil boom affected Oklahoma as dramatically as the land rushes of the preceding century. Although essentially an extractive industry, like farming, oil generated feedback in refineries, filling stations, and the manufacture of oil-field equipment. Oil and gas tax revenues also brought the state new wealth. Petroleum, combined with wheat and cotton, gave the state its first glimpse of self-sufficiency through an integrated economy.

However much oil as an abstraction affected the economy and society, its real importance was worked out in individual lives. Some fortunes, whether won or lost, were fabulous. Some of the money was squandered, but most of it went into the stream of capital that was developing the state and the nation. For every millionaire and philanthropist like E. W. Marland, there were scores of lesser-known but wealthy and generous men. In due course, they and their heirs returned some of their fortunes to the state through gifts for universities and museums and for the improvement of the small towns from which many came. Their philanthropies were insufficient to the state's needs; yet, they were uncommon, given the lack of stewardship associated with new money of any kind.

Few Oklahomans actually became truly wealthy through oil ownership, but the great discoveries made many landless people affluent. Oil-related industries built prosperous towns and ensured jobs for people who otherwise would have been poor. Thousands of small ranchers and farmers with royalties from a single lease were able to improve their homes, travel, send children to college, or buy livestock. The "stripper wells" that produced only a fraction of a barrel a day were to many Oklahoma farmers "what cows' teats are to Wisconsin dairymen. We milk them every day." [6]

The myth soon grew that Oklahoma Indians were all rich from oil leases. Many, like Jackson Barnett, did become overnight millionaires; still others prospered for a lifetime. But the discovery of oil was as great a tragedy to many Indians as removal or the allotment system had been. By the time of the great oil booms, many Indian allotments had passed to white owners through embezzlement, forgery, or deliberate mismanagement in the probate courts.

Only among the Osage were mineral rights reserved to the tribe as a group, with lease sales and royalties divided equally. With the discovery of the Burbank field in the 1920s, the Osage became the richest Indians in the world. Stories of their extravagant spending filled the national press. One correspondent who visited Pawhuska reported that Indians who owned ornate silver flatware still ate with their hands. They washed vegetables in cut-crystal bowls and stored baseball bats in cloisonné vases. But the Osage wealth also produced the cultural achievement of the Tall Chief ballerinas, Maria and Marjorie, and novelist-historian John Joseph Mathews.

A people unaccustomed to such wealth were victimized, as well as ridiculed. Between 1921 and 1923, systematic murdering and kidnaping alternated with legal deception, as whites plundered the remains of the Indians' inheritance. The Osage were primary targets, but many Creeks and Choctaws died mysteriously after marrying whites or making wills. No Indian earning royalties from his rightful allotment was ever completely safe from terrorism.

In the midst of all these booms, society often seemed a caricature of normality. Beginning with the discovery of oil at Red Fork in 1901, little settlements erupted in the wake of each strike. Almost overnight, as in the land runs, but with a different atmosphere, whole towns of cheap wooden or cloth construction appeared. Some buildings bore labels—"hotel," "res-

---

6. Richard Lloyd Jones, owner of the *Tulsa Tribune*, quoted in Frederick Simpich, "So Oklahoma Grew Up," *National Geographic* 79 (March 1941): 273–274.

taurant," "opera house"—all designed to separate men from their money with the minimum of fuss. Congestion, prostitution, violence were the hallmarks of oil towns. And the open saloon roared until accidents, absenteeism, and violence forced the operators to dry up liquor sources.

Most oil towns vanished quickly; but if their pool was substantial, they often became significant. Cushing changed from an agricultural trade center to a refining town. A few places like Wewoka boomed in the 1920s and used the revenue for permanent improvements, such as streets and public buildings. Keifer, the Glenn Pool boomtown, boasted a high school with a marble staircase, just before the bust. But Tulsa, with no oil of her own, became the most permanent of the boomtowns. Starting with little more than a three-story hotel—the Pig's Ear Cafe, which served good meals and had a bathtub in the hall—aggressive Tulsans set out to win over oilmen. They bridged the Arkansas River and persuaded four railroads to link them with the Glenn and Cushing pools and to refineries in Kansas. They drove the hogs away, paved the streets, put up office buildings, offered free construction sites to refineries and tool manufacturers. They established banks where a good geology report was acceptable as collateral for a man who wanted to sink a well. They did everything to change Tulsa from a tough cow town in Indian Territory to the petroleum headquarters of the world. In true boomer style, they set their sights on the great cities of the world as future peers and planned accordingly.

Profits from oil built palatial residences, as well as tasteful middle-class homes in Tulsa. A tradition of civic pride and a desire for public decoration developed there unequaled in the rest of the state. Oil millionaires used their money in diverse ways. Harry and Leta Chapman bequeathed millions to endow Tulsa University. Frank Phillips quietly paid off all the church mortgages in Bartlesville, home of Phillips Petroleum. His brother Waite endowed the Boy Scouts with Philmont, a vast New Mexico ranch, and added the Philtower, a Tulsa office building, to pay the bills. He bequeathed his art collection to Tulsa, with his Italian Renaissance home and gardens as a museum. The Thomas Gilcrease Institute's collection of nineteenth-century American art, rare western manuscripts, and Indian art was purchased with an oil fortune that began with royalties earned on a Creek allotment.

Such a record of philanthropy was encouraging, yet the great bulk of oil wealth went to private expenditure or reinvestment in the fields and the production system or, like so many other Oklahoma products, it was exported to eastern interests. Oil helped build Tulsa, but it was equally important in enriching distant entrepreneurs and interests in New York, Chicago, and Houston.

The often breath-taking glamor surrounding the stories of striking Oklahoma crude obscured the effects of an uncertain national economy as the 1920s closed. The rest of the nation began to feel the deepening depression in 1929 and 1930, but Oklahoma's economy seemed expansive on the surface. Chronic malaise in agriculture seemed almost normal. Oil prices fluctuated, but there was plenty of black gold, even at low prices. There was high unemployment in coal mining, but it had always been a boom-and-bust industry. Refining and subsidiary businesses seemed sound. Cities like Tulsa, Bartlesville, and Oklahoma City had budget surpluses. Boise City in the Panhandle was becoming a railroad shipping center. Its neighbor Guymon took on the look of prosperity that came with brick buildings and improved streets. Personal income was at an all-time high, except in the southeast quadrant of the state, where depression seemed uninteresting for being permanent. It was easy to ignore warning signals that the state's basic economy, under all the gloss of expansion, remained static.

The situation in agriculture was most ominous. Careless, wasteful agricultural practices had literally destroyed thousands of acres. Ugly red gullies defaced hillsides. Spindly crops straggled in exhausted soil, and dusty fields turned easily to powder in the summer sun. Flood damage was as extensive as periodic drought. Farmers who had plowed marginal lands to reap wartime profits continued to overproduce in the 1920s, merely to survive, as prices declined. They gave little thought to the disasters that would follow any weather change.

Despite agricultural problems, the national depression appeared first in the Oklahoma oil industry. The East Texas gushers that roared into production in 1931 signaled the end of

Oklahoma's supremacy in oil. In their first year, these new Texas wells produced more oil than all of Oklahoma's pools combined. When the price dropped to sixteen cents, then ten cents a barrel, oilmen followed the farmers' lead and simply pumped more.

Producing cheap energy and food for the rest of the country, Oklahoma's prosperity thus depended on an expanding national economy. When that faltered, as events of 1929–1931 made clear, the forty-sixth state faced intense danger. With an unstable extractive economy and an immature political structure, the state was destined to be a major casualty in any national depression.

The first stage of depression unfolded in familiar patterns. The prices of all produce declined, while debts appreciated, and farm foreclosures increased between 1931 and 1933. Retail sales dropped, along with business and factory employment, and the depression spared neither town nor countryside. Yet a certain stoicism pervaded the scene, especially among farmers. When blue northers raked the state, and there were six men for every job, many unemployed "decided that the hills of Cherokee County [were] not so bad after all." [7] Fortified with visions of fresh eggs and robust chickens for at least a subsistence diet, some 37,000 Oklahomans left cities for farms in 1930, while only 19,000 made the more usual change from rural to urban life. Most farmers stubbornly insisted that they would ride out the economic storm. Accustomed to winning in good seasons and losing when it failed to rain, they planted more land.

Weather, rather than Wall Street, brought the depression to Oklahoma in full force, making it seem both intensely personal and blindly impersonal in scale. In the fall of 1930, the *Oklahoma Farmer-Stockman* reassured readers that "the dry weather and hard times are but temporary." [8] Wheat farmers stoutly refused government relief. But by 1932, seed wheat refused to sprout, and even the weeds died from lack of moisture.

In January 1933, the calamity of blowing dust and violent

7. Letter to the Editor, from Mrs. A. B., *Oklahoma Farmer-Stockman* 43 (December 15, 1930): 862.

8. *Oklahoma Farmer-Stockman* 43 (September 15, 1930): 668.

weather fluctuations began in earnest. Strong dry fronts sand-papered the crops with fine dust, and static electricity burned tender shoots. The temperature rose to a record sixty degrees in February, then plunged a record seventy-six degrees in a few hours. Arctic winds swirled in, but contained no snow, and without moisture the wheat shriveled in the soil. By the end of 1933, some seventy dust storms were recorded at Goodwell.

With no rain in the state from February to July 1934, eastern Oklahoma's cotton and row crops were ruined, and only 3 percent of the western wheat crop was harvested. Although blowing dust diminished somewhat in 1934, it returned with full fury in 1935. These dust storms entered national folklore as examples of man at the mercy of nature. Awesome, majestic, frightening, they advanced on spectators as if they were rolling walls. Since the dust absorbed sunlight, the storms added the terrors of darkness to those of suffocation. In the black blizzard of April 14, 1935, people became lost in their own backyards. Travelers stranded in darkness at noon crawled along fences to farmhouses, or groped for ruts in the roads with bare toes. One man who was carefully holding on to his two small sons learned to his horror that he had only one child by both hands.

Man was not alone in his distress. Blowing sand blinded cattle, which ran in circles until exhausted or suffocated from inhaled dust. Newborn calves usually died within a day. Hordes of birds unsuccessfully tried to ride out the storms. Jack rabbits "huddled close to the ground, facing away from the storm, while the approaching eddies turned them into hillocks of dust and left only their twitching noses visible." [9] Caroline Henderson, a farm wife in Eva, recalled seeing plants sitting high above the surrounding earth, roots exposed by the wind's force. Cattle tracks made when the ground was frozen remained like tiny mesas as the surrounding soil blew away. Uncertain weather plagued the entire state with differing effects, but the northwestern quadrant bore the brunt of nature's revenge.

People reacted differently to the storms. Most fled for shelter, but others watched the displays of blue-gray, russet, and mauve colors that often preceded the "rollers." Dust affected every-

9. Hugh Moffett, "Dust Bowl Farmers," *Life* 23 (July 28, 1947): 96.

one's life, and Oklahomans responded with new varieties of the frontier humor that had softened hardships in earlier times. They told of the bachelor who used the sandblast coming through his keyhole to clean pots and pans. Men allegedly shot ground squirrels tunneling upwards through the air. And farmers mused that, since the wind was rotating the soil, there was no need of rotating crops.

Between 1933 and 1937, the Goodwell weather station reported 362 dust storms, an average of one every five days. The strongest fronts swept on into the eastern United States and even carried dust out over the Atlantic. But this pervasive and dangerous dust was only one aspect of the weather change. Tornadoes often followed the dust. And torrential rains falling on parched, hard ground ran off as destructive flash floods. Huge hailstorms often pummeled crops and destroyed buildings. In 1936 a strong earth tremor even shook Cimarron County. Rains early in 1935 coaxed a green cover over the soil just in time for a ravenous plague of hungry rabbits and grasshoppers. Like Job, of the Old Testament, the Oklahoma farmer had good reason to hate his life.

One bad year surprised no one; two seemed merely a longer sentence. But the succession of dust storms seemed endless and inevitably affected men's spirits and ambitions. In 1934 Margaret Bourke-White, writer and photographer, toured the drought-stricken plains and was impressed with people's optimism. A year later, she noticed distinct changes. The hopeful spirit was yielding to a "no use" syndrome. With another duster anticipated any minute, there was "no use digging out your chicken coops . . . no use trying to keep the house clean . . . no use fighting off that foreclosure." [10] By 1935, a steady stream of people were looking for an alternative to stoicism. Unemployment increased in the cities, and more and more marginal farmers sought a new frontier. A great exodus began.

In the wake of that heart-rending migration, an elaborate mythology arose, which obscured the facts and ultimately altered Oklahomans' self-image and the view of the state in the

---

10. Margaret Bourke-White, "Dust Changes America," *Nation* 140 (May 22, 1935): 597.

nation's consciousness. The national press inevitably capitalized on the "newsworthy" aspects of the depression, especially dramatic dust storms and migrants. The Dust Bowl became synonymous with drought. The term *Okie,* spat out like brackish water, connoted society's riffraff in search of relief checks in the golden west of California.

The news story that popularized the term *Dust Bowl* originated in Guymon, when Robert Geiger described the black blizzard of April 14, 1935, over the Associated Press wires. Geiger correctly included in the Dust Bowl area parts of Kansas, Colorado, New Mexico, and the Oklahoma-Texas panhandles. Texas and Cimarron counties in the Oklahoma Panhandle did receive the hardest dust storms. The most evocative and famous picture of the fray, of a farmer and his two sons struggling toward a barn in a dust storm, was taken in Cimarron County. And Dorothea Lange's pictorial chronicle of Oklahomans on the road to California created the impression that all of the depression's misery centered on the Sooner state. In short order, the nation's readers and newsreel watchers almost automatically agreed.

Yet, as so often in Oklahoma's history, the facts did not sustain the enduring myth. The cotton-tenant farmers of the southeastern counties, not the wheat farmers of the northwest, were the Okies whose images burned into the nation's retina. The boll weevil, low prices and excess production, high freight rates, and heavy debts all depressed the cotton industry in the 1920s. Mechanization and fluctuating weather compounded these problems. Even before the depression, many tenant farmers had moved on to other states. As the depression deepened, and various efforts at amelioration failed, the Oklahoma tenant, likely as not, packed his car with furniture and took his family in search of a new frontier.

That exodus was never significant among the wheat farmers. Most managed to hold on, however dispiriting the situation, because they owned their land. The population of Panhandle counties declined somewhat because of a lower birth rate and an increase in dust-induced deaths among infants and the elderly. Some wheat farmers moved to cleaner, nearby communities, but few left the state permanently. The case of Dietrich Ehrlich, a

Russian emigrant who abandoned his farm in Shattuck because of eye problems, was not unusual. When a freak duster destroyed his hay crop in Brighton, Colorado, he came home. If he had to endure the weather, he decided he might as well be in Oklahoma.

Most people who had invested their lives and fortunes in the high plains country seemed to agree with Caroline Henderson: "To leave voluntarily—to break all those closely knit ties for the sake of a possibly greater comfort elsewhere—seems like defaulting on our task. We may *have* to leave. . . . But I think I can never go willingly or without pain that as yet seems unendurable." [11]

The myth that drought and dust caused the migration persisted among migrants as well as in popular legend. In a Works Project Administration study of more than six thousand migrant households in California, 44 percent of the Oklahomans interviewed gave drought as the greatest single cause of migration. But the six Oklahoma counties with the highest percentage of families blaming drought were *not* in severe drought, and all had river water. Floods actually displaced more Oklahomans than did dust storms, especially in 1936 and 1937, as the dry cycle began to end.

But the drought and its symbol, dust, continued to grip the state's and nation's imagination. It was easy, in an industrial state, where men's policies seemed to create prosperity, to blame the same men and their systems for depression. But in a state like Oklahoma, where most people earned a living from the soil, drought-induced depression seemed a vengeful act of nature and a general explanation for society's ills. Oklahomans were ignorant of the forces restructuring the agrarian economy. They were equally unable to acknowledge their own wasteful farm practices. Catastrophe as an act of God thus seemed more explicable than the reality of men's stupidity or error.

More than 500,000 people fled the Dust Bowl states during the depression. Of these, some 300,000 settled in California. Although the phrase-mongers and publicists were reluctant to ac-

11. Caroline A. Henderson, "Letters from the Dust Bowl," *Atlantic Monthly* 157 (May 1936): 542–543.

cept any responsibility for creating the image of a "Golden State" that attracted so many people, more than 100,000 Oklahomans believed the glowing advertisements offering work and housing in an ideal California climate.

The Oklahoma migrants went to California for what it represented, success, and what it promised, self-sufficiency. They sought farms, not welfare checks. Few groups in American history ever believed so strongly in self-reliance or were so oriented toward the social conservatism that family, religion, and community represented. Nearly all prized independence and were inured to hard work and thrift. Rugged individualists, they frowned on accepting charity except in times of true crisis. "We ain't no paupers," one Oklahoma migrant told Dorothea Lange. "We don't want no relief. But what we do want is a chance to make an honest living like what we was raised." [12]

Traveling in family groups and remaining in Sooner enclaves where possible, the Oklahomans became more visible than their counterparts from other states. Fundamentalist religion sustained their sense of hope amid misfortune. The shack towns they established in the southern San Joaquin Valley and in the northern arm of California's great central valley represented better housing than most had ever known. To local officials, these makeshift homes were eyesores; but to the migrants, their whitewashed walls represented optimism for the future, in a place of their own. And whatever their success or failure in California, these migrants retained an affection for Oklahoma. "A fellow don't appreciate home until he comes to California," an Okie mused. [13] While few of them returned to Oklahoma, they believed life there to be slower, more congenial, and more friendly than in California.

In the broadest sense, the Oklahoma migrants were casualties of modernization. Neither vagabonds nor hoboes, they had simply dropped from the economy's margins. Oklahoma's economy was also stabilizing after a long period of booms and busts in

12. Dorothea Lange and Paul Schuster Taylor, *An American Exodus* (New Haven: Yale University Press, 1969), p. 135.

13. Walter J. Stein, *California and the Dust Bowl Migration* (Westport, Ct.: Greenwood Press, 1973), p. 64.

both agricultural and mineral production. This subsidence coincided with the Great Depression and the Dust Bowl years, causing thousands to leave the state. They left not so much from despair as from optimism and the hope of success elsewhere. The truly despairing did not migrate, but sank to subsistence living or welfare. And like the European immigrants of an earlier generation who contributed so much to the national economy, the Okies' labor helped to underwrite tremendous expansion in California.

The conditions that uprooted 100,000 Oklahomans also produced fundamental changes among those who remained. In strictly economic terms, the reduction of the farm population was beneficial. There was a rough, if ironic, justice to Will Rogers's remark that the Okie migration to California raised the cultural caliber of both states. Oklahoma agriculture simply could not support marginal farmers any longer. Their departure helped stabilize the total state agricultural system.

The Dust Bowl years also altered the frontier attitudes that nearly destroyed the state's terrain. Oklahomans began to see their eroded land as a monument to the cut-and-run views of the past. They began to plant grasses where their ancestors had burned ground cover. They grew trees, instead of felling them. They trapped water, rather than wasting it. And hardest of all, in a land where men judged themselves by the straightness of a furrow, they learned to plow in graceful arcs to save the soil. The disaster of the 1930s also forced many thoughtful state leaders to ponder the perils of an export economy. Stability and growth must clearly come through diversification, planning, and conservation.

Federal largess was not a major factor in recovery from the depression. By the time most government relief programs took effect, the rains had returned. Wheat and cotton acreage allotments curtailed production, and prices slowly crept upward in the late 1930s. Government subsidies and relief checks were important chiefly in helping people to avoid foreclosure and retain their land until the weather changed.

The oil industry, so dramatic an early victim of hard times, seemed the first sector of the economy to revive heartily. Governor Murray's closing of the state's wells until prices stabilized helped temporarily. But gasoline and auto sales began to revive in the mid-1930s. And under Governor Marland's leadership, the Interstate Oil Compact among the petroleum-producing states to limit production helped assure a stable market price.

By 1937, the worst seemed over. That year, a natural-gas boom began in the Panhandle. Increasing rains halted wind erosion. Starting in 1936, cane, sudan grass, and barley were planted widely as cover, and by 1938 the Soil Conservation Service noted that the land was recovering. After the harvest of 1939, incorrigible boomers and some more cautious folk were calling the dust a thing of the past. The wish doubtless fathered the thought, but time proved that optimism essentially correct.

While the physical scars of the Dust Bowl era faded rapidly, the image of Oklahoma formed during the period seemed etched forever on American thinking. The term *Okie* replaced *Oklahoman*. The term derived from news stories in California in 1935. Although Kansas and Colorado lost far more acreage to wind erosion than did Oklahoma and although thousands of people from Texas, Missouri, Arkansas, and Colorado joined Oklahomans on the great trek west, their pejorative nicknames did not become common parlance. How different the history of Oklahoma might be if newspapermen had written *Kansies, Arkies, Texies,* or *Colies* rather than *Okies*.

Uttered with the same venomous connotation as *kike, nigger, wop,* or *dago,* the epithet had profound effects on Oklahomans' self-image. The term and its symbolism repudiated the heroic frontier imagery of the past and cut the foundation from the vaunted ideals of individualism, self-help, and stamina in the face of adversity.

When John Steinbeck used a fictitious Oklahoma family to immortalize the plight of migrants and tenants, Oklahoma's spokesmen responded furiously. Steinbeck's novel repeated most of the errors of fact concerning the migrants' origins and ideals that no amount of correction seemed able to alter. But the state's spokesmen realized at once that this stereotype would dog their future. Somewhat unfortunately, they chose not to explain but to denounce it as a complete fabrication. Congressman Lyle Boren, son of a tenant farmer, denounced the book in the House of Representatives as ''a lie, a damnable lie, a black, infernal creation of a twisted, distorted mind.'' [14] Boasting that he had not read the ''obscene and inaccurate book,'' one *Oklahoma City Times* editorial writer condemned it as hearsay. Another declared: ''It's enough to justify a civil war.'' [15] Still other respondents adopted a good-riddance attitude, seeing the migrants as shiftless people who had failed to take advantage of the state's ''noble purpose and determination.'' [16]

Not everyone shared that self-righteousness. Many Oklahomans obviously wanted to understand and explore, if not explode, the book's myths. They thronged libraries and bookstores to buy or borrow copies. The owner of a large bookstore in Oklahoma City reported record sales. ''People who looked as though they had never read a book in their lives came in to buy it.'' [17] Standing-room-only crowds jammed the halls when the book was reviewed, dissected, refuted, and otherwise debated.

The Grapes of Wrath perpetuated many of the inaccuracies and myths surrounding the Dust Bowl days. Yet the essence of what Steinbeck wrote was true. Many Oklahomans had never shared in the state's fabled prosperity. The migrants' lives were more true to the facts than those of the apple-cheeked boys and golden-haired girls who frolicked in the hit musical *Oklahoma!* at about the same time. The migration symptomized great economic changes and revealed anew how many people remained at the mercy of obscure natural and social forces that they could no more control than they could stop the dust.

The 1930s were unhappy years in Oklahoma, especially for their residual adverse stereotype. The coincidence of William H. Murray as governor was also unfortunate for the state's reputation: ''Alfalfa Bill's'' embarrassing antics seemed to embody the pioneer heritage gone to ruin. Images were transposed: the sturdy yeoman now became the backward Okie. They and Mur-

14. U.S., Congress, Senate, *Congressional Record,* 76th Cong., 3rd sess., 1940, 86, pt. 13: 140.

15. *Oklahoma City Times,* May 4 and August 6, 1939.

16. Governor Leon Phillips's testimony in U.S. House of Representatives, *Interstate Migration Hearings,* 76th Cong., 3rd sess., 19–20 September 1940, pt. 5, pp. 2029–2030.

17. Martin Staples Shockley, ''The Reception of *The Grapes of Wrath* in Oklahoma,'' *American Literature* 15 (May 1944): 353.

ray seemed to typify Oklahoma to the rest of the nation and to many Oklahomans themselves. The pioneer had become the hick.

Oklahomans did learn some painful lessons about their past and future during the depression years. Because of the alternating ravages of drought and flood, they became almost obsessed with controlling water in the 1950s and 1960s. Senator Robert S. Kerr became adept at securing federal funds for flood control and water conservation projects throughout the state. His greatest monument became the Arkansas River waterway, boosted as Oklahoma's outlet to the sea.

In 1943, while surveying the widespread devastation of flooding in Oklahoma, Kerr became convinced of the primary role of water in the state's future. He also saw the economic development it could bring as a link between city and countryside. "Here was a ready made issue which no one in politics was using," he noted shrewdly.[18] Kerr's commitment to that and allied projects was total, and he literally altered the state's face and future. The navigation system, with seventeen locks in 448 miles of altered channel, included scores of reservoirs, dams, lakes, and recreation areas. Its projects extended into Kansas, Louisiana, and Missouri. In addition to navigation, the system provided flood control, soil and water conservation, some hydroelectric power, and recreation. Its impact on the state's economy was steady and enormous. As the *New York Times* noted in 1961, "New lakes not only make people happier, they have a direct effect on bank deposits."[19]

Water transformed Oklahoma after World War II, as oil had earlier. In addition to major lakes, the state built 1,800 small reservoirs and almost 200,000 farm ponds. Oklahoma's ratio of water to land exceeded that of Minnesota. At the same time, state agencies spent great sums on an outstanding park system, attractive both to Sooners and tourists.

These water policies produced many direct economic bene-

---

18. *Tulsa Tribune*, January 3, 1943. See William A. Settle, Jr., *The Dawning: A New Day for the Southwest, A History of the Tulsa District Corps of Engineers, 1939–1971* (Tulsa: U.S. Army Corps of Engineers, 1975).

19. *New York Times*, November 4, 1961.

fits, and helped refurbish some agricultural activities. Irrigation became more practical in some parts of the state. The cattle industry revived after the 1940s, as many tracts of land went back to range grass and as water supply became more predictable. South-central Oklahoma began to look as it had in 1889 and 1893, a new "Hereford Heaven" of blooded stock and horse farms. Beef and dairy cattle soon outnumbered people. In January 1971, the American Cattleman's Association predicted that Guymon would become the fat-cattle and slaughter capital of the nation. As the cattle industry prospered, so did rustling, this time in modern guise. Rustlers often used citizens' band radios and helicopters to locate and herd their quarry into fast trucks. The value that many Oklahomans placed on cattle was often amusing, if not amazing. When Governor Roy Turner's prize bull, "Old 81," died of old age in 1953, he was buried in a tile-lined vault with a stone marker befitting the sire of more than a million dollars' worth of blood stock that had enriched many southwestern herds.

Though cotton did not return to its old dominance, wheat production revived steadily. Planting of sorghum, soybeans, maize, alfalfa, peanuts, and broomcorn increased dramatically. Grain elevators dominated the skylines of Enid, Fairview, Cherokee, and other northwestern towns. Many a visitor remarked on their resemblance to the Gothic cathedrals that rose above European towns.

Mining activity also increased somewhat after the war, involving stone, clay, sand-gravel, gypsum, and volcanic ash. Coal did not recover, and Oklahoma became a net importer of it because her own stocks were unusually high in sulphur content. A new coal boom awaited improved technology that made both its recovery and burning environmentally safe. And while little new oil was discovered in the state, older fields were revamped and repressured to bring up deeper reserves. Oklahoma experts and roustabouts alike pioneered oil fields as far away as the Persian Gulf, Alaska, the Gulf of Mexico, and the North Sea.

The new level of activity in familiar endeavors such as farming, cattle-raising, and mineral production after 1945 was reassuring. But thoughtful Oklahomans understood, after both depression and war, that only a diversified economy based on manufacturing could function well. The first stages of industrialism exploited raw materials. The second now involved the proper use of labor, water, space, and fiscal policies

Manufacturing that used mineral and agricultural resources and the skilled labor trained in wartime industries grew rapidly after 1945. The making of glass and pottery, manufacture of cement and building materials from stone, metalworking, and food processing were all significant new industries in the 1950s and 1960s. Many garment plants were also established in small towns around the state because of an abundance of skilled women employees.

The most dynamic increases in manufacturing occurred in the transporation equipment industry. Shortly after the war, J. Paul Getty revamped Tulsa's Spartan Air Craft to manufacture house trailers. They were in great demand, both as expedients in a housing shortage and as leisure vehicles. Within a few months, Spartan was the nation's largest manufacturer of house trailers. It had models for the middle-income family, as well as one custom job with a raised throne for the king of Saudi Arabia.

New manufacturing plants were especially important to the state's smaller towns, still in danger of stagnating and becoming refuges for the elderly as young people left the state or moved to big cities. Although the state's over-all population continued to decline after 1945, that of its chief cities increased. Population shifts in Oklahoma continued to be rearrangements of the state's existing population rather than influxes of outsiders.

In the late 1960s, the state's business and political leaders actively sought to divide Oklahoma into districts for future planning. Local chambers of commerce and service groups joined in extolling the special virtues, resources, and talents of people in eleven of these districts. Recognizing that Oklahoma had an image problem, Governor Dewey Bartlett launched a national publicity campaign in the mid-sixties to give *Okie* a boastful connotation. Thousands of lapel buttons with the vertical legend "*O*klahoma *K*ey to *I*ndustrial *E*xpansion" were distributed. State agencies and businessmen alike joined the concerted effort to bring new industry to Oklahoma.

A favorable tax system, vocational training programs, and special inducements to interested businessmen slowly gained

success. Improved highways, space for expansion, and a relaxed life-style apparently supportive of "old-fashioned values"
also helped. Numerous national firms located regional headquarters in the state. American Airlines, Cities Service, Avis
Rent-a-Car went to Tulsa. A large Xerox plant and a huge
proposed General Motors fabrication facility chose Oklahoma
City. And many companies decided on smaller towns, both out
of necessity and for special reasons. Weyerhauser naturally built
pulp and milling plants in the forested southeastern counties.
But Westinghouse located a plant near Norman; Uniroyal at
Ardmore; Sylvania at Shawnee; and the nation's first iodine-
recovery plant was built near Woodward's salt plains.

By the early 1970s, this variety of industrial enterprise was as
prevalent throughout the state as were oil derricks, cotton gins,
and cattle pens. Oklahoma-based firms manufactured everything
from aero-space equipment to recreational goods. Hartshorne,
once a worn-out coal town, produced sophisticated electronic
equipment used in guided missiles. Enid turned out bicycles in
the shadow of her grain elevators. Oklahoma Indian tribes acquired a western-hat company at Lawton and announced plans
for a line of sporting goods and play-time products to be made
at Shawnee, Ponca City, and Anadarko.

Wind tunnels at Perkins; millwork at Ada; steel fabrication
and petrochemicals at Wetumka; a uranium plant at Sallisaw;
carpets at Pawhuska; sailboats at Henryetta; barbeque smokers
at Boley; dresses at Caddo; rods and reels at Broken Arrow; op-
tical lenses at Muskogee; and pecan harvesters at Madill were
dramatic testimony to the diversity of the state's changing industrial economy. Frederick, in southwestern Oklahoma,
seemed to sum up the whole trend. With a population of fewer
than 10,000 people in 1966 and an area of four square miles, it
hosted producers of helicopters, granite building materials, bras,
leather goods, and was the site for a cattle-feeding lot.

Industrial output and income rose steadily in the 1960s, and
quickened even during the recession of the 1970s. Investment in
new plants and equipment reached $87 million in 1967; $300
million in 1969; and it was more than $500 milllion in 1974.
That was not on the scale of Texas or California, but Oklahomans revealed little desire to follow in those giants' footsteps, at

least not without avoiding the problems that came with growth. Employment in manufacturing nearly doubled between 1953 and 1973, topping 152,000 in the latter year. In 1974, barge traffic through the Port of Catoosa on the Arkansas system jumped 600 percent as the state's largest wheat crop sailed to foreign markets.

Business executives inspecting possible sites for new plants were well aware of the state's central location, generally temperate climate, and low taxes. But the labor supply seemed to impress potential employers more than public facilities or tax incentives. In choosing Ardmore as the site of a large tire plant in 1968, Uniroyal executives mentioned the "competence and reliability" of the work force as the major factor in their decision.[20] Oklahomans retained a reputation for hard work and willingness to learn.

Many employers reported that the productivity of employees at their Oklahoma facilities was as much as one-third higher than in other states. McDonnell-Douglas, one of the nation's major aero-space contractors, reported after twenty years in Tulsa a below-average record of employee absenteeism. In former coal mining and lumbering areas of the southeast, residents falsely stereotyped as lazy and inefficient proved otherwise in the new furniture, clothing, and electronics plants located there. Jim Rice, owner of a firm producing sophisticated communications and telemetry equipment, found that "these folks don't want welfare. All they want is the chance to do a job."[21]

Oklahoma's modern version of the old factories-in-the-fields ideal revitalized many faltering rural communities. It also provided a new generation of young people with an alternative to emigration or big-city life. By the early 1970s the state population began to grow slowly. For the first time since the end of the oil boom, people from other parts of the country came in some numbers, and young Sooners elected to stay. The state's great variety of landscape, water resources, and unpolluted environ-

20. H. C. Neal, "Industry . . . People!!," *Oklahoma Today* 18 (Autumn 1968): 28–34.

21. Neal, "Industry . . . People!!," p. 34.

ment made it doubly attractive to many in search of a relaxed pace of living. That very environment, properly protected and nourished, should become the state's single greatest asset in the future. With renewed confidence that many of their traditional views are virtues and not vices, Oklahomans are trying to shape a modern economy without sacrificing the warmth of neighborliness.

In the years since 1945, Sooners have recaptured much of the optimistic spirit that marked the state's founding. Steady and diversified economic growth cushioned the state against recession in the 1970s. As an energy exporter, Oklahoma has dramatically improved both its general economic health and its fiscal soundness.

The social effects of this long curve of modernization are equally striking. Contrary to mythology, some 68 percent of the state's population lives in towns of more than 2,500. Half its people live in the urban areas surrounding Tulsa and Oklahoma City. Secondary cities such as Ardmore, Altus, Lawton, Enid, and Muskogee are growing. The major cities have undergone renovation, and they face new construction, on a scale to match the early Boomers' dreams.

Economics is more than making a living. Greater sophistication in economic activity is bound to require greater complexity in culture, education, and other intangible aspects of the state's life. Oklahoma faces a new set of frontiers, relating to life-style and purpose, quite as challenging as those frontiers that lured her first settlers.

Toward Tomorrow

KLAHOMANS do not seem conscious of their history. Like most Americans, they are oriented toward the future and appreciate history only in the vivid anecdote or visible relic. They seldom reflect on historic attitudes as shaping the future. That history is positive at one level, revealing the ways people and ideas prevail. Yet the story is also negative, showing the road not taken and the ideal not embraced. A sense of the past delineates the shape of things to come, since all change is rooted in history. It also reveals tasks that must be fulfilled to secure the state's proper future.

A general desire for cultural activity is the state's greatest present lack and future need. Oklahoma was always a culture exporter, sending promising children "abroad" for education and losing many of the bright people it trained at home. That was especially true in the fine arts and education, bit it was also a problem in industry and commerce. The phenomenon, typical of the South and the Southwest in general, was understandable, if not acceptable, while the state remained poor and outside the nation's mainstream. But that era of isolation is over. Oklahoma must emphasize her own native cultural qualities and encourage outlets for cultural ambition designed from national models. Oklahoma's economy is no longer provincial; her culture cannot remain so.

The state's urbanization and the immigration of outsiders should hasten cultural development. It is at least arguable that Oklahoma City, for instance, was more sophisticated and interesting culturally in the 1920s than since. Her population was more demanding of nonmaterial living, since she was in effect "born grown," as an urban area. Oklahoma City was on the railroad main line, drawing from New York-Chicago-St. Louis-

Kansas City to the east, New Orleans-Houston-Dallas from the south, and San Francisco-Denver from the west. In its first decades, Oklahoma City partook of most of the nation's culture that radiated out along those main lines. It boasted a firm sense of urban values and a self-conscous desire for the eminence of a vital city. It went to the theater, heard opera, and read the latest books as easily as it went to its varied and often enchanting amusement parks. The self-confidence and sense of direction that underlay these interests weakened under the impact of the Great Depression and the war years. An influx of rural people with different interests, not yet wedded to the ideal of a great city, impaired it further.

Tulsa was always the local epitome of "eastern" culture and took the lead within the state in establishing art centers, theaters, libraries, and other elements of "high culture." Most important, its tone was that of a highly self-conscious urban center linked to the tastes and standards of other urban models.

The relatively consistent growth that followed World War II pumped both people and money into the state's two major cities and into many other towns. Yet cultural facilities never equaled potential demand. Oklahoma remains far behind neighboring states in supporting cultural institutions of all kinds. The state's established wealth and growing corporations could easily fund them in the absence of government subsidy.

Nothing is more important within this broad cultural sense than a truly first-class system of education. Despite brave beginnings in territorial days, Oklahoma's commitment to education lagged far behind both its needs and its obligations. Hovering near the bottom of the list of states in support for any level of education, Oklahoma has taken pride in the amount it squeezed from the educational dollar, rather than the number of dollars necessary for quality.

Part of this inattention to education was rooted in the fear of the unusual individual that often accompanied the pioneer heritage. It was also one result of the old emphasis on practicality rather than creativity. The state must now encourage innovative and unusual talent if its sophisticated, complex economy is to grow and mature. And the outsiders needed for modernization will not likely come or remain if the educational system is not dramatically improved. The state needs a huge increase in support for common schools, higher education, and specialized training. It must fund without delay at least two universities of national importance. The Oklahoman's education has never been competitive in the national marketplace. It will not be competitive at home in the future if the educational system is not of the best.

The state's needs and obligations have altered much faster than her citizens or leaders comprehended. The basic fact of life in Oklahoma is the new population patterns that accompanied industralization. Oklahoma is no longer a state of isolated towns and farms. Its citizens' attitudes are shaped on national and international models through the media and information systems that have transformed American life in general.

Yet old attitudes inevitably remain, stubbornly determined to rule. Just as land drew Oklahomans in the 1890s, so it will shape their future. In the broadest sense, land remains the key theme in Sooner history. The disposition of natural resources in decades to come will determine whether or not Oklahoma becomes a major state. The old pioneer temptation to exploit the environment remains strong. A large state with a small population and much uninhabited land risks the temptations of destruction and waste. Lack of planning and overoptimism nearly destroyed much of Oklahoma in the 1930s. Then, nature seemed to blame; now, man's ambitions must be channeled. Oklahomans are justifiably proud of their lakes and waterways, the open spaces and wilderness areas. Yet the pull of profit is as strong as pride. The ugly disorder and lack of planning in the state's cities could as easily be the pattern of the future as any sensible planning. Large areas of the state can be turned into resorts, retirement communities, and playgrounds of the sort that have blighted her neighbors New Mexico and Arizona. Haste, greed, and simple unconcern, as much parts of the pioneer legacy as pride and self-reliance, jeopardize the state's greatest asset: the land itself.

Planning requires stronger government than Sooners have accepted in the past. Politicians must discuss frankly the state's immediate and long-term problems and must cast their answers in molds equal to the challenges. They must look to expanded expenditures in sectors that benefit the whole population. The windfall of high revenues from oil, gas, food, and fiber may allow political leaders to avoid tax increases. The coming question in government is new in the state's history: how to spend wisely on capital improvements that will sustain long-term development, rather than how to avoid taxation. Any suitable answer must rest on the genuine desire for excellence in education, culture, and an expanded personal expression. The broad processes of industrialization, as Americans in other sections have discovered, are remorseless. If men do not channel them, their effects will come in unhappy human terms.

Individual actions can alter and humanize these broad historic trends. The city dweller must demand an aesthetic environment. The businessman must pay a little more for an attractive office building. The politician must talk of larger questions than the price of blacktop. The millionaire must support universities, art galleries, and opera houses rather than mansions and stables. The educator must insist on a quality of learning good enough for the nation and the world, rather than for Oklahoma's past ambitions. The citizen of average or affluent means must pay a little more in taxes for general improvements rather than seek a larger boat or newer car for his driveway. These individual acts, combining pride and self-interest, can create a fresh sense of direction worthy of the '89ers and equal to the tasks of a sophisticated and complex future. The residual defensiveness epitomized in *Okie,* so often worked out in acceptance of the mediocre and the undistinguished, could easily yield before enlightened leadership and individual concern for larger ideals.

Oklahoma's past remains vivid, exciting, and unique. She will not abandon it lightly, nor should she. The question is, can she learn from it? The state is at a major, perhaps a final crossroads. The various systems that support her people have changed more rapidly than the population's perceptions. That gap can close if enough people care. Oklahomans should thus be careful of what they seek from tomorrow—continued disinterest in the era's most demanding tasks, or acceptance of an exciting, intensified life-style in a major state. They are likely to get what they demand.

Suggestions For Further Reading

The historiography of Oklahoma is unusual. There is considerable literature on some major questions, as in Indian affairs, but little on other important problems, as with general economic development and politics. Many good studies also exist as unpublished dissertations, not readily available to the general reader. This essay thus inevitably omits many valuable, detailed studies of the state's history. The Oklahoma Historical Society's *Chronicles of Oklahoma* (1921–), for instance, contains many articles that we cannot cite here.

Oklahoma history is understandable only as part of a region. Carl Frederick Kraenzel, *The Great Plains in Transition* (Norman: University of Oklahoma Press, 1955), is a good introduction to the geography that characterizes the state's western half and that forms so much of its stereotype. David F. Costello, *The Prairie World* (New York: Thomas Y. Crowell, 1969), is a brilliant evocation of the ecology and of man's impact on this special environment. The most perceptive analysis of man's cultural relations with this environment is Michael Frank Doran, "The Origins of Culture Areas in Oklahoma, 1830–1900" (Ph.D. diss., University of Oregon, 1974). Paul B. Sears, *Deserts on the March* (Norman: University of Oklahoma Press, 1947), remains a timely warning against disrupting the plains environment.

Of general state histories, the following remain useful, with varying degrees of emphasis and coverage: Edward Everett Dale and Morris L. Wardell, *History of Oklahoma* (New York: Prentice-Hall, 1948); Edwin C. McReynolds, *Oklahoma: A History of the Sooner State* (Norman: University of Oklahoma Press, 1954); and Arrell M. Gibson, *Oklahoma: A History of Five Centuries* (Norman: Harlow Pub. Co., 1965). Angie Debo's interpretive essay, *Oklahoma, Footloose and Fancy-free* (Norman: University of Oklahoma Press, 1949), is provocative and shrewd in analyzing the Sooner character.

Of the literature on Indian Territory, the following are useful in beginning: Robert E. Cunningham, *Indian Territory: A Frontier Pho-*

tographic Record by W. S. Prettyman (Norman: University of Oklahoma Press, 1957); M. Thomas Bailey, *Reconstruction in Indian Territory* (Port Washington, N.Y.: Kennikat Press, 1972); and H. Craig Miner, *The Corporation and the Indian: Tribal Sovereignty and Industrial Civilization in Indian Territory, 1865–1907* (Columbia: University of Missouri Press, 1976).

The writing on Indian civilization in Oklahoma is enormous, with numerous studies of each tribe and nation, and of their special problems. Perhaps the best place to begin is Angie Debo, *A History of the Indians of the United States* (Norman: University of Oklahoma Press, 1970). The book's bibliography is a good guide to more detailed studies. Grant Foreman, *Indian Removal: The Emigration of the Five Civilized Tribes of Indians* (1932; reprint ed., Norman: University of Oklahoma Press, 1972), is somewhat dated, but remains evocative. Among many valuable monographs on special problems, Rennard Strickland, *Fire and Spirits: Cherokee Law from Clan to Court* (Norman: University of Oklahoma Press, 1975), is excellent and deals with much more than its title indicates. Stan Steiner, *The New Indians* (New York: Harper and Row, 1968), has some relevant information on recent events in the Indian world.

Other aspects of population emigration into the state are equally fascinating and less well covered. The immigration of substantial European groups into Oklahoma is not well known, and Douglas Hale, "European Immigrants in Oklahoma, a Survey," *Chronicles of Oklahoma* 53 (Summer 1975): 179–203, is a good starting point. Gary Lynn Watters, "From Russia to Oklahoma: A Case Study of the Immigrant Experience" (Master's thesis, Oklahoma State University, 1975), is a good case study. Arthur L. Tolson, *The Black Oklahomans: A History, 1541–1972* (New Orleans: Edwards Printing Co., 1974), is not definitive, but remains useful.

There are many special studies of the range-cattle industry and of cowboy life in general, but the interested reader might well begin with the older works of Edward Everett Dale: *The Range Cattle Industry: Ranching on the Great Plains from 1865 to 1925* (1930; reprint ed., Norman: University of Oklahoma Press, 1960); *The Cross Timbers* (Austin: University of Texas Press, 1966); and *Cow Country*, 2nd ed. (Norman: University of Oklahoma Press, 1965). Many of Dale's shorter works are included in A. M. Gibson, editor, *Frontier Historian: The Life and Work of Edward Everett Dale* (Norman: University of Oklahoma Press, 1975). Angie Debo illustrated the way the frontier spirit lingered and influenced the modern state in *Prairie City: The Story of an American Community* (New York: Alfred Knopf, 1944). William W. Savage, Jr., *Cowboy Life* (Norman: University of Oklahoma Press, 1976), is an important book on that subject.

The origins of the modern state are charted in Roy Gittinger, *The Formation of the State of Oklahoma, 1803–1906* (Norman: University of Oklahoma Press, 1939). The first wave of white immigration is covered in Carl Coke Rister, *Land Hunger: David L. Payne and the Oklahoma Boomers* (Norman: University of Oklahoma Press, 1942). The complexities of the drive to statehood are difficult to compress, but relevant materials are in Amos D. Maxwell, *The Sequoyah Constitutional Convention* (Boston: Meador Pub. Co., 1953), and Irvin Hurst, *The 46th State: A History of Oklahoma's Constitutional Convention and Early Statehood* (Oklahoma City: Semco Press, 1957). There is a great deal of information on that subject in other works cited here.

Charles C. Alexander, *The Ku Klux Klan in the Southwest* (Lexington: University of Kentucky Press, 1965), is an excellent study with much relevant information on Oklahoma. The KKK in the state is covered well in Carter Blue Clark, "A History of the Ku Klux Klan in Oklahoma" (Ph.D. diss., University of Oklahoma, 1976).

The best general introduction to the complex story of prohibition is James H. Timberlake, *Prohibition and the Progressive Movement, 1900–1920* (Cambridge: Harvard University Press, 1963). Oklahoma is covered in Jimmie Lewis Franklin, *Born Sober: Prohibition in Oklahoma, 1907–1959* (Norman: University of Oklahoma Press, 1971).

The Socialist movement is well recounted in Garin Burbank, *When Farmers Voted Red: The Gospel of Socialism in the Oklahoma Countryside, 1910–1924* (Westport, Ct.: Greenwood Press, 1976). That complicated study may be supplemented with Howard L. Meredith, "A History of the Socialist Party in Oklahoma" (Ph.D. diss., University of Oklahoma, 1969). In many ways, the best and certainly the most personal view of socialism remains the memoir of the state's major socialist, Oscar Ameringer, *If You Don't Weaken* (New York: Henry Holt, 1940).

The oil industry has attracted many scholars, but no general detailed account of its operations in Oklahoma is available. Carl Coke Rister, *Oil! Titan of the Southwest* (Norman: University of Oklahoma

Press, 1949), is a good place to begin. Angie Debo, *Tulsa: From Creek Town to Oil Capital* (Norman: University of Oklahoma Press, 1943), reveals the impact of oil on that city. John Joseph Mathews, *Life and Death of an Oilman: The Career of E. W. Marland* (Norman: University of Oklahoma Press, 1951), is an excellent account of the kind of entrepreneur who operated in the industry's first stage.

The central event in the modern state's history is the Great Depression and accompanying Dust Bowl experience. Though we believe it has been greatly misunderstood, it remains a major part of the state's stereotyped image. Fred Floyd, "A History of the Dust Bowl" (Ph.D. diss., University of Oklahoma, 1950), is valuable for its treatment of the factual as well as social aspects of the problem. Guy Logsdon, "The Dust Bowl and the Migrant," *The American Scene* 12, no. 1 (1971), a publication of the Thomas Gilcrease Museum in Tulsa, is interesting. The best account of the entire problem is Walter J. Stein, *California and the Dust Bowl Migration* (Westport, Ct.: Greenwood Press, 1973). This well-researched and insightful book dispels many aspects of the "Okie" image.

State politics are discussed well in James Ralph Scales, "Political History of the State of Oklahoma, 1907–1949" (Ph.D. diss., University of Oklahoma, 1949), which still deserves publication though dated. Stephen Jones, *Oklahoma Politics in State and Nation, 1907–1962* (Enid: Haymaker Press, 1974), is really a study of the Republican party and is valuable for its maps of voting behavior. Three biographies are important to understanding Oklahoma politics, especially in relation to national affairs: Keith L. Bryant, Jr., *Alfalfa Bill Murray* (Norman: University of Oklahoma Press, 1968); Monroe L. Billington, *Thomas P. Gore: The Blind Senator from Oklahoma* (Lawrence: University of Kansas Press, 1967); and Anne Hodges Morgan, *Robert S. Kerr: The Senate Years* (Norman: University of Oklahoma Press, 1977). George Lynn Cross, *Blacks in White Colleges* (Norman: University of Oklahoma Press, 1975), is a good brief summary of desegregation in the state's life and politics. The most famous Oklahoman should probably be noted last. The writing about Will Rogers is voluminous, and the best introduction to this fascinating and enigmatic figure is Richard M. Ketchum, *Will Rogers, His Life and Times* (New York: Simon and Schuster, 1973).

Index

Agriculture: erosion of land, 11–13; as a business, 12; crops, 14, 65; from agrarian to industrial society, 94; after World War II, 136; early growth of, 147–149; after World War I, 149; and depression, 160; weather and dust storms, 161–164; soil conservation after Dust Bowl, 167–168; irrigation, 171. *See also* Cattle industry; Farmers

Ameringer, Oscar: socialist leader, 94–97

Ardmore (town), 60, 155, 174, 175

Arkansas River Waterway, 16, 138, 170

Asp, Henry, 81, 82

Atoka Agreement, 77

Bartlesville: site of first commercial oil well, 153; mentioned, 133, 159, 160

Bartlett, Dewey (governor): efforts to expand industry, 145, 172; as GOP governor, 146

Bellman, Henry: first GOP governor, 146

Black Mesa, 18

Blacks: and slavery among Indians, 27, 30; creation of Negro towns, 62; racism in constitution, 84–85; and socialism, 98; voting rights, grandfather clause, 99, 139; and the KKK, 104; prejudice toward, 138; and segregation, 138–139, 142; sundown laws, 139; and desegregation at University of Oklahoma, 139–143; as strike breakers, 152

Boley: all-black town, 62

Boomers: promote land, 47–49

Boren, Lyle (congressman): on *Grapes of Wrath*, 168–169

Boudinot, Elias C., 24, 29, 47

Bourke-White, Margaret: on Dust Bowl, 163

Branstetter, Otto: socialist, 95

"Bridge War," of Texas and Oklahoma,

127. *See also* Murray, William H. ("Alfalfa Bill")

Bryan, William Jennings, 82, 86, 95

Buffalo, 5, 9, 14, 37, 42

Buttram, Frank M., 124, 125

Cannon, Joseph G.: and single statehood, 76

Cattle industry: foundation for, 42; cattle drives, 43; ranching established, 44; conflicts with homesteaders, 45–47, 72; barbed-wire use, 46–47; after 1940s, 171

Cherokees: retreat of full-bloods, 17; hostilities among, 29; publications of, 31; refused allotments, 41; oil discovered, 153, 154. *See also* Five Civilized Tribes; Indians

—in Georgia: 1817 and 1828 treaties, 22; and constitutional government, 22; citizens against, 23; U.S. Supreme Court upholds, 23–24

—removal of: Treaty of New Echota (1835), 24; Treaty Party opposition to removal, 24; death of many, 25–26; settle in new land, 27; leaders murdered, 29

Cherokee Outlet: Cherokees retain, 35; ranching in, 44, 46–47; and 1893 land run, 54–55; mentioned, 39

Cherokee Run. *See* Cherokee Outlet

Cherokee Strip, 44, 50. *See also* Cherokee Outlet

Chickasaws: union with Choctaws, 27, 35; and hostile Indians, 28; loyalties divided in Civil War, 34; as coal miners, 152. *See also* Five Civilized Tribes; Indians

Choctaws: Chief Pushmataha, 27; union with Chickasaws, 27; pro-Southern in Civil War, 34; name Oklahoma, 35; as